The Political Economy of AIDS in Africa

Edited by

NANA K. POKU
University of Southampton, UK
and
Commission for HIV/AIDS and Governance
Economic Commission for Africa, Ethiopia

ALAN WHITESIDE
University of KwaZulu-Natal, South Africa

ASHGATE

Published by
Ashgate Publishing Limited
Gower House
Croft Road
Aldershot
Hants GU11 3HR
England

Ashgate Publishing Company
Suite 420
101 Cherry Street
Burlington, VT 05401-4405
USA

Ashgate website: http://www.ashgate.com

British Library Cataloguing in Publication Data
The political economy of AIDS in Africa. - (Global health)
   1.AIDS (Disease) - Economic aspects - Africa 2.AIDS
   (Disease) - Social aspects - Africa 3.AIDS (Disease) -
   Political aspects - Africa 4.Economic development - Social
   aspects - Africa 5.Africa - Economic conditions - 1960-
   6.Africa - Social conditions - 1960- 7.Africa - Politics
   and government - 1960-
   I.Poku, Nana, 1971- II.Whiteside, Alan
   362.1'969792'00967

Library of Congress Cataloging-in-Publication Data
The political economy of AIDS in Africa / edited by Nana K. Poku and Alan Whiteside.
     p. ; cm. -- (Global health)
   Includes bibliographical references and index.
   ISBN 0-7546-3897-9–ISBN 0-7546-3898-7
   1. AIDS (Disease)--Africa. 2. AIDS (Disease)--Social aspects--Africa. 3. AIDS
   (Disease)--Economic aspects--Africa. 4. Medical policy--Africa.
   [DNLM: 1. Acquired Immunodeficiency Syndrome--Africa. 2. HIV Infections--Africa.
3. Health Policy--Africa. 4. Socioeconomic Factors--Africa. WC 503 P7692 2004] I.
Poku, Nana, 1971- II. Whiteside, Alan. III. Series.

   RA643.86.A35P64 2004
   362.196'9792'0096--dc22

2003028034

ISBN 0 7546 3897 9 (Hbk)
ISBN 0 7546 3898 7 (Pbk)

Typeset by Martingraphix

Printed and bound in Great Britain by MPG Books Ltd, Bodmin, Cornwall.

Contents

List of Figures

List of Tables

List of Contributors

Carolyn Baylies
Reader, School of Sociology and Social Policy, University of Leeds

Morenike Folayan
Department of Preventive Dentistry, Obafemi Awolowo University Teaching Hospital

Daniel Low-Beer
Director of the Unit on Health and Population Evaluation at Cambridge University

Ryann Manning
Research Intern, Health Economics and HIV/AIDS Research Division, University of KwaZulu-Natal

Robert Mattes
Associate Professor of Political Studies and Director, Democracy in Africa Research Unit in the Centre for Social Studies at the University of Cape Town

Robert L. Ostergard, Jr.
Associate Director, Institute of Global Cultural Studies and Assistant Professor, Political Science and Africana Studies, State University of New York at Binghamton

Nana K. Poku
Research Director, Commission on HIV/AIDS and Governance in Africa, UN Economic Commission for Africa, and Reader, University of Southampton

Rand Stoneburner
Epidemiologist who has worked with Centers for Disease Control, the New York Public Health Department and the World Health Organization

Ian Taylor
Senior Lecturer, Department of Political and Administrative Studies, University of Botswana

Matthew R. Tubin
Graduate student, Department of Political Science, University of Pennsylvania

Alex de Waal
Director, Justice Africa

Douglas Webb
HIV/AIDS Advisor, Save the Children

Alan Whiteside
Director, Health Economics and HIV/AIDS Research Division, University of KwaZulu-Natal

Samantha Willan
Project Director and Researcher, Health Economics and HIV/AIDS Research Division, University of KwaZulu-Natal

List of Abbreviations

AfricASO	African Council of AIDS Service Organisations
AIDS	Acquired Immunodeficiency Syndrome
AIDSCAP	AIDS Control and Prevention Project
ANC	African National Congress
ANC	Ante-natal clinics
ARV	Anti-retroviral (drug)
ASOs	AIDS service organisations
AZT	Anti-retroviral drug aziothymidine, marketed as Zidovudine
CAFOD	Catholic Agency for Overseas Development
CBOs	Community based organisations
CHGA	Commission on HIV/AIDS and Governance in Africa
CISGHAN	Civil Society Consultative Group on HIV/AIDS in Nigeria
CSWs	Commercial sex workers
DFID	(British) Department For International Development
DHS	Demographic and Health Surveys
DPT	Diphteria, Pertusis, Tetanus (vaccine)
DRC	Democratic Republic of the Congo
ECA	Economic Commission for Africa
FAO	Food and Agriculture Organization (of the UN)
FDI	Foreign direct investment
FHI	Family Health International
GDP	Gross Domestic Product
GINI	Gazette International Networking Institute
GPA	Global Programme on AIDS (WHO)
HACI	Hope for African Children Initiative
HEAP	HIV/AIDS Emergency Action Plan (Nigeria)
HIPC	Heavily indebted poor countries
HIV	Human Immunodeficiency Virus
HSRC	Human Resources Research Council
ICASA	International Conference on AIDS and STDs in Africa
IDA	International Development Association (of the World Bank)
IDASA	Institute for Democracy in South Africa
IDPs	Internally displaced persons
IDUs	Intravenous drug users
IEC	Information and education campaigns
IFIs	International financial institutions
ILO	International Labor Organization
IMF	International Monetary Fund

INGOs	International non-governmental organisations
IP	Intellectual property
IPRs	Intellectual property rights
MTCT	Mother-to-child transmission
MTPI/II	First and second medium term plans (Nigeria)
NACA	National Action Committee on AIDS (Nigeria), also its state (SACA) and local government (LACA) arms
NACO	National AIDS Control Organisation (India)
NAP+	Network of African People living with AIDS
NASCAP	National AIDS/STDs Control Program (Nigeria)
NEPAD	New Partnership for Africa's Development
OAU	Organisation of African Unity
ODA	(British) Overseas Development Administration
OECD	Organisation for Economic Co-operation and Development
PACA	Presidential Action Committee on AIDS (Nigeria)
PhRMA	Pharmaceutical Research and Manufacturers of America
PLWHA	People living with HIV/AIDS
PMTCT	Prevention of mother-to-child transmission
PRGF	Poverty reduction and growth facility
SADC	Southern Africa Development Community
SADCC	Southern African Development Coordination Conference
SAfAIDS	Southern African AIDS Information Dissemination Service
SANASO	Southern African Network of AIDS Service Organisations
SANDF	South African National Defence Forces
SAPs	Structural adjustment programmes
SAPS	South African Police Service
SCF	Save the Children Fund
STDs	Sexually transmitted diseases
STIs	Sexually transmitted infections
SWAA	Society for Women Against AIDS
TASO	The AIDS Service Organisation (Uganda)
TB	Tuberculosis
TRIPS	Trade Related Intellectual Property Rights
UNAIDS	Joint United Nations Programme on AIDS
UNDP	United Nations Development Programme
UNHCR	United Nations High Commission for Refugees
UNICEF	United Nations Children's Fund
UNIFEM	United Nations Development Fund for Women
USTR	United States Trade Representative
VC(C)T	Voluntary counselling (and confidential) testing
WFP	World Food Programme
WHO	World Health Organisation

Acknowledgement

A big thank you to staff at the Commission of HIV/AIDS and Governance in Africa (CHGA) for their support in putting together this book: Fabian Assegid, Tekalign Gedamu, Atkilt Getahun, Maite Irurzun-Lopez, Virginie Mongonou, Bjorg Sandkjaer, Hemant Sunth, and Kumneger Tilahun.

This book is dedicated to Carolyn Baylies (1947–2003).

Acknowledgement

Introduction: Africa's HIV/AIDS Crisis

Nana K. Poku and Alan Whiteside

Across Africa HIV/AIDS is posing an unprecedented challenge to communities, nations and states: a challenge to human survival, human rights and human development. A distinctive characteristic of the pandemic is that it appears both as a **crisis** and a **systemic condition**. The crisis nature of the pandemic is evidenced by the speed with which HIV has spread across the continent. In some communities, infection rates have increased from 4 to 20 per cent or more in adult populations in less than a decade. In Cameroon, for example, the levels of infection have risen roughly ten-fold in just the last six years. Thus, before societies are even aware of the structural threat posed by the pandemic, their communities have been deeply penetrated.

The systemic dynamic HIV/AIDS is revealed in its associated morbidity and mortality, in increasing numbers of people, mostly healthy, productive young women and men, getting sick and dying. A 2000 survey in Bobo-Dioulasso, Burkina Faso, showed that infection rates among young girls aged 13 to 24 were 5-8 times higher than those among boys of the same age (UNDP, 2001). In lower prevalence situations, young men usually have higher infection rates than young women; as the pandemic progresses, an increasing number of women are infected. Crucially, in both groups – male and female – HIV/AIDS impacts most heavily on the most productive sectors of African economies, namely prime-aged adults, thus robbing these economies of scarce skills, depriving children of their parents and the continent of a generation in the prime of their working lives.

Policy responses over the past two decades have concentrated on the pandemic's first characteristic: namely, the need to decrease the level of prevalence among communities on the continent. This has imposed the imperative of targeting interventions aimed at modifying individual and community behavior through Information and Education Campaigns (IEC). Predicated on theories such as the health belief model, the theory of reasoned action, and the stages of change model, IEC campaigns have centered on improving risk perception, highlighting perceived benefits of behavior change, and influencing norms towards safer sexual practices. The messages are mainly aimed at influencing individual behavior with awareness messages like 'stick to one partner,' 'be faithful' and if that is not possible, 'use condoms.' At the heart of these messages is the assumption that people will go through various stages in considering the impact and their vulnerability to the pandemic: pre-contemplation, contemplation of change, determination for change, action for change and maintenance of that change. Uganda is often cited as a clear example of how effective behavior modifications strategies can be when applied properly (this volume, Chapter 12).

Clearly, behavior change to stop a sexually transmitted disease like HIV can and should work. However, the process necessitates changes in society's sexual norms, values and the creation of an environment which promotes the possibility of open and honest discussion of sexuality and dying. As such, the process is evolutionary, rather than revolutionary. The result is that, while being effective, behavioral modification strategies have had little impact on curbing the pace and intensity of HIV prevalence across the wider African continent. This is borne out in the general statistics from UNAIDS, which makes shocking reading: in ten countries on the continent, HIV prevalence among adults has exceeded 20 percent and it has risen above 10 percent in an additional eleven countries. An estimated 20 million African lives have been lost to the pandemic and a further 30 million are presently thought to be living with the virus. As a result, life expectancy at birth has fallen dramatically. In Malawi, Botswana, Mozambique and Swaziland, life expectancy is now less than 40 years, while for the continent as a whole it is 47 years – a figure not dissimilar to the continental average at the time of independence; in short order, wiping out progress made in life expectancy over four decades.

Against this background of declining life expectancy and increasing mortality, the overall population growth rate of the worst affected countries is expected to decline by 3 percent by 2010. As a consequence, the age pyramids of the most affected societies are expected to change dramatically, with a narrowing of the distribution in the working-age population and a consequent problem with respect to age dependency, with resulting larger numbers of youthful and elderly dependents. What this will mean for future generations is something we know very little about.

The Context of Vulnerability

In order to understand the scale of Africa's HIV crisis, one must proceed from the fact that it is complex, multi-faceted and influenced by many medical, social, economic, and cultural factors (see Chapters 1, 3, 5). Moreover, there is a great geographical variance across Africa regarding levels of HIV prevalence. South Africa counts 1,600 new infections a day, the highest rate by volume in the world, while in Namibia, Botswana, Zimbabwe, and Swaziland one in four adults carries HIV. In contrast, the general rates of infection in West and North Africa have been consistently lower, with countries registering between 0.5 and 5 percent prevalence rates among adults. Although the reasons for these regional variation are not fully understood, intense research (social and bio-medical) over the past two decades have helped to identify a number of dominant drivers facilitating the spread of HIV/ AIDS in Africa. A word of caution, however, must be entered here because the evidence is quite mixed with respect to the magnitude with which each of these groups of factors contribute to the spread and entrenchment of the pandemic across the continent.

Biological Factors

On the biological front, research points to three key factors as the proximate cause of Africa's high HIV infectivity. The first of these is the existence of undiagnosed and untreated sexually transmitted diseases among many Africans. Data for 2000 indicate that Africa has the highest incidence of curable STDs at 284 cases per 1,000 people aged 15–49 years, compared to the second highest of 160 cases per 1,000 people in South and South-East Asia (UNAIDS, 2000). There is now growing recognition of the public health implications of curable STDs (especially those causing genital ulcers) by virtue of their frequency of occurrence as well as their ability, when present, to facilitate the transmission of HIV (World Bank, 2000c). One study suggests that the presence of an untreated STD can enhance both the acquisition and transmission of HIV by a factor of up to ten (Mutangadura, 2000).

The second biological factor that has emerged in the recent literature as having some influence on the spread and transmission of the HIV is the low rate of male circumcision found in some African countries. A recent review of more than 25 published studies on the association between HIV and male circumcision in Africa found that, on average, circumcised men were half as likely to be infected with HIV as uncircumcised men. Moreover, a comparison of African men with similar socio-demographic, behavioral, and other factors found that circumcised men were nearly 60 percent less likely than uncircumcised men to be infected with HIV (UNAIDS, 2000a).

The final biological factor to be considered here pertains to the physiological vulnerability of women. Research shows that the risk of becoming infected with HIV during unprotected vaginal intercourse is as much as 2-4 times higher for women of all ages than men. Women are also much more vulnerable to other STDs. In comparison to men, women are biologically more vulnerable to HIV infection due to the fact that they have a bigger surface area of mucosa exposed to their partner's sexual secretions during sexual intercourse and semen infected with HIV typically contains a higher concentration of virus than a woman's sexual secretions.

Socio-Cultural Factors

Alongside the biological factors are a number of socio-behavioral factors which are either regarded as having or have been demonstrated to have, a major impact on the transmission of the HIV/AIDS in Africa. These factors tend to be derived from traditions and practices. Take the issue of multi-partner relationships. In most African societies, many people either do not, or cannot, limit their sexual activities to a single, infection-free lifetime partner (Schoepf, 1993). According one analyst (Hope 2001), some 30-50 percent of married women are currently in polygynous marriages. This state of affairs means that, for these women, the greatest danger of infection confronting them comes from their spouses, and it is most likely that the majority of female AIDS victims have been infected by their husbands (Caldwell et al., 1993, Orubuloye et al., 1997).

Apart from polygynous relationships, multi-partner sexual relations are also prevalent in Africa through sexual networking. Sexual networking is characterized by the prevalence of multiple (overlapping or concurrent) sexual partnerships. In particular, men's sexual networks seem to be quite extensive and appear to be accepted, at least tacitly, by the society at large. In many African countries, there is a general feeling that men may legitimately have multiple relationships, irrespective of their marital status, but women may not. This attitude is justified on the basis of culture. A study conducted in Nigeria, for example, found that the need for men to have sexual variation, and the assumed polygynous nature of man, were the two main reasons that men cannot be satisfied with one woman (Orubuloye et al., 1993). Similar findings and their implications for the spread of AIDS have also been reported elsewhere. Consequently, these high and repeated levels of infidelity render women more likely than men to be put at risk of HIV by their partner's sexual encounters. The consequences for a woman who remains faithful to an unfaithful partner can therefore be devastating. She not only finds herself at risk but also risks infecting her future children.

Poverty and HIV/AIDS

The setting of the HIV epidemic in Africa creates a downward spiral whereby existing social, economic and human deprivation produces a particularly fertile environment for the spread of HIV and, in turn, the HIV epidemic compounds and intensifies the deprivation already experienced by people on the continent. In this sense, although the relationship between poverty and HIV transmission is not simplistic, it is possible that all the factors predisposing Africans – particularly girls and women – to increased risk of HIV infection are aggravated by poverty (Sachs, 2001; Poku, 2002; Namposya-Serpell, 2000; Farmer et al., 1996; Kim et al., 2000). The following examples will perhaps suffice to indicate how poverty leads to outcomes which expose the poor to a higher probability of contracting HIV. Poverty, especially rural poverty, and the absence of access to sustainable livelihoods, are factors in labor mobility. Mobile workers are defined as those workers who work far away from their permanent places of residence and are usually unable to return home at the end of the working day. They therefore have temporary residences in the vicinity of their work sites and return home at various intervals. Such workers include, for example, truck drivers, road/dam/building construction workers, itinerant traders, soldiers, wildlife officers, seafarers, agricultural workers, miners and commercial sex workers. For these workers, being mobile in and of itself is not a risk factor for HIV/AIDS; it is the situations they encounter and the behaviors in which they may engage while they are traveling and living away from home that lead to an increased vulnerability to HIV/AIDS.

Decosas and Adrien note that migrants have higher infections rates than those who do not migrate, independent of the HIV prevalence at the site of departure or the site of destination (Decosas and Adrien, 1997). The mining community in Carletonville, South Africa, is a tragic and powerful reminder of how mobility provides an environment of extraordinary risk for HIV contraction. With a mine-working population of 85,000 people, of whom 95 per cent are migrant workers, Carletonville is the biggest gold-mining complex in the world. These migrant workers leave their families behind in rural villages, live in squalid all-male labor hostels and return home maybe once a year. Lacking formal education and recreation, these hardworking men rely on little else but home-brewed alcohol and sex for leisure. For these men, there is a 1 in 40 chance of being crushed by falling rock, so the delayed risk of HIV seems comparatively remote. Astonishingly, some 65 per cent of adults in Carletonville were HIV-positive in 1999, a rate higher than any region in the world (Williams et al., 2000).

Development Implications

We are at an early stage of understanding the structural ramifications of the HIV/ AIDS pandemic for the wider development capacity of African states, but it is clear that HIV/AIDS will greatly affect macro-economic performance in Africa. Existing estimates of the development implications – as measured by anticipated reductions in Gross Domestic Product (GDP) growth rates – as a result of these demographic shifts and other impacts are estimated to range between 0.3 and 1.5 percent annually. For African governments already struggling with many fiscal demands in resource-poor settings, the projected impacts of HIV/AIDS on growth rates do not make a compelling case for intervention strategies that are costly – at least in the short term. Not surprisingly, governments have taken the view that scarce resources should be spent on the full spectrum of public sector priorities. In reality, however, the costs of HIV/AIDS are much more dire than aggregate indicators demonstrate.

The real impact of HIV/AIDS must be examined in the context of the critical social and economic problems already experienced by countries on the African continent: poverty, famine and food shortages, inadequate standards of sanitation, health care and nutrition, the subordination of women and fiscal policies that do not allocate sufficient resources to the social sectors. These factors create a particular vulnerability, intensifying the spread of the virus, accelerate progression from HIV infection to AIDS and aggravate the plight of those affected by the pandemic. Economic need and dependency lead to activities that magnify the risk of HIV transmission and mean that many people, particularly women, are powerless to protect themselves against infection. In addition, HIV is unusual among infectious diseases in that it has extremely high fatality rate and – as noted above – because HIV-related mortality is disproportionately concentrated among the most economically active members of society. Moreover, the majority of HIV infections at any one time are asymptomatic and the full effects of HIV epidemic on mortality and orphanhood take decades to unfold. These factors are central to understanding the difficulties of mapping the long-term development implications of the pandemic. The time delay compromises our ability to monitor and fully capture the true nature of the threat posed by the pandemic. In turn, this also acts to slow down the nature of response needed to effectively safeguard societies and communities against the effects of the pandemic – thus delaying the rewards of action.

About the Book

The real impact of HIV/AIDS can only be understood in the context of the critical social and economic problems already experienced by countries on the African continent: poverty, famine and food shortage, inadequate sanitation and health care, the subordination of women and fiscal policies that allocate insufficient resources to the social sectors. These factors create a particular vulnerability to the devastating consequences of the epidemic. Economic need and dependency lead to activities that magnify the risk of HIV transmission and mean that many people, particularly women, are powerless to protect themselves against infection. Inequitable power structures, a lack of legal protection and inadequate standards of health and nutrition all further exacerbate the spread of the virus, accelerate progression from HIV infection to AIDS, and aggravate the plight of those affected by the epidemic.

The net effect of an AIDS-depleted society is a hollowing out of the state and social networks that are already under pressure from poverty and sundry other concomitant variables. At this stage of its history, it is difficult to visualize the devastating effect of the HIV epidemic as a critical challenge to state survival in Africa, but the vital signs are evident enough. Across the continent, the pandemic is reshaping social, political and economic life in way that have not been witnessed previously. As a result, all development activities are in a state of flux. Predicated on this, the contributors to this book have been chosen for their leadership in attempting to understand the broader ramification of the pandemic on specific components of Africa's political economy, with a view to affecting policy response to HIV/AIDS on the continent.

Chapter 1

Responding to AIDS in Crisis Situations

Alan Whiteside

For Southern Africa the AIDS epidemic is in and of itself a crisis. The argument in this chapter is that it is by no means the only crisis facing the region. There are multifaceted crises across much of the Southern Africa (which in this chapter is taken to include all mainland SADC countries). Of course a few countries are doing well in most areas while others are facing problems in most. The discussion will cover the HIV/AIDS epidemic, economic development, food production, governance and security. It suggests the crisis is driving the HIV epidemic and AIDS is magnifying the crisis in the region. Responding to AIDS and the many crises is crucial and must occur concurrently.

HIV/AIDS

HIV prevalence continues to rise in Southern Africa. This region is the epicentre of the epidemic. One third of the global population living with HIV are in the SADC countries. About 13 percent of the adult population of the SADC countries are HIV positive, although there is great variation: from 0.08 per cent in Mauritius to 38.5 per cent in Botswana. The most recent antenatal clinic surveys of women attending state facilities show the rates are continuing to rise, with an HIV prevalence rate of 24.5 percent in South Africa (2000) and 34.2 percent in Swaziland (2000). In Botswana, consistent prevalence rates of over 40 percent have been recorded in some antenatal centres. Even more worrying, the spread is far more uniform between urban and rural areas than was the case in East Africa, which previously had the highest rates of HIV infection. A review of the data from the (SADC) region shows the gravity of the situation.

As is discussed in other chapters in this book, HIV infected people will in the absence of affordable, deliverable and effective treatment, experience periods of illness that will increase in severity, frequency and duration, and they will eventually die. The estimated median period between infection and the onset of episodes of illness is about eight years and people will be sick for one to two years before they die.

AIDS is killing people at an age and in numbers that are without precedent. The nature of the disease means that Southern Africa is losing people who are educated, gaining experience and in many cases are parents. The long illness results in impoverishment of the survivors and many development gains are being lost. But AIDS is a crisis that both comes on top of and contributes to existing crises as is discussed below.

1

Economic Development

Economic development has been patchy in the region. Table 1.1 shows economic data up to 2000 as provided by the World Bank. Although GDP growth rates have for the most part been positive, the per capita gross national income tells a different story. Only in Botswana, Mozambique, Swaziland and Tanzania were citizens better off in 2000 than they had been in 1991. Per capita incomes have plummeted in Angola, the Democratic Republic of the Congo and Zimbabwe. There is no published data for the past two years, but the pages of the financial press suggest that economic development has stalled in most of the region. The global shocks of post 11 September 2001 and corporate misgovernment have pushed much of the world into recession. Closer to home the events in Zimbabwe have caused foreign investors to think carefully before committing resources to the region while the drought is hitting rural communities and agricultural output. Economic growth has not been sufficient or sustained, and in some countries there is evidence of economic contraction.

Table 1.1: Economic performance in the SADC countries (World-Bank 2002)

Country	GDP Growth Percent Annual change			GNI per capita US$			Total external debt per capita
	75 – 84	85 – 89	90 – MR	1980	1991	2000	1999
Angola	-	4.5	0.7	-	920	240	883
Botswana	11.5	10.6	4.8	1190	3080	3300	409
D R Congo	- 0.3	1.7	- 5.6	620	210	na $100 in 1998	241
Lesotho	5.2	5.3	4.2	490	590	540	326
Malawi	3.2	1.9	3.7	190	230	170	240
Mozambique	-	6.0	5.8	-	170	210	365
Namibia	-	2.5	4.2	-	2070	2050	108
South Africa	2.4	1.4	1.7	2540	3050	3020	591
Swaziland	3.2	9.7	3.4	970	1210	1290	253
Tanzania	-	-	3.0	-	180	280	245
Zambia	0.2	2.3	0.4	630	400	300	659
Zimbabwe	3.0	4.2	2.5	970	920	480	369

In World Bank terms South Africa and Botswana are upper middle income countries (although at the lower end: this category encompasses incomes from $2996 to $9265), Namibia and Swaziland are lower middle income countries ($756 to $2995) while the rest are low income ($755 or less) (World-Bank, 2000). What is most concerning, and this is not reflected in these figures is the slow down in economic development that has taken place in a number of countries over the past two years.

How do people actually feel about their economic status? The Afrobarometer surveys presented respondents with a list of basic needs and asked: 'In the last twelve months, how often have you or your family gone without (these things)?' Table 1.2 below displays the proportions of people who say that they 'sometimes' or 'often' do without (Bratton and Mattes). Most Southern Africans say they or their family have gone without basic necessities at least occasionally, if not frequently. They were most likely to have been short of cash income (on average, 66 percent in each country) and least likely to experience homelessness (9 percent). Between these extremes, significant proportions of people sometimes or often went without food (an average of 49 percent), medical treatment (46 percent), clean water (36 percent), and fuel for heating or cooking (36 percent).

'In the last twelve months, how often have you or your family gone without: _____? Was it often, sometimes, rarely or never?' (Percentage saying 'sometimes' or 'often' with reference to the previous twelve months) Again there are clear distinctions between Botswana (where people are best off, although likely to experience shortages of cash and food), South Africa where the greatest problem is cash, and the other countries surveyed. Worst off are Zimbabweans and Basotho. Poverty is a major issue in the region.

Table 1.2: Shortages of basic goods and services, Southern Africa, 1999–2000

	Botswana	Zimbabwe	Zambia	Malawi	Lesotho	Namibia	South Africa
Shelter	6	4	5	14	13	16	5
Enough fuel to heat your home or cook food	31	43	29	41	38	40	28
Enough clean water to drink and cook	16	46	30	47	50	41	24
Medicine or treatment you needed	16	38	49	58	69	54	38
Enough food	49	60	38	54	61	50	34
A cash income	52	77	69	69	80	71	47

Food Production

There is a food crisis in the region. At the end of 2002 there were about 15 million people facing food shortages in six countries: Zimbabwe, Zambia, Lesotho, Swaziland, Malawi and Mozambique. Interestingly senior UN staff recognise that food is only part of the problem; the heart of the issue is AIDS. In September 2002 James Morris, head of the World Food Programme (WFP), travelled round the region and in a series of press releases and speeches it was apparent how much AIDS was seen as the issue.

> What the mission team found was shocking. There is a dramatic and complex crisis unfolding in Southern Africa. Erratic rainfall and drought can be identified as contributing factors to acute vulnerability, but in many cases the causes of the crisis can be linked to other sources … Worst of all, Southern Africa is being devastated by the HIV/AIDS pandemic. HIV/AIDS is a fundamental, underlying cause of vulnerability in the region, and represents the single largest threat to its people and societies (Stephen Lewis October 4, 2002).

And

> Across the six countries visited, healthcare workers universally emphasised the lethal combination of hunger and HIV – how the convergence of the two calamities sharply increase peoples' vulnerability to infection and disease. … In every country visited the special envoy's team was confronted by a devastating mix of extreme hunger and severe shortcomings in agriculture, health, sanitation and institutional capacity (WFP September 2002).

What is ironic is that the data taken from the FAO and WFP websites (see Table 1.3 below) give as the main reasons for the emergency, drought, and civil strife – here there is no mention of HIV/AIDS, a stark contrast with the reports cited above.

The current food crisis comes on top of a general reduction in per capita food production in the region. This is shown in Table 1.4 below. Up to 2000 there was a decline in output in all countries except Malawi, Zimbabwe and Angola. The current drought is a recent phenomena, which means this impact is not yet being seen in these indicators. The disruption of farming in Zimbabwe is also not reflected.

Table 1.3: Countries facing food emergencies

Country	Reasons for emergency	Number of people facing food shortages	Food aid needed for 2002 (per tonnes)
Angola	Civil strife, internally displaced people (IDPs)	1.8 million	221,000

Congo, Dem. Rep. Of	Civil strife, IDPs and refugees	30,000	52,000
Lesotho	Drought in parts	445,000	147,000
Malawi	Drought in parts	3.2 million	208,000
Mozambique	Drought in parts	515,000	50,000
Swaziland	Drought in parts	144,000	15,000
Tanzania	Poor rains in parts, refugees	524,000	50,000
Zambia	Drought and floods in parts	2.329 million	225,000
Zimbabwe	Drought, farming disruptions	6.074 million	1,407,000
Total		15,061,000	2,375,000

Source: www.wfp.org

Table 1.4: Food production

Country	Food Production per capita index (average 1989 – 91 = 100)		
	1991	1995	2000
Angola	100	104	102
Botswana	104	92	78
D R Congo	99	90	65
Lesotho	81	80	81
Malawi	103	100	134
Mozambique	92	89	82
Namibia	100	96	78
South Africa	98	79	92
Swaziland	102	76	67
Tanzania	97	86	81
Zambia	95	82	81
Zimbabwe	94	68	101

Governance

How responsive and responsible are the governments of the region? Botswana, South Africa, Namibia and Tanzania have reasonably democratic and responsive systems of representation. Malawi, Zambia, Lesotho and Mozambique have moved in this direction. Swaziland, Angola, and the DRC are not democratic while in Zimbabwe, although there is an elected opposition, vote rigging and intimidation have been the order of the day.

Southern Africans have a poor opinion of government management. Afrobarometer surveys (Bratton and Mattes) asked a range of questions about the government's 'handling' of various policy areas, as is shown in Table 1.5. People are particularly negative about government performance at economic management. Only in Botswana does the government receive a positive rating in this area. Some governments receive favourable ratings for provision of education, basic services and services. The picture that emerges is of dissatisfied citizens, and the most dissatisfied are Zimbabweans.

Table 1.5: Public evaluation of government economic management, Southern Africa, 1999–2000

	Botswana	Zimbabwe	Zambia	Malawi	Lesotho	Namibia	South Africa
Creating jobs	52	20	26	32	38	47	10
Ensuring prices remain stable	41	14	28	8	20	38	17
Improving health services	69	35	37	46	50	62	43
Addressing educational needs	71	46	43	62	57	62	49
Managing the economy	60	16	33	25	36	45	28
Delivering basic services: water and electricity	69	36	40	65	35	55	61
Average	60	28	35	40	39	52	35

'Now let's speak about the present government of this country. How well would you say the government is handling the following matters? Would you say very well, fairly well, not very well or not at all well, or haven't you heard enough about this to have an opinion?' (percent 'fairly well / very well') Except in South Africa it is not known how most citizens rate their governments' handling of the HIV/AIDS epidemic. Here the recent Human Sciences Research Council study of HIV/AIDS found that 63.8 percent of those surveyed felt that 'political leaders are committed to AIDS', 68.9 said 'political leaders publicly recognise the importance of HIV/AIDS' but only 47.5 say the government is allocating sufficient resources for AIDS control (Mandela 2002).

The Security Crisis

Much has been written about the role of AIDS as a security issue. This is generally speculative and based on little information, this is not to criticise researchers – the facts are that there is very little information and we do not know how the epidemic will play out as a security issue. The regional context is that of the 12 countries; one (the Democratic Republic of Congo) is in the grip of ongoing civil war of varying intensity; four others – Zimbabwe, Namibia, Angola and Tanzania having actively committed troops to the conflict (either overtly or covertly) and one (South Africa) providing peace keepers. Angola is just emerging from a long period of bitter conflict.

The little evidence we have suggests that military forces tend to have higher levels of HIV infection than the general population. In addition conflict assists in the spread of HIV through movement of troops, increased sexual violence and refugees. There are currently 392,000 refugees in Congo and 470,000 in Angola, (www.infoplease.com/search/ipa/A0762539.html). Other concerns are: what happens in highly infected military units; how are national resources used? There is no evidence on how military (and for that matter police services) will react to high levels of infection, morbidity and mortality, this will depend largely on how the commands react to illness and what provision of care, including anti-retroviral therapy, there is. In the best settings army medical corps may provide high quality care and ensure troops are actively engaged in prevention; in the worst drugs may be rationed, soldiers discharged if found to be HIV positive. We do not believe that HIV will, by itself lead to greater instability but rather that it erodes the capacity of the uniformed services.

However, there are serious questions about the level of resources, both financial and human, being allocated to military expenditure. These are shown in Table 1.6. In South Africa many (not just AIDS activists) have been horrified by the signing of a controversial deal to purchase arms worth approximately $5.5 billion, money which is not therefore available for a range of other uses including social development.

Table 1.6: SADC military forces and expenditures

Country	Total armed forces in thousands (UNDP 2002)	Military expenditures in dollars	Political situation
Angola	108	1.2 billion	Civil war recently ended, involved in DRC
Botswana	9	61 million	No conflict

D R Congo	56	250 million	Civil war
Lesotho	2	34 million	No conflict
Malawi	5	9.5 million	Minor boundary dispute with Tanzania
Mozambique	6	35.1 million	No conflict
Namibia	9	104.4 million	No conflict involved in DRC
South Africa	63	2 billion	No conflict
Swaziland	-	19.198 million	No conflict
Tanzania	34	21 million	Minor boundary dispute with Malawi involved in DRC
Zambia	22	76 million	No conflict
Zimbabwe	40	127 million	Tense and unlawful involved in DRC

Responding to the Epidemic in Crisis

Having set the scene and shown that Southern Africa faces a multifaceted crisis the next part of the chapter addresses two key questions: To what extent is the crisis driving the HIV epidemic? And is AIDS adding to the crisis? These are difficult but important questions. The contention of the chapter is that the spread of HIV is assisted by the factures, schisms and inequalities in a society. Responding to HIV/AIDS offers a unique opportunity to get development processes right, and it is only by doing this that we can address the catastrophe facing the region.

Crisis as an HIV Driver

There is ample evidence to show that crises help drive the HIV epidemic (Barnett and Whiteside, 2002). Poverty and inequality increase the likelihood that poor women will be forced into commercial sex as a survival strategy. Orphans and vulnerable children are more likely to be exploited and this often includes sexual exploitation and abuse. Armed conflict and the movement of armies and refugees change sexual mixing patterns and rape is more commonplace, indeed there are instances where it has been used as a weapon. Poor agricultural policies and crop failure may result in rural urban migration and increased poverty. A lack of legitimacy means government messages may not be heard or acted on if they are.

Figure 1.1 shows some of the relationships between poverty and HIV. Although the most proximate determinants are biological, a person's sexual behaviour is next in line as it determines the number and type of sexual encounters he or she will have. However sexual behaviour is in turn determined by economic, social and cultural factors. For example, a truck driver on any of the major routes in Africa may be away for home for long periods. He might have sex with a commercial sex worker because he is bored; he feels his job is dangerous and he deserves some compensation; he is frequently away from his wife and family; he experiences peer pressure from his fellow drivers to engage in this activity; and he has the necessary money. The commercial sex worker, on the other hand, is driven by poverty and the need to feed her family. Each column also has an area where policy interventions can be imagined or actualised.

Determinants	Distal determinants		Proximal determinants	
	Macro environment	Micro-environment	Behaviour	Biology
	Wealth	Mobility	Rate of partner change	Virus sub-types
	Income distribution	Urbanisation	Prevalence of concurrent partners	Stage of infection
	Culture	Access to health care	Sexual mixing patterns	Presence of other STDs
	Religion	Levels of violence	Sexual practices and condom use	Gender
	Governance	Women's rights and status	Breast feeding	Circumcision
Interventions	Social policy – redistribution Legal Reform – Human Rights Taxation Debt relief Terms of Trade	Social Policy Economic Policy Legal Reform Employment legislation	Behaviour change communication	STD treatment
			Condom promotion and marketing	Blood safety Anti-retroviral therapy during pregnancy

Source: Barnett, Whiteside, Decosas, 2000

Figure 1.1: Proximal and distal 'causes' of HIV/AIDS

Figure 1.2 shows there are no simple causal relations between the epidemic and poverty. Botswana with the highest per capita income in Africa has the highest levels of infection. How can this be explained? Part of the answer may lie in the success of economic growth. Rapid economic growth brings its own problems – disruption, deprivation, disease and death. Quick growth disrupts traditional norms as cultures and people cannot adapt to the changes. In addition growth skews income distribution and changes distribution patterns.

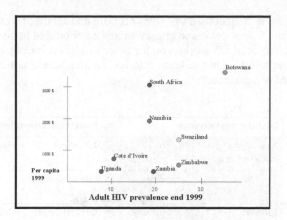

Figure 1.2: Wealth and HIV

But growth alone is not sufficient to explain the spread of the epidemic. There has been little real per capita growth in South Africa since 1994. In that year per capita income stood at R13,786, in 1997 it rose to R14,249 but by 1999 had fallen back to R14,013 (Nicholson, 2001). Yet the epidemic here has spread rapidly. The issue of income distribution is probably as important as economic growth. Although there has been a great deal of work in this area it has tended not to look at the relation between inequality and communicable disease in the developing world and specifically HIV/AIDS.

There is an additional wrinkle to the discussion. Economies may change without affecting the macro-indicators. Again we can look at the example of South Africa. Here the economy has been relatively stagnant in terms of per capita output, although in real terms output has grown. However this disguises fundamental changes in the structure. The primary (agriculture, forestry and mining) and secondary (manufacturing, electricity, gas water and construction) sectors are shrinking as contributors to GDP, while the tertiary sector (all services – banking, insurance, trade and tourism) is growing. This new structure of production has resulted in a real decline in the numbers in formal employment, from 5,576,000 in 1991 to 4,864,000 in 1999 (Nicholson, 2001). The unskilled have been worst affected. This is happening at a time when the economically active population is growing. A similar picture is seen in all African countries: formal employment is declining, informal employment increasing (and the tax base changing).

Of particular concern in South Africa at the moment is the food crisis. Stillwaggon has shown 'that HIV prevalence is highly correlated with falling calorie consumption, falling protein consumption, unequal distribution of income and other variables conventionally associated with susceptibility to infectious disease, however transmitted' (Stillwagon, 2000). The causal chain runs from macro-factors, which result in poverty through the community, household, individual and into the capacity of the individual's immune system. The biological mechanisms, which connect malnutrition and parasite infestation, depress both specific and non-specific immune responses by weakening epithelial integrity and the effectiveness of cells in the immune system. Protein-energy malnutrition, iron deficiency anaemia, vitamin-A deficiency, all poverty related conditions decrease resistance to many diseases, not just HIV.

It is argued by Barnett and Whiteside (Barnett and Whiteside, 2002) that, while crisis may be a major driver of the spread of HIV, it is the transition and the transition process that is the most dangerous period. This includes transition from good to bad (as may be happening in Zimbabwe) as well as from bad to good (as happened with the ending of apartheid in South Africa). The transition may be economic, political or social. Thus when an economy or political system implodes HIV will spread, but when peace returns with reconstruction and development, the behaviours that drive HIV become even more possible.

AIDS as a Crisis Driver

In order to understand how AIDS may be a crisis driver we begin by looking at its demographic impact. Essentially and simply AIDS causes people to fall ill and die and so is both changing the structure of the population and its life expectancy. The majority of HIV/AIDS infections occur in young adults – people who have completed their education and started their families. In South Africa, for example, the highest mortality among women is among those aged 25 to 29 and among men those aged 30 to 34 (Dorrington, Bourne et al.). The result is that in many countries, life expectancy will drop to below 40 years and population structures will change dramatically as is shown in the next two figures.

The social and political consequences of changing population structures across the region have yet to be fully appreciated or understood. However, it is clear that the premature death of so many adults will result in labour shortages – affecting household incomes and welfare, the productive sectors, and the provision of essential services – especially education, health, local administration, justice and security. Household capacity to care for children and older people is also being reduced. Here it is evident that AIDS is a crisis driver.

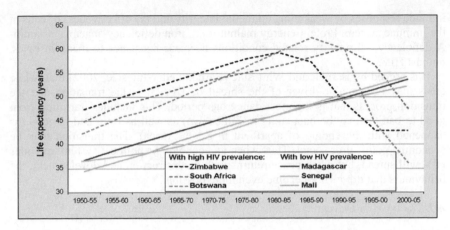

Figure 1.3: Life expectancy, selected African countries with high and low HIV prevalence, 1950–2005

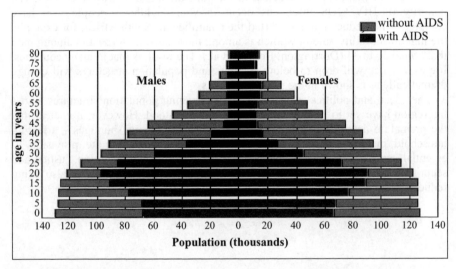

Figure 1.4: Projected population structure with and without the AIDS epidemic, Botswana, 2020

Economic Impact and Agricultural Production

AIDS causes people to be less productive. World Bank economist Rene Bonnel estimates AIDS has reduced Africa's economic growth by 0.8 percent in the 1990s (Bonnel, 2000). HIV/AIDS and malaria combined resulted in a 1.2 percentage point decrease in per capita growth between 1990 and 1995. There are two countries where rigorous analysis has been carried out: South Africa and Botswana (Arndt and

Lewis, 2000; BIDPA, 2000). In Botswana a report on the macroeconomic impacts of HIV/AIDS prepared for the Ministry of Finance and Development Planning, focused on GDP growth and per capita incomes from 1996 to 2021. It predicted GDP growth would fall from 3.9 percent a year without AIDS to between 2.0 percent and 3.1 percent a year with AIDS. After 25 years the economy will be 24 percent to 38 percent smaller. The South African studies suggest that annual GDP growth rates will be between 0.2 and 1.6 percent lower than would have been the case in the absence of AIDS.

It is increasingly recognised that conventional economics misses the complexity and full significance of the epidemic. When the epidemic was in its early stages projections based on scenarios computed 'with AIDS' and 'without AIDS' were reasonable, but such comparisons are no longer valid.

The impact of the disease cannot be treated as an 'exogenous' influence that can be 'tacked on' to models derived on the presumption that the work force is HIV-free. HIV/AIDS has become an 'endogenous' influence on most African countries that has adversely affected their potential for growth and development. In some cases, such as Zambia, Zimbabwe, and the region covering the former Zaire, the spread of HIV/AIDS may have already undermined their ability to recover economically (MacPherson, Hoover et al. 2000).

AIDS has the potential to push economies into decline and then keep them there.

At the company level work released at the XIV International AIDS Conference in Barcelona, Spain, in July 2002 by Rosen et al. (Rosen, MacLeod et al. 2002), provide the best analysis of the impact of AIDS on the private sector in recent years. The authors estimated the cost of AIDS to businesses and the benefits of prevention and treatment using company-specific data on employees, costs, and HIV prevalence for five large enterprises in South Africa and Botswana. This analysis is summarised in Table 1.7. The authors estimated the present value of incident (new) HIV infections with a 9–year median survival time and discount rate of 4 to 10 percent. The costs included sick leave; productivity loss; supervisory time; death, disability, and medical benefits; and turnover.

Table 1.7: Impact of AIDS: results from five South African companies

Sector	Heavy manufacturing	Agribusiness	Mining	Mining	Retail
Workforce size (number of employees)	>25,000	5,000–10,000	<1,000	<1,000	<1,000
Est. HIV prevalence 2002 (percent)	9.9	24.4	33.6	24.1	11.2
Cost per infection by job level (present value, 2001 USD)					
Unskilled/semi-skilled	32,393	4,439	10,732	9,474	4,518

Technician/artisan	50,075	6,772	17,972	14,097	11,422
Supervisor/manager	83,789	18,956	63,271	45,515	24,149
Average cost per infection (multiple of median salary)	4.3	1.1	5.1	2.9	0.9
Liability acquired in 2002 (future cost of incident infections) (percent of payroll)	5.0	2.4	9.4	5.9	0.9
Undiscounted cost of prevalent infections in 2006 (percent of payroll)		4.8	18.1	12.2	1.8

Source: Rosen, et al., 2002

Is there any evidence of the impact of AIDS on people's ability to work, outside of that from the private sector? Here we can turn again to the Afrobarometer data. As a measure of physical health, the survey asked respondents: 'In the last month, how much of the time has your physical health reduced the amount of work you would normally do inside or outside your home?' As a measure of mental health, the Afrobarometer surveys asked respondents: 'In the last month, how much of the time have you felt so worried or anxious that you felt tired, worn out, or exhausted?': the results are discussed in Chapter 8. It is evident that AIDS is beginning to bite into peoples' productive and reproductive capacities.

Responding to AIDS in Crises and Transitions

The idea that AIDS should be high on the agenda during times of crisis and change was first developed in the run up to the March 2002 Presidential election in Zimbabwe. It seemed that Mugabe might either give up power or be toppled. The thinking was that during times of transition, especially from bad to good, HIV/AIDS could be forgotten, but this is precisely when risk increases; responses should be planned; and any responses can have a long term impact. As it happens in Zimbabwe, the election was 'won' by Robert Mugabe and ZANU (PF). But the inevitable political transition has been delayed rather than prevented. At some point in the next few years Zimbabwe will have a new leadership and begin the long, slow and difficult process of rebuilding the nation, economy, society and rule of law. AIDS threatens this and we should be planning now how to deal with the epidemic in and after the crisis.

A transition should be an opportunity to undertake AIDS interventions around both prevention and impact and should be seized with both hands. Such interventions can link with embedding democracy and good governance practices in the country in the post-transition phase. If the response to HIV/AIDS is appropriate then it will, in turn, reinforce democratisation and the building of civil society. Times of transition offer opportunities for AIDS interventions and HIV prevention that have been lacking. In the cases of South Africa, Mozambique and Namibia this opportunity was lost. It should not be missed in future.

It can be argued that many of the successful interventions in Uganda (and increasingly evident in Zambia) were due to the political environment, which followed the taking of power by Museveni in Uganda. Zambia is the other African country where recent data seems to indicate a decline in HIV prevalence, especially among the younger age groups and it may be significant that it has seen the government change through peaceful democratic elections. Re-building civil society through various fora and forms is one of the best ways to respond to the epidemic and as such should be encouraged. The transition in Uganda was one of the major factors, which lead to the control of the AIDS epidemic.

The SADC region has the unenviable position of being the epicentre of the epidemic. It is also a region in crisis. There is currently a security crisis in the DRC and to a lesser extent in Zimbabwe, but this has the potential to escalate. Angola is just emerging from a long running civil war. In much of the region economic growth has stagnated and there seems little prospect of growth in the short term. There is a crisis of governance in that the citizens in the SADC countries have little contact and even less faith in their government's ability to deliver. All this is dramatically amplified by the food crisis. The crises in the region are at least in part due to the HIV/AIDS epidemic and that HIV/AIDS will deepen the crises and make the prospects of recovery remote. Indeed one of the real dangers is that HIV/AIDS interventions in turn have even less chance of success. The overwhelming preoccupation is with economic and social survival. But there is a window of opportunity to respond to HIV/AIDS. In countries in transition or that may undergo transition (such as Zimbabwe), HIV and AIDS must be a priority both for donors and the new government. Governance and democracy can both embed HIV interventions and be embedded by HIV interventions. In countries in crisis, whether the crisis is a single issue such as lack of employment, or multiple such as countries where the government is regarded as illegitimate, or where there is starvation and civil unrest, we need to understand how AIDS is contributing to the crisis; how response to the crises should also respond to AIDS and how long term HIV prevention depends on stability, equality and development. For example in situations of transition there are concrete suggestions as to what can be done. It is to be hoped that the donor community, Ministries of Foreign Affairs, SADC and other pan-African organisations and intelligence organizations of major donor countries are engaging with the opposition parties about their plans for a post-transition government. Actions that might be considered are reviewed below.

HIV/AIDS should be placed on all the agendas; indeed there are a number of crucial players in the field who would be receptive to having this put on their agenda. There should be an AIDS component in all interventions both emergency and long-term that are put in place in the post-transition stage. This means that whatever authorities and committees are being established by the donor community should be charged specifically with looking at the impact of AIDS on the country and how it can be responded to. Given the concealment of the scale of the epidemic and the demoralizing effect this has on a society, immediately after a transition there should be a major campaign to make people and politicians aware of the scale of the problem. Giving the disease a name is absolutely crucial. Where there is a vibrant network of people living with HIV/AIDS this should be engaged with, and should be developed.

AIDS is cutting away at the key people in the country in terms of skills and leadership. There ought to be put in place an emergency process for training up people and making sure that key skills are available. In addition where there have been major outflows of skills consideration could be given to attracting these people to return. Donors should consider an innovative way of providing health care and support to the key people in the country. This might be done through getting nominations as to who should receive scarce resources. If this is done at the community level, then it could be extremely valuable. Not only will key leaders in the community be given the necessary treatment to ensure their continued survival for at least a period but traditionally the community will have come together to make these decisions which is of itself a community building activity.

One of the results of both the transition and the AIDS epidemic will be that there are large numbers of children and orphans who are unsocialised, uncared for, unloved and have very little future. We would see this is as one of the priority interventions for the donor community and we would urge that there be provision of massive training and support and existing orphans support programmes ought to be scaled up as rapidly as possible.

What about AIDS as a cause of crises? Here little has been done, and the first step must be to understand the bi-directional causality. If this is done then the next steps will follow. For example can food aid be of a type that will help people to stay alive longer – i.e. add micro-nutrients. Can we look carefully at how we target our support? The reality is that much of Southern Africa is facing larger problems than at any time in the recent past. It is clear that AIDS has contributed to this and makes recovery difficult in the short term and potentially impossible in the long term, unless its importance is recognised.

References

Arndt, C. and J. D. Lewis (2000). *The Macro Implications of HIV/AIDS in South Africa: A preliminary assessment*. IAEN Conference, the World Bank.

Barnett, T. and A. Whiteside (2002). *AIDS in the Twenty-First Century: Disease and Globalisation*. Basingstoke, Palgrave Macmillan.

BIDPA (2000). *Macroeconomic Impacts of the HIV/AIDS Epidemic in Botswana*. Gaborone, Botswana Institute for Development Policy Analysis.

Bonnel, R. (2000). *HIV/AIDS: Does It Increase or Decrease Growth? What Makes an Economy HIV-Resistant?* International AIDS and Economics Network Symposium, Durban, South Africa.

Bratton, M. and R. Mattes 'Popular Economic Values and Economic Reform in Southern Africa.' *Afrobarometer* Paper No. 10.

Dorrington, R., D. Bourne, et al. 'Some implications of HIV/AIDS on adult mortality in South Africa,.' *AIDS Analysis Africa* 12(5).

Lewis, Stephen (October 4, 2002). *Luncheon Speech to Conference on HIV/AIDS and 'Next Wave' Countries*, UN Special Envoy for HIV/AIDS in Africa at Centre for Strategic and International Studies Washington, DC.

MacPherson, M. F., D. A. Hoover, et al. (2000). *The Impact on Economic Growth in Africa of Rising Costs and Labor Productivity Losses Associated with HIV/AIDS*, Harvard Institute of International Development.

Mandela, N. (2002). *HSRC Study of HIV/AIDS South African National HIV Prevalence, Behavioural Risks and Mass Media Household Survey 2002*. Cape Town, Human Sciences Research Council.

Nicholson, J. (2001). *Measuring Change: South Africa's Economy since 1994*. Durban, South Africa, University of Natal.

Rosen, S., W. MacLeod, et al. (2002). *Investing in the epidemic: The impact of AIDS on businesses in Southern Africa*. Abstract 1505, XIV International Conference on AIDS, Barcelona, Spain.

Stillwagon, E. (2000). 'HIV Transmission in Latin America: Comparison with Africa and Policy Implications.' *South African Journal of Economics* 5(68): 985–1011.

UNDP (2002). *Human Development Report*. Oxford, Oxford University Press.

WFP (September 2002). 'Southern Africa Crisis Worsens: 14.4 million people in dire need', World Food Programme.

World-Bank (2000). *Development Report 2001*. Oxford, Oxford University Press.

World-Bank (2002). *African Development Indicators 2002*. Washington, World Bank.

www.wfp.org.

Chapter 2

Legitimate Actors? The Future Roles for NGOs Against HIV/AIDS in Sub-Saharan Africa

Douglas Webb

Any analysis of the political economy of HIV/AIDS in sub-Saharan Africa will ultimately recognise the crucial role of organisations beyond the government. This wide spectrum of organisations loosely clustered as 'non-governmental organisations' (NGOs), in reality forms an interconnected web of affiliations and sometimes competing agendas. At the lowest scales this web constitutes recognised individuals who may be officially registered in some capacity, through to community based organisations (CBOs), again of varying degrees of organisational complexity and status, through to national and finally international NGOs (INGOs) with operational bases within sub-Saharan Africa.

The 'mushrooming' of national and sub-national NGOs in the past 15 years in response to the epidemic is in itself a large scale behavioural response. While the cooperation of individuals in combating a common external threat is well recognised, the rise of the AIDS related NGOs or AIDS service organisations (ASOs) has been on an unprecedented scale. Arguably no other single issue has galvanised civil society cooperation in so many different contexts on such a scale before. Depending on the mandate of the NGOs under question, their reach and coverage may well exceed that of the state when looking at areas of service provision such as health, welfare and rehabilitation.

But where are NGOs in sub-Saharan Africa headed, given the realisation that the scale of the HIV/AIDS epidemic is overwhelming? The rise of NGOs holds clues as to their future, but challenges within this future are considerable. The rise of NGOs working on HIV/AIDS in Africa is explored here, focusing on the critical determinants of state inaction and neglect, combined with the tenuous accountability, in many contexts, of state actors to their populations. Where governments have been supportive of NGO activity the recognition of the crisis within public sector capacity is central, but historical political factors continue to dominate in most government-NGO relations.

International financial support and the mobilisation of civil society has created an African NGO collective centred on HIV/AIDS. Its overall organisation is in a state of flux, with national NGOs attempting to overcome any lingering divisions to combine into national mutually supportive networks, while INGOs are increasingly forming consortia to respond to donor needs for consolidated funding channels. An exploration of these processes uncovers the weaknesses which remain; the struggle to go to scale with interventions outside of a state infrastructure, and the lack of any real political engagement with both state actors and macro-financial decision making.

The struggle to act at scale has moved INGOs especially into the position as advocates for wider socio-economic and political change and this trend is examined in some detail. Central to this emergent function is the problem of legitimacy. This role cannot be overemphasised and it is arguable that the very future of the NGO role in HIV/AIDS is dependent on this legitimacy; its definition, widespread recognition and ultimately absorption into the body politick of the response to the epidemic itself. It is argued here that this legitimacy rests on the twin pillars of the need to represent a genuine constituency and on the ongoing definition of intervention 'best practice'. The ultimate transfer of ownership of this activism to the African NGO collective has to be the goal but will be extremely difficult, as the complex agenda is riddled with diverse interests and lacks a distinct lobbying force in the south to take it forward independently.

The Rise of NGOs and State Neglect

Many questions surface when addressing the role of NGOs in the political economy of HIV/AIDS. While their proliferation in sub-Saharan Africa is apparent, the causes of this are not initially clear. There are, however, three evident political processes at play. Firstly, the rise of NGOs has been in direct response to the inaction or neglect of the state where a clear mandate to act has been dismissed. Secondly, NGO proliferation has been in response to the absence or limited nature of government credibility with its own constituency, leaving a vacuum of representation at local levels. Finally, and more rarely, governments have encouraged NGO activities in HIV/AIDS.

State neglect can be described in a variety of ways, but is most commonly associated with initial denial then silence from political leaders on the issue.[1] This indifference has not been confined to sub-Saharan Africa – President Clinton has mirrored Presidents Mandela and Kenneth Kaunda by vocalising concerns only after the period of office tenure has finished. The tokenistic budgetary allocations to HIV/AIDS, the piecemeal way in which the public sector has itself addressed the epidemic and the lingering association between AIDS and something which is seen to be inherently 'foreign' are other common signs of neglect. It is not unfair to allege that African governments have not sought to 'own' the response to the epidemic and the lack of responsibility has been wholesale and thorough. At the International Conference on AIDS and STDs in Africa in Lusaka in 1999, for example, not one head of state attended. President Chiluba's opening address to delegates was cancelled due to his attendance at a funeral of one of his ministers. At the beginning of the 21st century little has changed. The indigenously produced New Partnership for Africa's Development (NEPAD) was warmly welcomed in 2002 by donors but only made passing mention to HIV/AIDS, arguably the key development issue on the continent. The newly constituted African Union (2002) was chaired by a South African president, Thabo Mbeki, who himself had demonstrated considerable ambivalence when faced with the fundamentals of the disease.

State Responses: The Crises of Constituency and Capacity

In some sub-Saharan states the indifference of government to the epidemic has reflected its lack of any constituency, or tenuous link with its population, leading to an absence of any definable accountability to those most affected by the pandemic. Countries racked by conflict would be central here, notably Angola, Mozambique (pre-1992), the Great Lakes region and swathes of West Africa such as Liberia, Sierra Leone and Côte d'Ivoire. This problem of state mandate is still a key constraint in many countries and will remain so for an extended period.[2]

Understanding early governmental and NGO responses to the epidemic in apartheid South Africa, for example, is impossible without seeing state and civil society in a violent (but ultimately political) negotiation. Early NGO activity on AIDS in South Africa in the late 1980s and early 1990s was founded in two distinct lobbying groups, the trade unions in the case of the Progressive Primary Health Care Network on the one hand, and the north American style activism of the white gay lobby on the other. The National Party's indifference to the epidemic was replaced in 1994 with the ANC's squeamish attitude to matters sexual. The resultant impasse allowed the epidemic to escalate unhindered in a context dominated by reconciliation and the search for political unity. Post-apartheid donor activity busied itself with reconstruction and the thorny issues associated with a rampant sexually transmitted infection were left well alone. Government endeavours when they were adequately funded in the mid to late 1990s floundered in accusations of incompetence and corruption. As a result, the political struggle for democratisation has been replaced with a struggle to engage community activism with combating rampant sexual violence, social dislocation and ultimately HIV/AIDS itself. The highest profile (and often controversial) of these efforts is the NGO LoveLife initiative, itself grounded on considerable North American funding.

Government 'inaction' is intertwined with the prevalent and growing crisis of public sector capacity in southern Africa. Rapid public sector contraction, best described in the cases of education and health, has itself been nurtured by ongoing, macro-economic crisis. Resources connected with debt repayments still flow from the south to the north, away from the development of preventative services, while privatisation of those very same state services often means that poor people cannot afford to access them even where they do exist. Although some debt cancellation is happening, the burden of servicing debt continues seriously to hamper the abilities of these countries to respond to the epidemic. For example, an estimated 21 per cent of Zambian adults are HIV positive in 2002 yet Zambia is spending 30 per cent more on debt than on health. The Government of Malawi plans to allocate around $2.40 of domestic resources per head of population to its national HIV/AIDS strategic plan. Yet, in 2002 it transferred almost $5 per head to creditors in debt payments. Fully 13 of the 26 countries receiving debt relief are still spending more on debt than on public health.[3]

The State as Host: NGO and Government Cooperation

In other contexts the rise of NGOs relates to the active encouragement of the state. Histories of the epidemic to date in Uganda and to a lesser extent Senegal, for example, tell the story of political openness (and subsequently openness within social discourse) and nurturing of a civil society response, eagerly fostered by concerned donors. The honey pot which was Uganda to donors in the mid to late 1980s and early 1990s saw at the time the highest HIV prevalence rates in the world. While the relationship between declining HIV prevalence since 1992 and the activities of NGOs remains a point of debate, analysts concede that a critical factor in the success was a government aware of the problem as well as its own limitations, combined with the willingness of President Museveni to adopt the response to the epidemic as a personal crusade. Uganda remains the cradle of maturing NGO responses to the epidemic, developing and innovating models of community based dialogue, destigmatisation, care and support which are appropriate across sub-Saharan Africa, and this is in no small part due to the courageous leadership shown by the president. This leadership has been, however, largely and sadly absent from the continent, except where finances allow for such a response, as is arguably the case in Botswana. The fact that 13 countries in sub-Saharan Africa currently have the national AIDS commission/council chaired by either the president or a senior deputy is encouraging, but real multi-sectoral responses within governments are less easy to identify.[4]

The growing realisation in the international community of the incapacity and subtle disinterest of the African state has no doubt fuelled the growth of the NGO sector. Aware of this, governments have rhetorically embraced (rather than actively supported) NGO functioning in recent years. The widespread support given to NGOs by donors has been a constant source of tension within key government ministries. Many donors, accountable to foreign constituents rather than the people or governments of beneficiary countries, have often favoured expediency in the form of direct partnerships with NGOs (the US Agency for International Development being the key example). While this makes sense regarding financial accountability, government coffers and plans remain largely under-funded. The solution may well lie in the increasing viability of states sub-contracting NGOs using donor dollars. This maintains a veneer of central control for government while bypassing the crisis of public sector capacity. Its long-term sustainability, however, lies in the support that NGOs can provide government rather than vice versa, and the development of NGO capacity must not be at the expense of that within government and public sector ranks.

Where state and NGO relationships remain fragile, as in parts of southern Africa, this state acceptance of NGOs has been delayed by a lingering association between NGOs and anti-state activism; a legacy from the 30 years of struggle for regional political independence. The evolution of the Southern African Development Coordination Conference (SADCC) into the Southern African Development Community (SADC) in the early 1990s and the later development of the Organisation of African Unity (OAU) into the African Union has signified a dramatic shift in the African political landscape. The urgency to realise post-colonial political unity (and transform apartheid South Africa and Namibia) has been replaced with a collective engagement in developmental aims. This in turn has freed civil society to organise itself towards causes which are themselves not overtly political. HIV/AIDS has become one of the principal rallying points, intertwined with activism related to human rights, gender equality, access to services and the needs of families and individuals directly affected by the disease. The critical role played by mission hospitals in galvanising this response is recognised (such as the Salvation Army hospital at Chikankata in southern Zambia), but it was not until the establishment and formal recognition of secular AIDS focused NGOs, led by The AIDS Service Organisation (TASO) in Uganda from 1986, that the potential for a widespread and relevant NGO response was evident. The crucial ability of NGOs to mobilise communities and foster interpersonal dialogue is now gaining recognition in epidemiological analyses.[5] This role, arguably, is beyond the capacities and reach of the state, necessitating an organised but locally-focused civil society response. NGOs increasingly mirror democratisation at lower geographical scales through their work with communities, emphasising citizen participation and responsibility, within a wider struggle for equity and social justice.

NGOs as Specialist but Team Players

In appraising the roles of NGOs at the start of the third decade of the epidemic there are some major challenges to overcome. The first concerns the way that the rapidly expanding number of NGOs organise themselves, in an environment where increased specialisation and consortia development are becoming the dominant trends. NGOs working on AIDS are each under pressure to differentiate themselves from other actors, through defining their 'comparative advantage', while at the same time being coerced into forming strategic affiliations by donors looking to disburse larger and fewer grants.

While the initial responses of NGOs centred on a witnessing and support role of those directly affected by HIV/AIDS, the overall mandate has arguably moved on. There is a stratification process evident where welfare-based CBOs and NGOs continue to directly support small to medium numbers of people with HIV prevention and basic care, while larger organisations have started to address political and policy responses to the epidemic. This division of roles has led to both an increased diversity of specialisms and a bewildering complexity within the NGO response. Realising that the coverage of this existing response is low and predominantly urban centric, combined with the indifference of the state as described above, NGOs have had to reappraise their roles if impact at any appreciable scale is to be realised. This challenge of scale has resulted in two key processes. Firstly, the establishment of ASO networks at national and regional scales has allowed NGOs to coalesce, if not operationally, but certainly in terms of (1) solidarity towards a common cause, (2) a critical mass to allow representation at political or lobbying levels, such as the UN Theme Groups on AIDS, and (3) a mechanism to exchange experiences and share learnings, most often through national level conferencing. National AIDS networks exist now in most countries in sub-Saharan Africa, with regional grouping also emerging, notably the Southern African Network of AIDS Service Organisations (SANASO). The potential of these networks as political entities remains unfulfilled however, as the divergent concerns of members, combined with a lack of investment in high level management and infrastructure has prevented a consistent, forceful and persuasive presence at the policy table.

The second process consists of INGOs forming consortia in operational and funding terms. An example of this new trend in HIV/AIDS interventions is the Hope for African Children Initiative (HACI). This privately funded initiative, started in 2000, consists of six separate international agencies; Plan International, Care International, the World Conference for Religion and Peace, the International Save the Children Alliance, World Vision and the Society for Women Against AIDS (SWAA). While such alliances facilitate the disbursement of ever-larger amounts of donor money, the challenge of scale remains critical, as better coordination in itself does not necessarily imply a greater coverage of programmes. The tendency of donors such as USAID and the British Department For International Development (DFID) to seek NGO consortia funding relationships represents a desire to encourage NGO consolidation into a viable and large scale alternative to government as primary grant recipients. The funding behaviours of donors, however, are likely to remain unpredictable as long as they are caught between pressures to develop government capacities at the same time as fostering a structured civil society response to the pandemic. NGOs, while becoming adept at second guessing the intentions of donors, need to present themselves as supporters of the national, (state defined) responses while being core to the empowering of civil society responsibility which African governments have traditionally been keen to suppress.

NGOs as Advocates and the Search for Legitimacy

The emergence of the advocacy role of NGOs has been dramatic in recent years and worthy here of some attention. There are three strands to this advocacy, which together constitute the search for legitimacy: (1) the representation of minority groups within a larger and nebulous civil society, (2) the articulation of good/best practices in HIV prevention and HIV/AIDS care, and (3) developing activism beyond a pre-existing, northern dominated, human rights agenda.

Representing the Marginalised?

Do NGOs represent those vulnerable and affected by HIV/AIDS? AIDS is a condition of the marginalised, feeding off discrimination and inequality. This is now recognised as a truism at all geographical scales including the global, with sub-Saharan Africa the marginalised continent in the global economy.

NGOs are in the dual position of serving while representing these marginalised groups. These can be (vulnerable) children, women, widows, the elderly, the sick, the destitute, the abandoned, those impacted by natural calamity or those experiencing any one of a multitude of forms of discrimination. NGOs representing the rights of children have an additional claim to legitimacy in that children as minors are excluded from democratic processes. While democratic principles do not literally apply in the case of NGO function, they are implicit within this dual service delivery and representative role and the links with processes of democratisation are clear. Representation of the marginalised to demand better services, education, information, livelihood options, condoms etc, is a political act that implicitly both challenges and complements the state authority and function. Where democratic processes have either broken down or are very fragile, state actors are not accountable to their constituents, and a void is created where interests are pursued through other means. State inaction in the face of AIDS has necessitated the empowerment of an alternative and representative group, partly as a result of failures within democratisation. While NGOs strive to fulfil this role, politically strengthening through forming national and international associations and networks, the development of a 'constituency' on which their claim to legitimacy depends, still remains tenuous. While representation of constituency is under dispute, the voices of NGOs can be effectively mute as a result. INGOs, conscious of the importance of the place of advocacy within their own profile (and hence maintenance of a financial support base), increasingly seek out media attention and associated opportunities to put across a message. Whilst committed policy makers within governments welcome genuine and considered contributions to policy debate, INGOs need to be careful not to equate 'profile' with their degree of influence within such debates.

Seeking structural change implies more than designing and effecting 'projects', which are the traditional staple of medium and small size NGOs. The deliberate move towards advocacy has meant deliberate politicisation. For NGOs, advocacy has been defined as;

> The strategic use of information to democratise unequal power relations and to improve the conditions of those living in poverty or who are discriminated against. Advocacy may therefore include direct lobbying, public campaigning, public education, capacity building and creating alliances in order to achieve desired changes in people's lives.[6]

The search for legitimacy outside of any democratic process becomes problematic, and the claim shifts to representation through processes of mobilisation of a 'community' or in effect, a self contained constituency. Precedents from North America and Europe from the 1980s onwards concerned the representation and galvanising of the gay community, and AIDS issues naturally fitted within a pre-existing gay rights agenda. Even today, the northern NGOs' attention on access to treatments has its roots within earlier activism related to accessing AZT in the late 1980s.

Challenges now in North America (and arguably parts of Western Europe) relate to the civil society representation of a much larger group, the heterosexual black and Hispanic population where HIV has taken hold. In the developing world, such a ready-made, self-identified constituency akin to the gay movement simply does not exist. CBOs and NGOs have instead had to seek constituency in small geographically defined areas (such as hospital catchments, villages or sub-urban districts) or more commonly the especially vulnerable within those areas, such as widows, orphans, migrant workers, out of school youth and sex workers. This trend is extreme in some contexts, such as in Maputo, Mozambique, where in the late 1990s, 26 separate NGOs were catering for the needs of fewer than 1,000 street children.[7]

Realising that legitimacy depends on engagement, NGOs have pioneered methods of community mobilisation in HIV prevention and care work, producing manuals and handbooks, and treating target group engagement as a development sub-discipline in itself. While principles of mobilisation have been well known in terms of agricultural extension and drought mitigation, and qualitative methods have been adapted from market research techniques, the surge in their application to issues of sexual health was initially limited to family planning promotion. More recently, mobilisation around improving gender relations, challenging risky sexual mores and gender-based violence has been spurred directly by the advent of the HIV/AIDS pandemic. Recognising the practical implications of beneficiary consultation and the related endorsement of project design, NGOs have subliminally exploited this connection in the pursuit of legitimacy. Cynical exploitation of this process has resulted in the phenomenon of 'briefcase NGOs' where donors are duped into supporting an institution which is sometimes no more than a legal façade. While this is an inevitable by-product of a donor-supported process, improving means of accountability between donors and locally based NGOs will hopefully keep cases of fraud to a minimum. As the legitimate process of advocacy develops, resources are increasingly being switched from 'projects' to the building of 'capacity', networks, 'resiliency'[8] and momentum, and away from concrete outputs, on which NGO activity used largely to be judged.[9] Intended beneficiaries of these processes may in the short term fail to see concrete changes, and INGOs in particular must better communicate to beneficiary groups the principles underlying their work – long term empowerment resulting in sustained and wide scale changes. The 'project' approach towards HIV prevention and care adopted by NGOs is being questioned by those frustrated by evident lack of impacts at any scale, and instead move to questions of governance, state accountability, and engagement of civil society in political change.

This attempted representation by national and sub-national NGOs of constituents of populations at risk is recognised by some, but not all. Implicit support comes from donors and INGOs who are investing increasing amounts of resources in the development of a strong and independent national NGO profile. At the same time, the Joint United Nations Programme on AIDS (UNAIDS) and the cosponsoring UN agencies are now calling overtly for more NGO engagement in policy dialogue. UNAIDS has NGOs sitting on its Programme Coordinating Board as both members and observers, and Kofi Annan's ushering of NGOs to the policy table, most markedly at the UN General Assembly Special Session on HIV/AIDS in June 2001, has set the tone for improved NGO relations with the UN.[10] The benefits of this are mutually recognised if never mentioned explicitly. For the NGO collective, entry points into international policy discussion and thus their potential influence are clearer-cut and more numerous, while for the UN, so often shackled by the wishes and whims of member governments, an alternative mouthpiece in the form of NGOs can drive forward a mutually beneficial agenda. The UN's recognition of this is unequivocal:

> A strong civil society flourishes in an environment in which the State allows for such nongovernmental organization participation. In an activist mode, civil society organizations must be empowered by law and daily practice to organize, publish and collect information, while having legal recourse to the courts and, if necessary the option to demonstrate. As active participants in policy and programming design and implementation, they must be at the table, right from the beginning.[11]

This shifting and delicate consensus is now often contained and represented through rights-based conventions and statements of commitment, most notably now the UN Declaration of Commitment on HIV/AIDS (2001). At the same time, NGOs are free to operate in areas beyond UN mandate (such as some conflict zones) where the UN is reliant on partnerships with NGOs to have any operational, albeit indirect, presence.

As bilateral donors and, increasingly, charitable foundations and the UN, encourage the expansion of the NGO sector through political support and most crucially ever larger funding agreements, their legitimacy is most challenged through the actions (rather than the words) of governments within countries most affected by HIV/AIDS. While overt accusations of subversion are confined to countries where democratisation processes are failing the most (such as Zimbabwe), the relationship between NGOs and African governments is most often mediated by external institutional actors rather than being direct. In HIV/AIDS policy dialogue, national and regional AIDS conferences provide useful fora for dialogue but not decision making, as the real decision makers (ministries of finance and planning) are not there. The freeing of resources for state services and HIV prevention is possible within the ongoing poverty reduction strategy processes, but these potential allocations are small (ten countries have budgeted five per cent of their debt savings for AIDS activities[12]) and the continued absence of ministers of finance and their delegations from critical fora and discussions on AIDS mean that the converted continue to talk to themselves. The UNAIDS-designed process of developing the National Strategic Framework on AIDS at national level mandates government to consult with NGOs but this dialogue occurs once every four years and annually at best. The inclusion of NGO representation on national level UN Theme Groups on AIDS is optional and sporadic, and recent analyses of the involvement of NGOs on the Country Coordination Mechanisms of the Global Fund to Fight AIDS, TB and Malaria suggests that consultation has generally been no more than tokenistic.[13]

At the Cutting Edge: NGOs, 'Best Practice' and Technical Legitimacy

Politically excluded at national level, but gaining credence internationally, NGOs have had to depend increasingly on technical legitimacy for their influencing. In reality, this entails the ability of NGOs to engage in the process of 'best practice' articulation. The meaning of the term 'best practice' is unclear, as is the reason why the term has shot to prominence within HIV/AIDS discussions so quickly. One possible explanation is that 'best practice' is seen as a means of addressing the lack of consistency or quality control in monitoring and evaluating HIV/AIDS interventions. This in turn relates to the overall lack of institutional accountability within responses to the pandemic. A signpost pointing to 'best practice' is, also, immediately attractive, but there is a growing tension between and within NGOs to meet the standards of 'best practice', arguably at the expense of what may be 'good' or 'effective' practice.

UNAIDS sees one of its main tasks as identifying 'best practice' projects and examining how and why they work. UNAIDS claim that 'best practice is not reserved only for 'ultimate truths' or 'gold standards'.[14] For UNAIDS, best practice means accumulating and applying knowledge about what is and what is not working in different situations and contexts. 'In other words, it is both the lessons learned and the continuing process of learning, feedback, reflection and analysis. At its most basic, best practice suggests a simple maxim: "Don't re-invent the wheel: learn in order to improve it, and adapt to your terrain to make it work better".' UNAIDS summarises the best practice process as the means to 'identify and describe the lessons learned and the keys to success of any given project, programme or policy'. Best practice submissions come from a variety of sources. These include UN system staff, NGOs, government representatives and agencies, community groups, individuals, small and mass media. Submissions usually arrive in the form of electronic files, often with supporting documents. Others are handwritten and come from non-governmental, community organisations and independent researchers. Some are gleaned from journals, project reports, even newspapers and magazines. Some have been accepted for publication almost verbatim, including some better-known projects that are often *held up* as examples of best practice. 'Surprisingly few have been rejected outright, probably because almost all efforts to respond to the epidemic have something to teach us.' Recognising that this novel approach could invite criticism, UNAIDS explains:

> While some of the practices have been the subject of formal evaluation processes, most have not. This may seem odd in a publication devoted to best practice, but there is a reason for it that is based solidly in the reality of the HIV/AIDS epidemic. Formal evaluation of the kind practised by academic and government institutions is often a slow, complicated and expensive process that can take more professional time and cost more than the actual process being evaluated. The majority of practices detailed in this summary were orientated towards action rather than methodological purity. Many were formed by grassroots organizations and individuals, few of which have the resources or in-house expertise for formal evaluation.

But the explanation of best practice (and ultimately the blueprint for intervention design) given by UNAIDS is problematic. While correctly pointing out the reality of interventions in resource poor settings, there is still an evident ambivalence towards quality control in assessing the efficacy of interventions. Even where an intervention is conducted in a resource-poor setting, this does not imply that assessments of efficacy should be necessarily different in a qualitative sense. This leads to an assumption or acceptance that something is 'best' if it is informed by previous experience and contributes to further learning. While this reflective process remains important, the subjective use of the term 'best' devalues it and obscures the ultimate collective aim of interventions, i.e. a process leading to permanent zero HIV incidence (in any one context).

NGOs faced with imported standards associated with the articulation and implementation of best practices have experienced some key associated but unforeseen problems. This subtle pressure may actually militate against effective responses to HIV/AIDS prevention and care. The reliance upon physical documentation within the learning (and accountability) process derives more from western-centric concepts of knowledge acquisition and sharing, in contrast to more traditional oral methods of knowledge aggregation, analysis and transfer. The latter would implicitly be the *modus operandi* of most community based organisations (CBOs) and smaller NGOs in sub-Saharan Africa, resulting in a widespread lack of appreciation within CB/NGOs of the need for documentation, combined with a lack of basic skills in their production to externally defined standards of acceptability. As a consequence, documentation and reporting remains the greatest source of angst within NGO-donor partnerships.

As the body of knowledge of 'what works' grows, the pressure on donors to avoid funding projects with little or no impact increases. Smaller NGOs are thus under increasing pressure to justify high-quality, sustainable, cost-effective programmes by conducting expensive and time-consuming evaluations. Small and medium size NGOs often enter into agreements with donors with a certain degree of ambivalence if stringent reporting is required. CAFOD, for example, reports that the push for greater accountability is adversely affecting their relationship with partners – often long term relationships built on principles of solidarity and mutual trust.[15] Pressure from donors on Zambian NGOs is also reported to be increasing, creating concern that resources may be diverted from education and care work into impact assessment, research and evaluation.

Yet there remains uncertainty as to what information is required for evaluations, who should produce it and how, and perhaps most importantly, who should pay for it. The resulting paradox is that there is more and more need for information on effective responses to the epidemic, aggregated to a mythical collection of best practices, but the source of this information lies within institutions with little or no capacity or interest for research and documentation. When the *raison d'etre* of so many smaller CB/NGOs is the need for urgent, welfare-based responses to an unprecedented epidemic, the priority accorded to diligent reporting is unsurprisingly low.

This fact is well known to the INGOs who have strategically started to dabble with advocacy in the national and international arena regarding HIV/AIDS. The desire to engage, with the maximum degree of legitimacy, has been hampered not so much by the need to represent a constituency, but by the absence of evidence. While at large scales, INGOs mention their constituents in terms of the 'poor', 'those affected by HIV/AIDS'[16], 'the disenfranchised', 'older people'[17], 'patients' and the even more nebulous 'orphans and vulnerable children'[18], the argument often fails on the lack of evidence rather than the vagaries within the definitions of the subjects. This lack of evidence of what constitutes an effective intervention, or analysis regarding the impacts of national policies, stems from another crisis alluded to above, that of information itself. Intuition has played a greater role than hard evidence in the development of HIV/AIDS interventions in sub-Saharan Africa, as the monitoring and evaluation, research and analytical capacities have remained under-nurtured and seen to be secondary to imported research capacity, most notably from North America. While some INGOs are trying to reverse this trend of under-investment, such as Family Health International and the International HIV/AIDS Alliance, the continued dominance of external academic institutions, most often engaged on a consultancy basis, exemplifies the ongoing crisis of capacity within NGOs and African universities north of the Limpopo. Institutional centres of capacity within sub-Saharan Africa, such as the Regional AIDS Training Network in Nairobi, the Harare-based Southern African AIDS Training Programme, and the coordination role of the African Council of AIDS Service Organisations (AfricASO) in Dakar, will, over time, become crucial to filling the capacity gap of African

NGOs. The irony within the capacity crisis is that much indigenous talent is recruited for international service by INGOs and the UN system, who themselves seek 'local' knowledge to increase their own legitimacy as well as reap the benefits of the Africa based experience.[19]

Activism and Advocacy from within Africa

Efforts to generate an indigenous and rigorous knowledge base in sub-Saharan Africa are underway and this is to be welcomed. INGO investment in the capacities of their own staff, as well as in partner organisations and public sector personnel, are becoming a common feature of programming, often under the guise of 'mainstreaming'.[20] This will be have to be a long term investment, not only because the base point is so low, but that AIDS continues to ravage the very institutions that are mandated or committed to respond. Investment in research and evaluation capacities will, however, take some time to provide the knowledge base that is so desperately needed. Possibly as a consequence of this, some INGOs are forced to rely on a secondary evidence base consisting of previously published reports rather than direct from local experience and knowledge. Issues of most concern have been access to (anti-retroviral) treatments, the structure and operations of the Global Fund to Fight AIDS, TB and Malaria, negotiations relating to the Trade-Related aspects of Intellectual Property Rights (TRIPs), behaviours of the private (especially the pharmaceutical) sector,[21] World Bank led poverty reduction strategies and other macro-funding behaviours of the G8. While the issues addressed are of global relevance, the alluded to constituency of sub-Saharan Africa and its inhabitants is often explicit but rarely directly challenged.

External representation on the international policy agenda is the norm due to the lack of an organised counterpart of the south, representing the south. A key challenge for the northern-based INGOs within this international advocacy process is thus garnering a relationship with NGOs in the south to the extent that claims for legitimacy, built on the twin pillars of representation and evidence base, are actually real. This has been difficult beyond immediate funding relationships and genuine representation based on a shared advocacy agenda is rare. For example, representatives of the UK Consortium on AIDS and International Development met with southern NGO representatives at the International Conference on AIDS and STDs in Africa (ICASA) in Burkina Faso in 2001 with the explicit aim of forging working relationships in support of a UK based awareness raising campaign. The failure to achieve this was based on different agendas and confusion of funding relationships within such an agreement. Representation is difficult within Africa also; at an INGO co-sponsored international workshop in Namibia, in late 2002, of 20 country teams planning responses to the impacts of AIDS on children, there was not one child present.

An additional limitation on African NGO activism is that the 'independence' of NGOs is not always possible to maintain when funding relationships with bilateral donors remain so crucial to both international and African NGO existence. This is even more pertinent in the case of private sector donations. Indirect affiliation through funding binds, however subtly, any NGO to the political profile and (commercial) agenda of the donor. In extreme cases, NGOs can be little more than covert actors in executing a governmental foreign policy, or expanding/maintaining a market position. Any loss of independence on the part of an NGO inevitably questions the legitimacy of their claim, emphasising the critical need to be seen to be in an empathetic tie with the beneficiaries, 'target group' or indeed 'constituents'. NGOs of the south are financially dependent on the north, and this can only hamper the development of a truly independent, activist, southern collective.

Southern-based activism akin to organised responses in the north is almost entirely absent. Where it does exist, the institutions and individuals concerned are often over-exposed and held up to be representative (with little evidence for this) of a much wider movement. The high levels of international attention received by the Treatment Action Campaign and the activism centred around Nkosi Johnson in South Africa, are testament to the fact that genuine and organised activism around AIDS in sub-Saharan Africa is minimal. While information orientated pressure groups do exist, such as the Harare based Southern African AIDS Information Dissemination Service (SAfAIDS), direct 'confrontation' with governments north of the Limpopo is rare. Northern INGOs, seeking legitimacy both within sub-Saharan Africa and the international policy arena, need to find ways to facilitate and harness the considerable degree of experience, concern and genuine anger which is evident within Africa-based civil society organisations, perhaps most crucially within the Network of African People living with AIDS (NAP+) and its national branches. While accusations of tokenism and spats of friction with governments may ensue in some cases, it is clearly the emerging role of NGOs, in seeking structural changes, to empower those most marginalised, both despite, and in spite of, the evident failings of democratisation.

Conclusion

The central place of NGOs within the response to HIV/AIDS in sub-Saharan Africa is not in dispute. State incapacity and indifference has created a void of service provision and meaningful societal engagement. The aim of a coordinated response at national level with government providing an enabling policy environment for NGO function is possible and arguably most realised in Uganda. As this complementarity evolves at different speeds in different countries, the onus on NGOs to define their roles in terms of their capacities and technical niches has never been greater, given their surge in numbers and their increasingly complex relationship with state actors. The skills of NGOs to do this are limited, however, and expertise in information management and communications are perhaps most crucially limited. INGOs must play a role here, at the same time galvanising a collective and representative voice which has legitimacy at the national and international levels in policy debates. As INGOs themselves take this challenge on board, the quest for legitimacy, based on representation and evidence, will determine their success or otherwise in influencing. One of the by-products of the globalisation debates has been a crystallisation of who the key global institutional players are in the response to the HIV/AIDS pandemic, both in sub-Saharan Africa and beyond. NGOs know who they are, and in this post-Seattle world, the knocks on the doors are getting louder.

Notes

1   This denial was described early on the epidemic – a good review being Renee Sabatier's *Blaming Others*, written in 1988 with Panos.
2   See *HIV and conflict: a double emergency*, Save the Children, 2002, and *Combat AIDS; HIV and the World's Armed Forces* Healthlink International/Panos, 2002, London.
3   Data compiled in the *Stop AIDS Campaign Briefing Paper*, UK Consortium on AIDS and International Development, October 2002.
4   UNAIDS (2002) *Report on the global HIV/AIDS epidemic*, Geneva.
5   Stoneburger, R., Low-Beer, D., Barnet, T., Whiteside, A. (2002) *Enhancing HIV prevention in Africa: Investigating the role of social cohesion on knowledge diffusion and behaviour change in Uganda*, unpublished paper.
6   Roche, C. (1999) *Impact Assessment for Development Agencies: Learning to Value Change*, Oxfam, p. 192.
7   From authors' own research with UNICEF Mozambique, 1998.
8   Mallmann, S.A. (2002) *Building resiliency among children affected by HIV/AIDS*, Catholic AIDS Action, Windhoek, Namibia.
9   See Michael Edwards' *Future Positive; International Cooperation in the 21st Century* (Earthscan, London, 1999) for an in-depth look at the broader role of NGOs and civil society engagement.
10 For example, see the UN Non-Governmental Liaison Service (2001) *Voices from Africa 10; NGO Responses to HIV/AIDS*, Geneva.
11 UNAIDS (2002) op cit. p. 179.
12 UNAIDS (2002) op cit.
13 International HIV/AIDS Alliance (2002) *NGO Participation in the Global Fund*, review paper, October 2002, Brighton.
14 UNAIDS (2000) *Summary booklet of best practices*, Issue 2, UNAIDS, Geneva. Following quotes come from this document also.
15 Webb, D., Elliott, L. (2000) *Learning to Live; monitoring and evaluating HIV/AIDS programmes for young people*, Save the Children UK, London.
16 Grainger, C., Webb, D., Elliott, L. (2001) *Children Affected by HIV/AIDS: Rights and responses in the developing world*, Save the Children UK, Working paper no. 23, London.
17 HelpAge International (n.d.) *Ageing Issues in Africa: A Summary*, London.
18 International HIV/AIDS Alliance and Family AIDS Caring Trust (2002) *Expanding Community Based Support for Orphans and Vulnerable Children*, Brighton.
19 This represents a difficult dilemma for INGOs and the UN who are fully aware of the paradox it creates regarding institutional capacity within Africa. As one senior UNAIDS official remarked to me when we discussed this 'you are damned if you do and you are damned if you don't'.
20 Holden, S. (2002) *Development Work in a time of AIDS: the Challenge of Mainstreaming AIDS in Development and Humanitarian Programmes* (working title), Oxfam publications, forthcoming.
21 Voluntary Services Overseas (2002) *Street Price; making medicines affordable for poor countries*, VSO position paper, London.

Chapter 3

Confronting AIDS with Debt: Africa's Silent Crisis

Nana K. Poku

In less than a generation, HIV has become one of the leading killers on the African continent, but its long-term impacts on the continent's already fragile development capacity threatens to be particularly devastating. In both men and women, the virus is impacting heaviest on the most productive sectors of African economies – prime-aged adults – robbing these already besieged economies of scarce skills, children of their parents and a continent of a generation in the prime of their working lives (Poku 2002; Whiteside 2002). Crucially, these losses – in both human capital and intergeneration knowledge – are taking place against a background of declining economic capabilities with its related structural indebtedness; weak states with their deteriorating infrastructures; and societies already reeling from two decades of adjustment pressures. Herein lies Africa's predicament: on the one hand, how to respond effectively to the multiple demands of HIV/AIDS, whilst on the other, struggling with a debt overhang which is undermining investments in social welfare. In what follows, I will argue that any effective engagement with HIV/AIDS in Africa must simultaneously engage with the continent's economic decline, if it is to be effective and sustainable.

AIDS in the Context of Economic Retrogression

The latest economic indicators from the African Development Report 2002 underline the extent of the continent's economic decline. The Report's celebrated headline growth of 3.5 per cent in Gross Domestic Product (GDP) in 2002 compared to 3.2 per cent in 2001, belies the systematic decline observable in real per capital GDP growth from 1.0 per cent to 0.8 per cent in the same period – see Figure 3.1 (ADB 2002). In developmental terms, this means that the combined economies of Africa actually shrunk by 0.2 per cent in the 12 months up to the end of 2002. To put this in context, all other regions are already outperforming Africa, and efforts to redress this poor performance over the past two decades have not been successful – see Table 3.2. In 2002, for example, the average Gross National Product (GNP) per capita in the Organisation for Economic Co-operation and Development (OECD) countries was $28,086, compared with $528 in Africa. This means that the industrialised countries are roughly 51 times wealthier than African states. Assuming that the OECD countries could stop stretching this development gap further, and hoping that African economies could grow at an annual rate of 3.5 per

33

cent over the coming years, it would take the continent some 135 years to reach today's level of wealth enjoyed by OECD countries.

The scale of the continent's economic decline is brought into even sharper focus by looking at the latest indicators from the United Nations Development Programme (UNDP). According to this data, some 80 per cent of the low human development countries – these are countries with high population growth rates, low income, low literacy, and low life expectancy – in 2002, are located in Africa (UNDP 2002). There are only eleven African countries in the middle category – Algeria, Botswana, Egypt, Gabon, Libya, Mauritius, Morocco, Seychelles, Swaziland and South Africa; five of which have a combined population of just 4.6 million – Mauritius, Seychelles, Botswana, Gabon and Swaziland. The remaining 41 countries on the continent are in the low human development category. This, however, does not tell the entire story. There are 55 countries in this category, which means African countries account for 85 per cent of the category. Even more telling, is that, of the 30 countries with the lowest human development indices, 26 (or 89 per cent) are African. Not surprisingly, poverty has increased at a faster rate on the continent than anywhere else in the world. With a fifth of the world population, the continent is home to one in three poor persons in the world (World Bank 2002) and four of every ten of its inhabitants living in what the World Bank classifies as 'a condition of absolute poverty.' More worrying still, Africa is the only region in the world where both the absolute number and the proportion of poor people are expected to increase during this millennium (UNDP 2000).

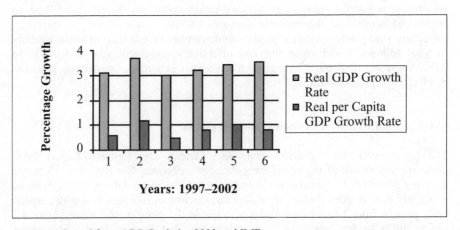

Source: Adopted from ADB Statistics 2002 and IMF

Figure 3.1: Economic indicators in Africa, 1997–2002

The report also highlights a number of equally depressing statistics about the general state of the continent. Take for example, the continental situation with respect to health, food, nutrition and education. The percentages of the population having access to health services, safe water and sanitation are 59, 45 and 31, respectively;

and average calorie supply per capita is only 92 per cent of the daily requirement of the World Health Organisation (WHO). In the sphere of education, only 49 per cent of adults can read and write while the enrolment ratio for all levels is 35 per cent, suggesting a very low level of human capital formation. Critical as the general situation is, it is even worse for children and women. The mortality rates for infants (under twelve months) and children (under five years) are, at 101 and 160 respectively, again the highest of all regions in the world. The percentages of children who are underweight, wasted and stunted are 31, 13 and 44 respectively. Trained medical personnel attend only 40 per cent of births and only 49 per cent of one-year-olds are fully immunized. The literacy rate of women is only 60 per cent of that of men and the corresponding figure for mean years of schooling is 40 per cent that of men. Similarly, the gaps in school enrolment are also wide, the figures being 85 per cent, 67 per cent and 35 per cent for primary, secondary and tertiary level education, respectively. While the life expectancy of women is higher than that of men, other indicators of health are biased against women. Maternal mortality rate is 700 per 100,000 live births, and only 64 per cent of women get prenatal care (UNDP 1999a). There have also been reversals in school enrolment ratios and increases in school dropout rates relative to the appreciable gains made in the 1960s and 1970s.

Beyond this general depiction of Africa's economic retrogression and decline lies an unfolding story of human misery. If we remove territorial boundaries from our cognitive map, we are left with the picture of people across the African continent attempting to pursue basic subsistence within the hostile and unpredictable environment of the national and global economies. Households are attempting to secure these basic needs in conditions of extreme adversity, as governments and state managers either fail to, or are unable to, pursue policies that will increase the human security of their citizens. Indeed, in the process of globalisation, Africa has simply been left behind, in terms of any of the spoils of the process. Moreover, many of the features of modern societies, which Africans have been exposed to are withering: trucks no longer run because there are no spare parts and roads have become impassable due to degradation and neglect. A recent World Bank report described the continent's predicament in the following way:

> Many institutions are deteriorating, both in physical and in their technical and financial ability to perform efficiently. although the picture varies from country to country, even those with good [development] records in the 1970s and 1980s are now facing serious difficulties. In short, the economic and social transformation of Africa, begun so eagerly and effectively in the early years of independence, are now being halted and reversed.

Any account of the continent's condition must attempt to unravel what is cause and what is effect. It is precisely at the level of interpretation, however, that one must be careful not to resort to simplistic causalities or reduce its plight to a series of causal or tautological clichés, most of which carry distinct racist connotations. Clearly, decades of domestic economic mismanagement with its associated corruption, violence and resultant debt, cannot be overlooked. But in emphasising these factors, we must also be careful not to overlook the fact that the continent has also been a victim of particularly bad advice. Kwesi Asante of Ghana, spokesperson of the

United Nations Office for Emergency Operations in Africa, summarised the position this way:

> Africa's problem – Africa's biggest problem – is too many people going around the continent with solutions to problems they didn't understand. Many of these solutions are half-baked. But this is not to put all the blame on the North. Some Africans don't understand the African problems (Poku 2003).

James Wolfensohn, the president of the World Bank, pursues the theme further, noting:

> We…. have failed in Africa, along with everybody else. We have not fully understood the problems. We have not identified the priorities. We have not always designed our projects to fit…. But we will continue to try (Poku 2003).

This admission of failure by Wolfensohn belies the true culpability of the World Bank and other international financial institutions (IFIs) in shaping contemporary Africa's disheartening reality. Over the past two decades, African governments have had to adopt Structural Adjustment Programmes (SAPs) as a crucial prerequisite to receiving vitally needed loans from these IFIs – particularly International Monetary Fund (IMF) and the World Bank. The immediate context for these was the continent's unsustainable debt overhang and its deepening economic state in the early 1980s. The volume of world trade, which had expanded at 5.7 per cent yearly in the 1970s, virtually stagnated between 1981 and 1983, with average annual GNP growth rate of African's trading partners falling from 4.4 per cent in the 1970s to 1.8 per cent between 1980-81. Similarly, the growth in demand for primary products and for fuel dropped between the 1970s and 1981 from 2.0 to 0.5 (IMF, 1989a). With the sharp downturn in commodity prices and the increase in the prices of manufacturing products, the overall terms of trade of Africa fell by 7 per cent between 1981 and 1985 (IMF 1989a). Nominal interest rates on the foreign debt mushroomed to record high levels of 18-20 per cent during 1980-83. The decline in nominal rates observed since then has not been paralleled by a commensurate decline in real interest rates. Because of the debt crisis of 1982, gross capital flows declined sharply after 1983. Net capital flows dropped even more dramatically, from $10 billion in 1982 to about $2.5 billion in 1985. These external shocks produced immediate adverse effects on inflation and, in turn, created balance of payment problems.

Against this background, SAPs were designed to initiate two crucial developments in African economies: fiscal stability and economic growth. The IMF was charged with the former and its primary aim was to reduce short-term disequilibrium, especially budget and balance of payment deficits and inflation; while the World Bank sought to deliver the latter by reorienting the structures of African economies for greater efficiency and growth potential in the medium-term. In practice, this distinction was blurred because the World Bank programmes were almost never implemented without an IMF programme in place. The impact on the ground was a critical tension between the demand management approach of the IMF on the one hand, and the supply-oriented thrust of the World Bank on the other.

Two decades on, there are no signs of these programmes achieving their desired objectives. Yet, their socio-economic impacts have been particularly devastating. Table 3.1 shows the knock-on effects of SAPs for essential services on the continent. The cumulative impact has been a severe deterioration in basic services in adjusting countries. Cuts in government expenditure, for example, have forced up the costs of primary education and health care beyond the reach of many ordinary Africans (Wallace 1999). Similarly, rushed privatisation has resulted in the laying off of tens-of-thousands of workers (Tangri and Mwenda 2001); the removal of price controls and the devaluation of the national currency have resulted in the cost of living spiralling (Bayart 2000). Moreover, 'the promotion of exports for debt repayment and the cutting of public expenditure on welfare in a region where 280 million people are undernourished; where there is 1 doctor for nearly 55,000 people, compared with 1 for 400 people in industrial countries; and where nine out of the ten HIV infected people worldwide reside, is a scandal' (Poku 2002).

Perhaps the most insidious aspect of all is the relationship between adjustment programmes and the spread of HIV/AIDS. Peter Piot, the director of UNAIDS, puts the position this way; 'structural adjustment raises particular problems for [African] governments because most of the factors which fuel the AIDS pandemic are also those factors that seem to come into play in structural adjustment programmes' (Piot 2001). The state of Africa's health care system is a particular point in mind. At a time when up to 70 per cent of adults in some hospitals are suffering from AIDS-related illnesses – placing extreme pressure on health services – many African countries are still cutting health expenditure in order to satisfy IMF and World Bank conditionalities. For example, in Tanzania – where over half a million children are orphans as a result of AIDS (UNAIDS 2002) – the government spends only around US$3.20 per person per year on health provision, a quarter of what the World Bank itself estimates is necessary to provide basic care (World-Bank 2002). The Tanzanian government spends in excess of three times more on debt servicing each year than it does on health care – see Table 1.2. Similarly, in Malawi where nearly 16 per cent of the population are either living with HIV or AIDS, where there is only one doctor for every 50, 000 people, government spending on health care was dwarfed by debt repayment by two to one – see Table 3.2.

Table 3.1: Circle of decline and vulnerability: the impacts of SAPS on African societies

Policy	Policy Response	Domestic Impact	Implications for the spread of HIV/AIDS
To reduce government expenditure	Introduce user fee for health services	Reduce access to health services; decline in general health of the population	Reduced awareness of health issues, including HIV/AIDS; poor general health; reduced treatment for opportunistic infections, particularly STDs

	Introduce user fee for education	Children, particularly girls, removed from schools; marginalisation of large section of population to informal sector like prostitution with associated risk	Reduced education; increased illiteracy; increased risk of HIV transmission due to poor educational knowledge. Particular vulnerability of women due to lack of formal education
	Decrease spending on health and education	Reduce quality and quantity of facilities; lack of equipment; fewer and less trained staff	Increased vulnerability to infection
	Public sector redundancies and wage freezes	Unemployment; staff shortages leading to reduced quality and quantity of education and health services	Increased vulnerability to infection
	Removal of price subsidies on food, fuel and other basic commodities	Reduced quality and quantity of food; declining calorie consumption per head	Poor health means greater vulnerability to infection, increased in informal sector activities with increased risk of HIV infection
	Reduced civil services	Reduced administrative capacity	Governments less able to promote AIDS prevention
To increase export earnings	Promote large export-orientated projects	Workers migrate to jobs from home; decrease food production; restructure domestic production patterns leading to decrease in consumable food for domestic societies; rural to urban migration	Workers more likely to engage in risky behaviour with increased risk of HIV/AIDS contraction; spreading of HIV through migration; returning migrants infecting local communities

Table 3.2: Debt to health and education profile: selected African countries

Country	Percentage of Adult Population with HIV/ AIDS *	Percentage of Govt. Spending on primary education **	Percentage of Govt. Spending on Health ***	Percentage of Govt. Spending on Debt Servicing 2001****
Malawi	15.5	15.8	14.5	34
Mozambique	13.0	20.2	11.1	57
Rwanda	8.9	9.2	9.8	32
Tanzania	7.8	25.4	14.9	42
Uganda	5.9	21.1	9.3	39
Zambia	21.5	14.6	12.6	62

Various sources: * UNAIDS 2002 (December), ** World Bank (various sources), *** WHO (2002 Health Reports), **** UNDP/World Bank figures

In aggregate terms, the total long-term debt of the continent stood at US$315 billion in 2000 (World Bank 2001). Although this figure is quite modest by global standards – Brazil, for example, owed more than US$120 billion at the end of 2000 – compared to the continent's ability to repay, the debt is enormous. Africans can pay off the debt only with earnings in foreign currency; that is, they must use money from exports, from aid or from new foreign loans. Take the case of Ethiopia, one of the poorest countries in the world. Its debt of US$10 billion ($179 a person) at the end of 1999 may not seem like much compared to the US$98 billion the American government released for emergency response to ground-zero after the terrorist attack of 2001. But Ethiopia's debt is almost thirteen times the amount the country earned in exports in 1997. Ethiopia used the equivalent of 45 per cent of its US$783 million in export earnings on debt payments. Even after such a crushing payout, Ethiopia's debt is still unsustainable. Or consider the trade-offs with investments in health care. In 2000, 75 per cent of the world's new AIDS infections were in sub-Saharan Africa. So were four-fifths of all deaths from AIDS that year. Yet among all African countries only South Africa was spending more on health care than on debt service. For most African countries, the entire annual health budget is less than US$10 a person. Health care, moreover, is only one of the urgent needs requiring investment. This perverse anomaly is reducing the already limited ability of governments across Africa to provide even the basic levels of health care for their people at a time when the pressures of HIV/AIDS threatens to overwhelm existing health services (Sachs 2001).

The potent mix of debt and adjustment makes it virtually impossible for any African country to treat those with the virus effectively, or to undertake successful campaigns to reduce high-risk behaviour while also providing essential resources in the fight against the pandemic. Hence, why some presidents as well as governmental technical and consulting staff deliver messages which, at the very least, can be characterised as ambiguous. In this vein, the former president Lissouba of Congo-

Brazzaville regularly evoked his country's determination to confront the pandemic during interviews with foreign press, while not hesitating to characterize HIV infection as the primary symbol of social and political disorder in his country in 1993 and 1994. More recently, in July 1999, the president of Kenya declared war on AIDS, while affirming in the same speech his staunch opposition to all initiatives to promote condom use in his country.

Indeed, until very recently a culture of indifference and denial existed among Africa's ruling elite regarding HIV/AIDS. Even where denial was conquered, the types of intervention proposed and pursued by governments often exacerbated the problem. As recently as the 15 August 2000 (some 15 years since the first reported HIV case in his country) President Bakili Muluzi of Malawi was calling on his police force to intensify swoops on known brothels to slow down the spread of AIDS. So convinced was the President of the relationship between high prevalence and the sex industry that he proposed to give police greater powers to restrict the 'civil liberties' of known prostitutes and their clients. Similarly, in Swaziland, Tfohlongwane Dlamini, the chairman of the powerful Swaziland National Council Standing Committee, told delegates at a recent conference that HIV-afflicted people, 'should be kept in their own special place if we want to curb the spread of the disease'. The statement followed an earlier parliamentary debate where Swazi King Mswati III called for HIV-positive citizens to be 'sterilized and branded'.

At one level it is not difficult to see why African leaders have opted to play this dual game. In many of the countries worst affected by HIV/AIDS, poor economic management, high inflation, rampant corruption, and deteriorating infrastructure are commonplace, and conflicts and population displacement are far from rare. The contribution of AIDS to this generally grim picture is to further exacerbate the already precarious situation on the continent. In Zambia and Zimbabwe, for example, HIV-infected patients occupy 50 to 80 per cent of all beds in urban hospitals. The services provided meet only a fraction of the needs. Yet spending on AIDS care is crowding out spending on other life-saving, cost-effective programmes. On average, treating an AIDS patient for one year is about as expensive as educating 10 primary school students for one year. Not surprisingly, governments have taken the view that scarce resources are better spent on rival health priorities.

> In reality, this argument is less effective than it sounds because often measures to fight AIDS also serve other medical and social objectives. Better post-maternity counselling, for example, can cut mother-child HIV transmission; it also reduces infant mortality more generally. Equally, treatment of venereal diseases such as syphilis slows the spread of HIV; it is also good in itself. In the end, a determined effort against AIDS is likely to advance other health objectives as much as it diverts resources from them.

Adjustment and Poverty: The Context of Vulnerability

To be clear, SAPs do not cause HIV or AIDS, but they do create an extremely fertile environment for the spread of HIV/AIDS – see Table 3.1. Of particular interest here, is the correlation between adjustment programmes and poverty on the one hand, and poverty and vulnerability to HIV/AIDS on the other. Africa's experience with SAPs shows a strong correlation between their implementation and a rise in poverty (van de Walle 2001). Poverty is closely linked with high unemployment, hunger and malnutrition, lack of basic services, inability to pay for or access health care, disintegration of families, vulnerability, homelessness and often hopelessness. Mainstream biomedical literature has long documented the methods by which this combination of factors can undermine the body's specific and non-specific immune response (Farmer 1999; Kim, Millen et al. 2000). Hence, we know that protein-energy malnutrition (general calorie deficit) and specific micronutrient deficiencies, such as vitamin A deficiency, weaken every part of the body's immune system, including the skin and mucous membranes, which are particularly important in protecting the body from STDs, including HIV (Jakab 2000). Moreover, in an environment of poverty, parasite infestation plays a dual role in suppressing immune response. It aggravates malnutrition by robbing the body of essential nutrients and increasing calorie demand; and in addition, the presence of parasites chronically triggers the immune system, impairing its ability to fight infection from other pathogens.

One of the key societal legacies of poverty in Africa is the existence of undiagnosed and untreated sexually transmitted diseases among many Africans. Data for 2000 indicate that Africa has the highest incidence of curable STDs at 284 cases per 1,000 people aged 15–49 years, compared to the second highest of 160 cases per 1,000 people in South and South-East Asia. There is now growing recognition of the public health implications of curable STDs (especially those causing genital ulcers) by virtue of their frequency of occurrence as well as their ability, when present, to facilitate the transmission of HIV (World Bank 2000b). One study suggests that the presence of an untreated STD can enhance both the acquisition and transmission of HIV by a factor of up to ten (MEDILINKS 2001). Such viral STDs are relatively uncommon in rich countries because of the availability of antibiotics. Yet, in Africa, even when the poor have access to health care, the clinics may have no antibiotics to treat those STDs that act as cofactors for AIDS. Sub-Saharan Africa is not the only region where malnutrition is associated with HIV/AIDS. Among all low and middle-income countries, HIV prevalence is strongly correlated with falling protein and calorie consumption.

Alongside STDs is the perennial issue of poverty-induced migration. A by-product of commodity specialisation – a central facet of SAPs – is the focusing of African economies on the production of specific products. The plantations, mines and industries, though development enclaves from one point of view, have required and attracted massive quantities of labour not only from the traditional rural areas, but also from neighbouring and regional states. The dislocation of so many millions of people from their traditional places of residence significantly increases their probability of contracting HIV or indeed, passing the virus on. Decosas and Adrien note that migrants have higher infection rates than those who do not migrate, independent of the HIV prevalence at the site of departure or the site of destination (Decosas and Adrien 1997).

The mining community in Carletonville, South Africa, is a tragic but powerful reminder of how mobility provides an environment of extraordinary risk for HIV contraction. With a mine-working population of 85,000 people, of whom 95 per cent are migrant workers, Carletonville is the biggest gold-mining complex in the world. These migrant workers leave their families behind in rural villages, live in squalid all-male labour hostels and return home maybe once a year. Lacking formal education and recreation, these hardworking men rely on little else but home-brewed alcohol and sex for leisure. For these men, there is a 1 in 40 chance of being crushed by falling rock, so the delayed risk of HIV seems comparatively remote. Astonishingly, some 65 per cent of adults in Carletonville were HIV-positive in 1999, a rate higher than any region in the world (Williams, Gilgen et al. 2000). When these men return back to their families, they often carry the virus into their rural communities. A study in a rural area in the South African province of KwaZulu-Natal, for example, showed that 13 per cent of women whose husbands worked away from home two-thirds of the time were infected with HIV (Morar, Ramjee et al. 1998). Among women who spent two-thirds of their time or more with their husbands, no HIV infection was recorded (Lurie, Williams et al. 2000).

Poverty structures not only the contours of the pandemic, but also the outcome once an individual is sick with complications of HIV infection. A strong feature of HIV infection is that it clusters within families, often resulting in both parents being HIV-positive – and in time falling sick and dying. Poor families have a reduced capacity to deal with the effects of morbidity and mortality than do richer ones, for very obvious reasons. These include the absence of savings and other assets that can cushion the impact of illness and death. The poor are already on the margins of survival, and are unable to deal with the costs associated with HIV/AIDS. These include the cost of drugs – when available – to treat opportunistic infections, the cost of transport to health centres, reduced household productivity through illness and diversion of labour to caring roles, loss of employment through illness and job discrimination, funeral and related costs, and so on. In the longer term such poor households never recover even their initial level of living, since their capacity is reduced through the loss of productive family members through death and migration, and through the sales of any productive assets they once possessed. As a result, a true process of immiseration is now observable in many parts of Africa, particularly southern Africa.

Take this powerful image from a field worker in Zambia:

> In the field you are often led into somebody's home. The first thing that hits you is that the patient will be on the floor. If that household was not poor before HIV/AIDS infected somebody, then by the end of the first few years, poverty will come to the household as all of their assets are sold off to pay for healthcare. Children have been taken out of school – daughters, particularly – to become caregivers. Invariably, the person you have come to see will be on the floor without a blanket or a pillow. If you look around that mud hut for food, you won't see it, and you won't smell people cooking. There is no food (Poku 2003).

There is thus enormous strain on the capacity of families to cope with the psychosocial and economic consequences of illness, such that many families experience great distress and often disintegrate as social and economic units. Even where they do not, by eliminating the breadwinners – often both parents – the process further exposes the rest of the family members to poverty, which then increases their chances of contracting the virus. This is particularly so for young women, who will often be forced to engage in commercial sexual transactions, sometimes as casual sex workers, as a survival strategy for themselves and their dependants. The effects of these behavioural patterns on HIV infection in women are only too evident. In part, this also accounts for the much higher infection rates in young women, who are increasingly unable to sustain themselves by other work in either the formal or informal sectors.

HIPC and HIV/AIDS

Against this background, the introduction of the Heavily Indebted Poor Countries (HIPC) initiative in 1996 by the World Bank and IMF appeared as a step in the right direction – not least because it seemed to recognize the impossibility of resolving the continent's debt crisis by simply postponing payments (the now infamous rescheduling policies of the late 1980s and early 1990s). Some debt, creditors acknowledged, would have to be cancelled, including debt owed to the multilateral institutions themselves (which accounts for almost one-third of Africa's total debt). Creditors agreed that, in principle, as much as 80 per cent of external debt could be cancelled. The unanswered questions, however, were under what conditions, how much, how fast and who would pay for it. Typically, the international financial institutions imposed rigid economic adjustment programmes as a condition for participation in HIPC. By September 1998 only eight countries, including five in Africa, had qualified for debt relief packages adding up to about US$6.5 billion. Uganda was the only African country that had actually reached the 'completion point', receiving about US$650 million in debt reduction (Cheru 2001). To supplement World Bank and IMF funds, 15 donor countries (not including the United States) had paid or pledged about US$300 million for the initiative by late 1998.

In view of the challenges facing Africa, it was clear by the end of 1998 that the HIPC initiative was not even close to meeting the continent's needs for debt cancellation. It was in this context – not to mention intense NGO pressure – that at the G7 meeting in Cologne in June 1999 the leaders of the industrialized countries announced the HIPC II initiative. This initiative proposed incremental, but noteworthy steps towards the modernization of the original HIPC initiative. Chief among these was the proposal to grant larger reductions of the total accumulated debt (the 'debt overhang'), quicker reductions in debt service payments, and finally placing poverty reduction at the heart of the enhanced new framework. The devil, however, was in the detail (Cheru 2000). Eligibility for debt relief under the enhanced HIPC initiative was made conditional upon 'good performance' in the implementation of an enhanced structural adjustment programme (to be renamed the poverty reduction and growth facility – PRGF) for a period of three years instead of six years under the original HIPC (Cheru and Figueredo 2000). Having reached the decision point after the first three years of good economic performance, the country must then demonstrate that its debt-servicing requirement is unsustainable, following designated threshold values with respect to the ratio of debt to exports, and the ratio of debt to fiscal revenues. If the country finally qualifies for relief, its debt-servicing payment is brought down to what is deemed within the terms of the initiative to be a sustainable level, only after reaching the completion point, or a further three-year waiting period.

This less than generous arrangement would still leave the qualifying country diverting a sizeable portion of its scarce foreign exchange earnings towards debt servicing for an indefinite period of time. Moreover, while expenditures on education and health services will be expanded under the new HIPC, the structural factors that induced poverty were not addressed by conventional structural adjustment programmes. More worryingly, while debt relief is important in the short run, the extent to which additional fresh resources would be available for HIPC countries is not certain. Debt relief alone is not going to be enough to put these marginalized countries on a path of sustained growth.

Not surprisingly, there exists a great deal of scepticism about the willingness of Western creditors, in particular the multilateral development banks, to break the chain of debt-bondage of the HIPC countries, not to mention about the adequacy of funding for HIPC to wipe the slate clean. Conditionality and external control remain the core guiding principles of the enhanced HIPC initiative, despite the claims of the architect of the plan that poverty eradication is its real objective. Moreover, linking debt relief to successful implementation of 'good governance' is a major mistake and is bound to delay much-needed relief to countries desperately in need of fresh resources to fix collapsed social systems.

Zambia is a clear case in point. It is one of the worst HIV-infected countries in the world, with a prevalence rate of 21.5 per cent among its adult population – see Table 3.2. The annual number of deaths has been increasing slowly and will reach 127,000 per annum or nearly 350 per day by 2005 (Ministry-of-Health 1997). This means that one in five of Zambians now over the age of 15 will die at a young age from this disease, mostly over the next five to ten years. The overall impact of the virus on life expectancy is particularly noteworthy: life expectancy, which stood at 54 years a few years ago, has plummeted to 37 and is expected to decline in the coming decade to 30 years. As adult mortality from AIDS rises, people with essential skills account for a significant percentage of HIV/AIDS-related deaths. Teachers, accountants, civil servants and other professionals are dying in large numbers (UNECA 2000; UNAIDS 2002). As a result, labour productivity has been diminishing and HIV/AIDS is now the central concern of firms. One review of 33 businesses in Zambia showed a dramatic increase in average annual mortality from 0.25 per cent in 1987 to 1.6 per cent by 1992. Barclays Bank of Zambia has lost more than a quarter of its senior managers to AIDS. On a large sugar estate, 55 per cent of the deaths between 1992 and 1993 were HIV-related. Part of the reason for increased absenteeism is the time employees spend attending funerals. Additional training costs will be incurred as labour turnover increases and businesses will have to pay out more in medical care, salary compensation for the families of the deceased, and funeral grants.

Zambia belongs to the category of the HIPC zone wherein the debt burden has been a major contributor to the persistence of underdevelopment. It has taken a heavy toll on public budgets, severely shrunk the resources available for development and greatly reduced the prospects for growth. Even before HIV/AIDS became recognised as the greatest threat to human development in Zambia, the country's external debt was regularly serviced at the expense of vital social programmes. Thus, finding lasting solutions to Zambia's debt can open up a strategic opportunity to contain the threat of the HIV/AIDS pandemic to sustainable human development. The total external debt of Zambia stood at US$6.5 billion in 1998. Of this, 46 per cent is owed to the multilateral institutions, such as the IMF, the World Bank and the African Development Bank. Because multilateral debts are 'preferred and exempt' debts, they cannot be rescheduled or cancelled, and they take precedence over other debts. Debt service payments falling due in 1998 amounted to US$123 million and were paid to creditors accordingly: US$89 million to multilateral and US$30 million to Paris Club creditors – composed largely of western governments. The US$123 million in debt service payment was about 69 per cent of the funds budgeted for the social sectors. Yet no nation can develop without educated and healthy citizens, no matter how faithfully it may meet its debt-servicing requirements.

The Zambian government has pursued a policy of debt forgiveness and rescheduling in order to reduce the country's debt burden. During the period 1992–7, various creditors extended debt relief amounting to a total of US$1.873 billion, of which US$1.44 billion was provided by the Paris Club creditors, and the balance by both non-Paris Club and commercial creditors. The multilateral creditors have offered no debt relief. It is possible now that Zambia can qualify for debt relief under the enhanced HIPC initiative, if the government successfully fulfils numerous macroeconomic and governance conditionalities that creditor countries are demanding. At the earliest, the government can hope for real debt relief three years from now. Like many other countries on the continent, Zambia's progress towards qualification for debt relief under the enhanced HIPC initiative hinges largely on the government's capacity to show real and tangible progress on the promise it made during the last consultative group meeting to institute fundamental governance reform. While there is little wrong with this in principle, the fear is that the critical resources needed to tackle the AIDS pandemic might be held up indefinitely if progress on governance reform falters. As a consequence, the excellent work that NGOs and civil society are doing with meagre resources to prevent the spread of HIV/AIDS will be completely wiped out. In the context of the pandemic, action is needed now; not three years down the road, by which time millions more Africans will have been infected with or died of the HIV virus.

As other highly indebted countries struggle to meet the criteria for HIPC relief, it is time to face the facts. The case of Zambia has, perhaps more clearly than any other, laid bare the myth of HIPC debt relief. Even with the full application of the HIPC initiative, Zambia's debt crisis will not be lessened, its government will be no more able to address the national health emergency and its people will be no less tied into a cycle of deprivation. On average, countries that receive HIPC relief see reductions of only about one-third in their debt service payments. As Kofi Annan, Secretary-General of the United Nations, concluded in a September 2000 report, 'the enhanced HIPC Initiative does not provide an adequate response to HIPCs' debt problems', and therefore 'a bolder approach will have to be taken'. The current debt relief framework has failed Zambia, just as it has failed other highly indebted poor countries across Africa and throughout the developing world.

The Moral Calculus of Inactivity

Table 3.3 illustrates the magnitude of Africa's economic challenge. Other regions of the world have demonstrated a much greater ability to attract FDI over the past few years (arguably over the past two decades) than Africa. The table does not fully reveal the highly selective patterns of FDIs. Of the US$18.52 billion FDI that flowed into Africa during the 1990s, just two countries (Angola and Nigeria) accounted for US$11.672 billion – both of them lucrative mining or oil-producing countries (ADB 2002). If South Africa is excluded (both as a recipient and a source of FDI), five other countries accounted for another US$4 billion – Republic of Congo, Côte d'Ivoire, Equatorial Guinea, Namibia and Sudan – leaving the remaining 40 countries of the continent to compete for just US$3.275 billion in FDI flows over the decade (Sadik 2002; UNDP 2002). According to African Development Indicators 2002, official aid has followed a similar selective trend over the past decade and is falling in terms of total volume. Aid levels in 1999, for example, were US$10.8 billion compared to US$17.9 billion in 1992, when development assistance to Africa reached its highest ever levels.

Table 3.3: Foreign direct investment (as percentage of global FDI flows), 1997–2002

Indicators	1997	1998	1999	2000	2001	2002
Developed countries	56.8	69.8	77.2	79.1	80.1	
Developing countries and economies	39.2	27.2	20.7	18.9	18.0	
Asia	22.4	13.8	9.3	11.3	11.2	
Latin America	14.9	12.0	10.3	6.8	6.8	
Africa	2.3	1.2	1.0	0.7	0.7	
Africa (as a percentage of developing countries)	5.88	4.63	4.72	3.78	3.87**	3.11**

Source: ADB Statistics Division and IMF
Note: * UCTAD data 2002 ** UNDP2002

Not surprisingly, many organizations – particularly UN agencies working in Africa, such as the United Nations High Commission for Refugees (UNHCR) – have repeatedly pointed to the unequal treatment of Africa by the donor community. For example, in 1999 donors provided less than three-fifths of the US$800 million the UN requested for emergencies in sub-Saharan Africa. Similarly, the World Food Programme announced in September 2000 that it would curtail its feeding programme for nearly 2 million refugees in Sierra Leone, Liberia and Guinea after receiving less than 20 per cent of requested funding. An emergency appeal in the summer of that same year to feed and shelter at least 600,000 Angolans who had been displaced in that country's long-standing civil war – a number nearly equal to Kosovo's refugees – brought minimal initial response and predictions of mass starvation. In the Great Lakes region of Congo, Burundi and Rwanda, the UN estimated it would need US$278 million to take care of nearly 4 million people crowded in refugee camps. By late October 2000, only 45 per cent of that amount had been donated. By contrast, Kosovo and Bosnia have been able to generate one of the biggest international responses in recent memory.

The reason for the differing responses by the international community is simple: Kosovo and Bosnia were 'loud crises' unfolding in front of television cameras and affecting largely people of European descent; the HIV/AIDS pandemic in Africa and the developing world is a 'silent crisis' affecting largely poor black people (mainly Africans), who, in the eyes of the Western media, are constantly portrayed as being in a state of permanent crisis. Indeed, racism must not be underestimated in any analysis of why the Western nations have responded so half-heartedly to the AIDS pandemic. The position is perfectly summarised by Salih Booker, director of the Africa Fund/American Committee on Africa, when he concludes that 'AIDS is a black plague; it is mainly killing black people . . . And that is the cruel truth about why the world had failed to respond with dispatch' (Booker 2001). Consider this cruel irony: the World Bank – as a sponsor of UNAIDS – is charged with funding strategies to alleviate poverty and to reduce HIV infectivity in the developing world. Yet it could write concerning the pandemic that 'if the only effect of the AIDS pandemic were to reduce the population growth rate [in developing countries], it would increase the growth rate of per capita income in any plausible economic model'. Moreover, the Bank has developed the idea of 'disability-adjusted life year', or DALY, to measure the number of years lost to illness and death. 'By this calculation,' reported the *Washington Post*, 'a country that spent US$1,000 a year to save the life of someone earning US$500 a year would suffer a net economic loss .'

Conclusion

Although the proximate cause of Africa's AIDS crisis is HIV, the underlining societal causes are much broader and familiar. Across the continent, poverty structures not only the contours of the pandemic but also the outcome once an individual is infected with HIV. Thus, until poverty is reduced there will be little progress with either reducing transmission of the virus or creating an enhanced capacity to cope with its socio-economic consequences. It follows that sustained human development is an essential precondition for any effective response to the pandemic in Africa. Herein lies Africa's predicament: how to achieve the sustainable development essential for an effective response to the pandemic under conditions where the pandemic is destructive of the capacities essential for the response – namely, killing the most economically productive members of the continent's people. Simple answers to this problem do not exist, but recognition of its nature is a step towards its solution. The next step has to be the development of policies and programmes that address the interrelationships between poverty and development and actually to put in place those activities that can make a difference for development outcomes. Central to these activities are programmes that address poverty today so as to facilitate socio-economic development tomorrow.

The recent WHO Report puts the position this way: 'With bold decisions in 2002, the world could initiate a partnership between rich and poor [countries] of unrivalled significance, offering the gift of life itself to millions of the world's dispossessed and proving to all doubters that globalization can indeed work to the benefit of all humankind' (Sachs 2001). Central here is the perennial problem of Africa's overwhelming debt and the necessity of its unequivocal cancellation. To be sure, debt cancellation is not a panacea for Africa's AIDS crisis, but it is a hugely important step in enabling the continent's states to engage more effectively with the challenges posed by HIV/AIDS. With the best will in the world, no country can physically afford to make the investments necessary in social services while being forced to give priority to debt repayments. The argument that cancelling the debt of African countries would foster financial irresponsibility by debtors does not hold up. On the contrary, it is necessary for countries on the edge of economic marginality to take responsibility for the use of future resources – however limited – in the fight against HIV/AIDS.

Moreover, a mechanism could be devised whereby the conditions of debt cancellation would be determined by a governance structure that incorporated civil society and elected governments in the affected states. This would be a particularly powerful safeguard against corruption and would expose domestic strategies to public scrutiny in both debtor and creditor countries. Clearly, any such strategy must be driven by political will, within both lender states and their omnipresent institutions of economic governance – mainly the IMF and the World Bank. Ominously, the rhetoric of political will on the part of these bodies has not been supported by context-relevant strategic initiatives – such as total debt cancellation for the heavily indebted countries confronting the modern incarnation of Dante's inferno that is AIDS. Yet unless these dominant players mobilise quickly and effectively, the future prospects for Africa look decidedly gloomy. In this sense the moral calculus of inactivity could be beyond computation.

References

ADB (2002). *African Development Report 2002*. Oxford, African Development Bank (ADB).

Bayart, J.-F. (2000). 'Africa in the world: a history of extraversion.' *Afr Aff (Lond)* **99**(395): 217-267.

Booker, S. a. W. M. (2001). 'Global Apartheid'. *The Nation:* pp.11-17.

Cheru, F. (2000). 'Debt Relief and Social Investment: Linking the HIPC Initiative to the HIV/AIDS Epidemic in Africa: The Case of Zambia'. *Review of African Political Economy* (No. 86): pp.519-535.

Cheru, F. (2001). *Uganda's Experience with the PRSP Process: What are the secrets of its success?* Addis Ababa, Report prepared for the UN Economic Commission for Africa.

Cheru, F. and R. Figueredo (2000). *Debt Relief and Social Investment: Linking the 'HIPC' Initiative to HIV/AIDS Epidemic in Africa, post-Mitch Reconstruction in Honduras and Nicaragua, and The Convention On The Worst Forms Of Child Labor*. Geneva, United Nations High Commission For Human Rights.

Decosas, J. and A. Adrien (1997). 'Migration and HIV.' *AIDS* **11**(supp. A).

Farmer, P. (1999). *Infections and Inequalities: The Modern Plagues*. California, University of California Press.

Jakab, E. A. M. (2000). *Louis Pasteur: Hunting Killer Germs*. London, McGraw-Hill.

Kim, J. Y., J. V. Millen, et al., Eds. (2000). *Dying for Growth: Global Inequality and the Health of the Poor*. Monroe, ME, Common Courage Press.

Lurie, M., B. Williams, et al. (2000). *HIV Discordance Among Migrant and Non-Migrant Couples in South Africa*. 13th International AIDS Conference in Durban, UNAIDS.

MEDILINKS (2001). African Statistics: Cost of HIV/AIDS, Malaria & TB to Africa, http://www.medilinks.org/Features/Articles/Statistics%20in%20Africa%202001.htm.

Ministry-of-Health (1997). HIV/AIDS in Zambia: Background, Projections, Impacts and Interventions. Lusaka, Central Board of Health.

Morar, N. S., G. Ramjee, et al. (1998). *Safe Sex Practices among Sex Workers at Risk of HIV Infection*. 12th World AIDS Conference, Geneva, 6/28 – 7/3, Poster 33287, UNAIDS.

Piot, P. (2001). 'Aids and Human Security'. address given at the United Nations University.

Poku, N. K. (2002). *Living with High Seropositive Rates: Africa*. New York, Background paper commissioned by the Social Science Research Council, New York.

Poku, N. K. (2002). 'Poverty, Debt and Africa's HIV/AIDS Crisis.' *International Affairs* **78**(3): 531-46.

Poku, N. K. (2003). *The Politics of Africa's AIDS Crisis*. Cambridge, Polity Press.

WHO. (2001). *Macroeconomics and Health: Investing in Health for Economic Development*. Geneva, presented to Gro Harlem Brundtland, Director-General of the World Health Organization: 213.

Sadik, A. (2002). 'The Economic Implications of Globalization for the GCC Countries.' *Globalization and the Middle East*. H. Dodge. United Kingdom, Royal Institute of International Affairs. pp. 83-112.

Tangri, R. and A. Mwenda (2001). 'Corruption and cronyism in Uganda's privatization in the 1990s.' *Afr Aff (Lond)* **100**(398): 117-133.

UNAIDS (2002). *Report on the Global HIV/AIDS Epidemic*. Geneva, UNAIDS.

UNDP (2002). *Human Development Report*. Oxford, Oxford University Press.

UNECA (2000). *HIV/AIDS and Economic Development in Sub-Saharan Africa*. Addis Ababa: African Development Forum 2000, United Nations Economic Commission for Africa (UNECA).

van de Walle, N. (2001). *African Economies and the Politics of Permanent Crisis*. New York, Cambridge University Press.

Wallace, L., Ed. (1999). *Africa: Adjusting to the Challenge of Globalisation*. Washington, International Monetary Fund Publication Service.

Whiteside, A. (2002). 'Poverty and HIV/AIDS in Africa.' *Third World Quarterly* **23**(2): 313-332.

Williams, B. G., D. Gilgen, et al. (2000). *The Natural History of HIV/AIDS in South Africa: A Biomedical and Social Survay in Carletonville*. Johannesburg, Centre for Scientific and Industrial Research.

World Bank (2000b). *Intensifying Action Against HIV/AIDS in Africa: Responding to a Development Crisis*. Washington, DC, World Bank.

World Bank (2001). *Africa Development Indicators 2000*. Washington DC, World Bank.

World Bank (2002). *Africa Development Indicators 2002*. Washington DC, World Bank.

Chapter 4

AIDS-Related Famine in Africa: Questioning Assumptions and Developing Frameworks

Alex de Waal

Introduction

The concurrence of a generalised AIDS epidemic and acute food insecurity threatens to spring a number of unpleasant surprises on southern Africa in the years ahead. This chapter examines some of the implications of the 'new variant famine' framework (de Waal and Whiteside 2003), and how they compel us to re-examine a range of assumptions about the nature of famine and the trajectory of the HIV/AIDS epidemic.

The 'new variant famine' hypothesis posits that AIDS selectively impacts upon certain key aspects of the smallholder agrarian economy, creating a new profile of vulnerability to famine and a new trajectory of failing to cope when famine does strike. Note that it does *not* claim that HIV/AIDS is the major, still less the sole, cause of food production decline. It is a much more subtle and complex process whereby inequalities are exacerbated and a new class of destitute people is created, who are vulnerable to starvation. New variant famine contrasts with traditional or 'old variant' drought-famine, which killed individuals (mainly young children and the elderly), but did not threaten the basic economic and social viability of society. Agrarian societies in Africa and elsewhere could be said to have achieved a mutual adaptation to a range of threats such as drought-induced epidemic hunger. Like a familiar virus, that causes harm and pain, drought-famine did not threaten the fundamental viability of that society. Mortality in drought famines such as the west African Sahel in the early 1970s was low and transient (Caldwell 1977). Communal adaptations to the threat, such as spreading family members over wide areas and different ecological and economic niches, and the survival skills of individuals such as knowledge of wild foods and how to prepare them, contributed to an impressive resilience. The sociological study of famine in the later 20th century is marked by scholars' admiration for the survival capacities of African farmers (de Waal 1989, Mortimore 1989, Swift 1993, Davies 1995).

In an AIDS-impacted society, this is changing. We face the prospect of a 'new variant famine', a food crisis with a different profile and a different trajectory. It will not look like a 'traditional' famine but, insofar as a substantial section of the populace will face extreme hunger, destitution and raised death rates, it will fit the criteria for being a famine.

'New variant famine' threatens to emerge even when there is no food production shortfall, to lead to mass destitution, to become a chronic condition, to kill adults as well as children, and to increase the level of HIV transmission. Our existing models for food security and famine response—and our projections for the course of the HIV/AIDS epidemic—are all unable to cope with this. Many assumptions about both famine and the HIV/AIDS epidemic need to be questioned, and throughout this chapter, such assumptions will be highlighted. The first assumption we must overturn is that we have reliable guides to what will happen.

Challenged assumption number 1: the past is a guide to the future

Four general themes will recur. The first is that AIDS is not 'a shock like any other' (Baylies 2002). It has distinct characteristics that render it particularly deadly to agrarian livelihoods in ways that are markedly different to other shocks such as drought. For reasons to do with the source of capital in intra-household accumulation, the constraints on labour availability and use, and the irreducible demands of caring for children and the sick, the smallholder agrarian sector is structurally highly vulnerable to the effects of HIV/AIDS. Hence, we must recognise that rural households afflicted by both AIDS and food insecurity are not 'coping' but 'struggling' (Rugalema 2000). Even though rural areas typically have HIV rates considerably lower than cities and towns, the impact of those relatively modest rates may be more detrimental to social and economic resilience. The impact of a given level of HIV prevalence will translate into different socio-economic outcomes depending on the nature of the livelihood system. In many cases, the high level of structural vulnerability means that even relatively low levels of HIV lead to high impacts. A simple correlation between HIV prevalence and impact is the next assumption we challenge.

Challenged assumption number 2: lower rural HIV rates mean that rural areas are less affected by the epidemic

A second theme is that the impact of AIDS is complex and systemic, and compounds livelihood systems that are already under severe stress due to poverty, environmental scarcity, and unfavourable integration into a globalised trading system. The 'causes' of any episode of food insecurity are a range of elements in this complex system, including drought or commodity price collapse, exacerbated by the impact of HIV/AIDS. Third, statistical aggregates are often misleading: the AIDS-poor may be invisible in overall figures for food production and availability, income per capita, and dependency ratios. These misleading aggregates have helped planners overlook reality for too long, and means that those who are wedded to food balance approaches to measure famine are likely to miss the crisis. Lastly, we are late: the problem has been neglected for too long. Unfortunately, reality testing of the 'new variant famine' hypothesis against the encroaching crisis in southern Africa will precede conventional academic testing: the disaster has begun to hit us before we understood what it was.

This chapter utilises a simplified four-component model of food insecurity to structure discussion. The components are the following:

1. Food production decline;
2. Vulnerability to entitlement collapse;
3. Resilience in the face of external shock;
4. Morbidity and mortality during food crisis.

The HIV/AIDS epidemic affects each one of six components. Moreover they are interrelated. The analysis of this chapter will deal with each. The chapter will not address the additional questions of how HIV/AIDS may interact with other causes of famine (economic crisis, environmental decay, conflict), and what sort of responses may be effective.

Food Production Decline

A generalised HIV/AIDS epidemic in an agrarian society leads to a selective food production decline among the afflicted. This is not primarily, or even at all, an overall decline, but rather the decreased capacity to grow food by households afflicted by AIDS, leading to a food emergency in slow motion.

The first study of the probable impact of HIV/AIDS on farming systems was commissioned by Britain's Overseas Development Administration (ODA) in the late 1980s and published a few years later (Barnett and Blaikie 1992). In broad terms, its predictions have stood the test of time. Illness and death of productive adults impoverishes households in terms of assets, cash income and food production. Across sub-Saharan Africa, household and community-level studies have replicated essentially the same results (Baier 1997, Kwaramba 1998, Toupouzis 1998, Rugalema 1999, Webb and Mutangadura 1999, Baylies 2002, Food Economy Group 2002). These studies show a consistent pattern of adverse impacts (Haddad and Gillespie 2001, FAO 2002):

1. Reduction in area of land under cultivation;
2. Declining yields;
3. Decline in crop variety and changes in cropping patterns;
4. Decline in livestock production;
5. Decline in post-production operations including storage, processing and marketing;
6. Loss of agricultural skills;
7. Shift in the structure of household expenditures to neglect agricultural inputs.

However, there is an important paradox at work. Micro-level studies consistently replicate these depressing results, but it remains extraordinarily difficult to discern measurable effects of HIV/AIDS on food production at a national or regional level. There is a marked disconnection between what we know from household and community studies, and what we observe in aggregate figures. There are several probable reasons for this. A first set of reasons concerns time and data. HIV/AIDS causes a food emergency in slow motion. AIDS mortality lags several years behind HIV infection, and the impact of the epidemic lags still further. Discerning the impact of HIV/AIDS requires a long time series of good quality data. Such data are either unavailable or of insufficient quality for the necessary analysis. And simply because 2002/03 is witnessing the first-ever AIDS-related major food crisis, agricultural statisticians have not looked for AIDS factors in production data. Related to this is a second factor, which is the impact of other variables such as rainfall, market prices, and political instability which may cause greater year-to-year fluctuations in production and create both 'noise' in the data and an overlying systemic crisis that disguises the impact of HIV/AIDS.

These factors point to the way in which HIV/AIDS exacerbates existing problems. Drought, adversely structured international markets, decline in marketing infrastructure and other factors are all important contributors to the crisis. Underpinning all these factors is the extreme poverty of large segments of the southern African rural populace.

The complexity of the impacts of HIV/AIDS contributes to a second set of measurement problems, namely non-linear interactions. As mentioned above, HIV/AIDS impacts different livelihood systems differently. The type of climatic-agricultural system is one determinant: those with unimodal rainfall patterns and time-concentrated labour demands are more vulnerable than those with well-spread rainfall. Those with strict gender divisions of labour (for example where women are prohibited from ploughing) are likely to be more vulnerable than those with more flexibility. Another complicating non-linearity is the compounding factor of a bad rainfall year. Household-level labour shortages may cause difficulties in a normal year, when the rains are good and planting can be spread over a longer time, but be disastrous in a poor rainfall year, when planting must be concentrated in a short time period. A fourth complexity factor is the way in which the impact at the household level of AIDS differs according to the impact stage (Barnett and Blaikie 1992: 89). At an early stage, for example, households may shift production away from cash crops towards cereals, thereby actually increasing food production. This has been documented in Zambia (Baylies 2002). At a later stage, households may reduce cereal production and shift instead to roots such as cassava and sweet potatoes. In this regard, time series data for cassava production are suggestive, implying a reversal of former agricultural development trends.

Table 4.1: Cassava production in selected countries

	1990	1993	1996	1999	2000
Malawi	144,800	216,000	534,500	895,000	900,000
Mozambique	4,590,400	3,511,200	4,734,000	5,352,800	5,362,000
Zambia	640,000	744,000	744,000	970,800	815,200
Zimbabwe	95,000	130,000	150,000	170,000	175,000

Source: FAO

The final reason and most important reason for the statistical invisibility of AIDS-related production decline is the selective impact of the epidemic. Certain households are affected severely, and others less so. A minority may even prosper, taking advantage of their neighbours' distress. For example, women widowed by AIDS may lose their land to relatives and neighbours. It is possible that the new owners may be more productive than the recently dispossessed, thus actually increasing overall food production in the locality, alongside selective destitution of the afflicted. Inequalities are exacerbated. This inequality factor is the most important adverse outcome of the epidemic. In a chronically food insecure country, any increase in inequality ipso facto implies an increase in the number of very poor and food insecure households.

The inequality induced by the HIV/AIDS epidemic means that we can expect AIDS-related food crises even when there is no overall food production or availability deficit in a country. In this context, we should recall Sen (1981), who points out that famine is the phenomenon of some people not *having* enough food to eat, not when there has not *been* enough food to eat. South Asian famines have often been concentrated in certain vulnerable classes without there being a general food availability decline. In Ethiopia, transport problems, poor marketing infrastructure, interruptions in communications by war and low purchasing power by the poor have also led to famine conditions even when the country appears self-sufficient in food. Across most of Africa, however, governments and international organisations continue to assume that food crises are driven by food production declines. Historically this has been a broadly valid assumption. The food balance sheet approach to identifying food crises and responding to them remains dominant. This approach sums the food available in a country, from production, storage and commercial imports, puts it against the total food needs of the population, and identifies a food gap to be filled. In the era of AIDS, this approach is no longer defensible. Food production declines, such as have occurred in southern Africa in 2001–03, are a feature of a poor and drought-prone region, and will be a contributory cause for future food crises. But AIDS-related famines may occur in the absence of such declines, and may continue despite food production rebounds.

> Challenged assumption number 3: African famines are caused by a food production decline

Two additional factors contributing to production decline are worthy of mention. One is the decline in the quality of land management (Barnett and Whiteside 2002: 234–5), which may contribute to pest infestations, soil erosion and other problems. There are no studies yet on the quality of maintenance of irrigation systems during the AIDS epidemic, but it is plausible to expect decline. A second factor is the decay in key institutions such as agricultural extension services and marketing cooperatives, which suffer high rates of staff attrition, lower efficiency and declining morale. For example, in Malawi the number of deaths among the Ministry of Agriculture and Industry staff rose from about 0.45% to 1.1% annually between 1996 and 1998 (Government of Malawi/World Bank 1998).

Vulnerability to Entitlement Collapse

The key point that emerges from the foregoing section is that HIV/AIDS creates a new category of very poor that may be invisible in statistical aggregates. These people cannot be readily defined geographically (as with a drought, a flood or a war), nor politically or ethnically (as with a civil conflict) nor in terms of their structural position in the economy (as with, for example, South Asian famines related to a collapse in the real incomes of certain occupational groups). AIDS is creating little pockets of destitution, like the holes in a Swiss cheese. This also represents a reversion to a pre-modern profile of poverty. In his classic study of the African poor, John Illiffe (1987) argued that before colonialism, poverty in Africa was:

> the structural poverty characteristic of societies with relatively ample resources, especially land, and that characteristic of societies where such resources are scarce. In land-rich societies the very poor are characterised by those who lack access to the labour needed to exploit land (perhaps because they are incapacitated, elderly, or young) and the labour of others (because they are bereft of family or other support). [By contrast,] In land-scarce societies the very poor continue to include such people but also include those among the able-bodied who lack access to land (or other resources) and are unable to sell their labour power at a price sufficient to meet their minimum needs (p. 4).

Whereas the transition from land-rich to land-scarce poverty occurred in Europe and Asia, it did not take place in pre-colonial Africa. Many traditional African concepts of poverty are closely related to having no relatives. With capitalist labour relations in South Africa, a new kind of poverty emerged, namely the structural poor who are deprived of land or other assets that will enable them to utilise their own labour for a livelihood. Writing in the 1980s, Illiffe concluded that the transition to a new kind of structural poverty was underway. With HIV/AIDS, the traditional 'lack of labour' structural poverty has returned with a vengeance.

This new category of the 'AIDS poor' may be defined by a modest revision to Amartya Sen's entitlement theory (Sen 1981). Sen presents entitlement theory with the following, simplified two-dimensional model. The starvation set of an individual is defined as in the figure below. A person plunges into starvation either through a fall in the entitlement bundle or through an unfavourable shift in the exchange entitlement mapping. Figure 4.1 is drawn from Sen's own simplest-case example (Sen 1981: 47–8), which involves pure trade and only food and non-food items. With a price ratio between non-food and food items reflected by the incline of the line AD, the individual x lies outside the starvation set S1 (defined by the region OAD). If, either through a fall in endowments (move to x_i) or a less favourable exchange between non-food and food items (an increase in the incline of the line, AD to BD), then that individual falls within the starvation set (original, S1 or expanded, S2).

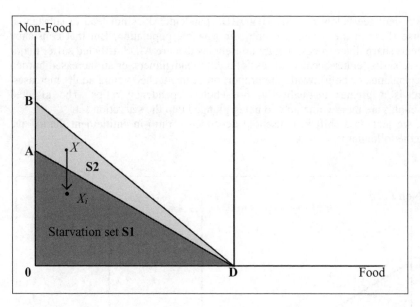

Figure 4.1: Illustration of 'classic' entitlement theory

This analysis points to certain remedies: increasing endowments (moving x upwards) or improving the terms of trade between labour and food (lessening the incline BD).

Agrarian livelihoods are in fact better represented by a three-dimensional model, which includes an additional axis to represent assets and claims (cf. de Waal 1990). Assets include both productive (land, plough, oxen, domestic livestock) and unproductive (jewellery), while claims include social networks. This does not fundamentally change the argument presented here. In a three-dimensional model, additional remedies could be to increase the productivity or monetary value of assets or expand the remit of social claims.

What Sen, and other theorists of famine, did *not* analyse was vulnerability based on household-level scarcity of labour. Even though this was self-evidently a vulnerability factor at the household level, his working assumption was that overall societal dependency ratio would not change adversely during famine, and thus this variable could be held constant, and thereby discounted as a causal factor. Entitlement theory can easily be adapted to allow for an adverse shift in dependency ratios among substantial numbers of households as a contributing cause for the collapse in a household or community's entitlement to sufficient food. In the affected households, each productive individual simply has to be more productive to a specified degree in order to feed her or his dependants, and those with fewer endowments will find this impossible to do. The difficulty that arises is the *practical* one of identifying vulnerability scattered throughout society in this way, rather than the *theoretical* one of understanding why it has occurred.

We shall see below that the HIV/AIDS pandemic does not lead to substantial adverse shifts in the dependency ratio in a whole population. But that constancy conceals sharp divergences: mature households that are AIDS-afflicted suffer major adverse shifts (either because of loss of adult breadwinners, or an increased burden of dependants, or both), while the proportion of unattached young adults increases. There is a greater inequality in household dependency ratios. The affected households are more vulnerable to being plunged into the starvation set.

If we include a shift in household dependency ratio in entitlement theory, we have the following:

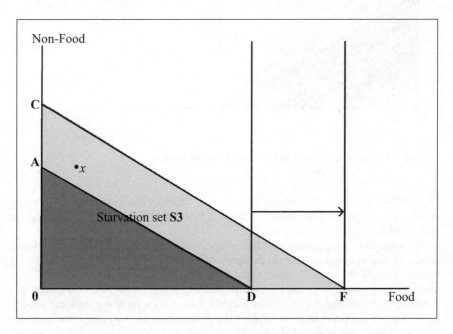

Figure 4.2: Illustration of 'dependency ratio-revised' entitlement theory

Let us take x to represent an average household in a particular community. This is represented simply by moving point D—the food needs of the household—to the right. Even with an unchanged endowment and no change in the exchange between non-food and food items (the incline CF is the same as AD), the household x now falls within the expanded starvation set S3, defined by OCF. Note that this illustration takes no account of the possibility that the household is further afflicted by the illness and consequent lower productivity of its working members, in which case the shift is even more adverse, as the incline of the line CF would become steeper (not shown in the figure). This analysis does not supplant the remedies identified by classic entitlement theory but adds an additional one: lessening the burden of dependants.

HIV/AIDS has the potential to affect every component of household entitlement (Rugalema 1999). On each axis there is a double effect. Affected households lose assets and deplete claims, while also losing the skills and labour necessary to utilise them effectively. Households lose cash income while also needing to spend more on care, treatment and upkeep for dependants. Households need to produce more food to feed a greater number of dependants (orphans and sick adults) while suffering labour shortages. Such households simply cannot reproduce themselves. Even without an external shock such as a drought, they are not 'coping', but stuck in a downward spiral of impoverishment (Rugalema 2000). They cannot utilise development programmes or exploit market opportunities. In this context, the idea that 'relief' is a short-term emergency measure before 'development' can resume must be questioned.

> Challenged assumption number 4: stricken households and communities just need short-term relief so that they can resume development

Just as new methodological and analytical tools are required to identify the food production declines in AIDS-afflicted households, they are also needed for the identification of the dependency dislocations in impacted populations. As mentioned, demographers do not predict overall adverse changes in dependency ratios. However, as the population pyramids for high-prevalence countries show, there are substantial shifts within the adult population. Specifically, there are more young adults and fewer mature adults, and more men than women. This represents a 'dependency disjuncture': the adults who do most of the work of supporting dependant children and the elderly are relatively scarce, while those who are least socially engaged are relatively plentiful. A crude proxy for this is the ratio of the labour force to the total population. Table 4.2 presents projections for labour force contraction in southern Africa.

Table 4.2: Projected labour force losses in Southern Africa due to HIV/AIDS

	Overall labour force		Agricultural labour force	
	By 2005	By 2020	1985–2000	1985–2035
Botswana	-17.2	-30.8	-6.6	-23.2
Lesotho	-4.8	-10.6		
Malawi	-10.7	-16.0	-5.8	-13.8
Mozambique	-9.0	-24.9	-2.3	-20.0
Namibia	-12.8	-35.1	-3.0	-26.0
South Africa	-10.8	-24.9	-3.9	-19.9
Tanzania	-9.1	-14.6	-5.8	-12.7
Zimbabwe	-19.7	-29.4	-9.6	-22.7

Sources: Columns 2 and 3, Husain and Badcock-Walters, 2001: 13; columns 4 and 5, FAO 2002

The overall population is expected to decline only marginally over this period. These figures represent a substantially smaller workforce supporting a substantially larger number of dependants. Note again that vulnerability will be a product of inequality: these overall figures represent losses concentrated in a minority of households. A supplementary measure of vulnerability will be the proportion of households that have seriously adverse dependency ratios, for example 'sibling households' that lack any adult, and those with just one adult and several children.

An additional methodological tool is the 'effective dependency ratio' (EDR), which includes sick adults among the dependants. Households with an adverse EDR are seriously at risk of impoverishment and hunger. It is a unique and tragic feature of HIV/AIDS that the period of sickness of a person living with AIDS may be more stressful and impoverishing than the bereavement itself. Studies show that dying of AIDS causes more distress to a household than dying of other causes (Kwaramba 1998).

Challenged assumption number 5: stable dependency ratios mean we do not have to worry about labour scarcities

---

These two methodological innovations, the dependency disjuncture and EDR, are profoundly gendered in a way that conventional dependency ratio calculations are not. Any measure of social engagement and participation in care activities will necessarily place greater emphasis on women's work. The burden of production, care and coping is falling disproportionately on women, who are not only overburdened by these tasks, but disproportionately vulnerable to HIV and AIDS.

Resilience and Livelihood Coping Strategies

The second main plank of the 'new variant famine' hypothesis is that it entails a new trajectory of outcomes of famine, and specifically a steady descent into destitution with less chances of a post-crisis recovery.

Livelihood coping strategies in the face of food shortage have been widely studied (de Waal 1989, Davies 1995) and are credited with enabling southern Africa to avoid famine despite the serious drought of 1991– 2 (Eldridge 2002). In the era of HIV/AIDS, however, we need to examine the assumptions on which effective coping strategies are based. There are six key premises. Three are definitely called into question by HIV/AIDS, and for the other three, it is plausible that they are, but we do not currently have data.

A central assumption in coping strategy theory is that reducing consumption is viable. In old-style famine adults reduced their food consumption and simply went hungry. They routinely ate one meal a day or perhaps one every two days, and these meals chiefly consisted of carbohydrates, often cereal substitutes such as roots or wild grains. The physical resilience of rural adults meant that, with the exception of nursing mothers, their wellbeing was usually ignored by relief agencies. With a concurrent generalised epidemic of HIV/AIDS, adult malnutrition has very different implications, which will be discussed in the following section.

Challenged assumption number 6: adults can withstand protracted malnutrition without adverse consequences

The next assumption is that kinship networks work. The generosity of the African 'extended' family has long supported individuals who have fallen on hard times. Rural people typically migrated to cities for assistance during drought. But, with HIV/AIDS, we see two distinct differences. The first is a reversal of the flows of assistance. In the private sector, some employers are 'shifting the burden' of HIV/AIDS by withdrawing health benefits (Rosen and Simon 2002). In the public sector, salaries and benefits may be theoretically available, but simply not paid on time, or at all. Urban people living with HIV and AIDS may also return 'home' to rural areas to end their lives and be buried. As a result, impoverished rural people have an additional burden (which may in fact be the major economic impact of the disease in some areas) and cannot count on urban networks for support. The second difference is that kinship networks are saturated in caring for children orphaned by AIDS. The escalating numbers of these unfortunate children means that hungry rural families are unlikely to find relatives ready to support them, by sharing food or taking in children for the duration of the famine. Kindness has its limits.

Challenged assumption number 7: the African kinship network operates as an effective safety net

Another unstated assumption is that households have sufficient labour to undertake alternative activities for earning income and food. In traditional famines, dependency ratios improved on account of lower fertility and the deaths of young children (Watkins and Menken 1985). This made possible activities such as foraging for wild foods, working on farms and income-generating activities such as collecting firewood. Many of these activities involve travelling long distances on foot. The amount of work necessary to earn sufficient calories to sustain a family increased: but usually not to breaking point.

Household-level labour scarcities change this. If breadwinners are occupied with caring for children and sick adults, or are sick themselves, this may not be possible.

Challenged assumption number 8: rural people will exploit whatever coping strategies are available

The importance of these three assumptions can be seen in the following figure, which represents the trajectory of livelihood coping strategies by households threatened with famine. First, households resort to the 'high resilience' strategies that do not impair their chance of returning to their former livelihood, such as reducing consumption, utilising support networks, and gathering wild foods. Only when these fail, or are impossible to follow, do they pursue activities that impede their future recovery, such as working during the planting season, selling essential assets, or abandoning their land altogether. In most agrarian societies in Africa, it was a truism that two or more years of drought were needed before households reached this point.

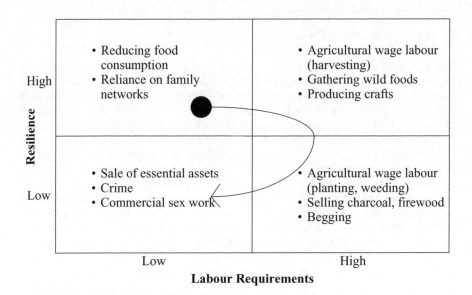

Figure 4.3: Trajectory of livelihood coping strategies

In the era of AIDS, the two preferred strategies (in the top left quadrant) may be dangerous or inoperable, while high-labour activities (in the right quadrants) may be constrained or impossible. The velocity of decline may be much faster. There is evidence in support of this from Uganda (Baylies 2002: 620, quoting Seeley (1993) and Donahue (1998)), where three stages of 'coping' have been identified: first, using kinship welfare mechanisms, second, disposing of key assets, and last, household dissolution.

> Challenged assumption number 9: African famines are slow-onset because coping strategies provide delay destitution and starvation for many months

Another assumption, that must be questioned but cannot at this point be overturned, is that the market in fall-back activities will not collapse entirely. Working on farms for money or food is possible if there are sufficiently many farmers that are not poor to provide employment; selling firewood depends upon a demand by urban households, etc. In any situation of widespread distress, unskilled wage rates will plummet, because labour supply increases and demand contracts. But even in the worst drought famines, wages were usually sufficient to feed an individual and one or two children. This may change. But to date, the macro-economic trajectories of AIDS-affected economies have not reached this point. In most cases, although the economy may be growing less fast or shrinking somewhat, it has not collapsed entirely, so that labour markets are still functioning.

Note that this also holds for commercial sex work. The model of coping strategies presented would predict that the supply of commercial sex workers would increase much more rapidly than in an old-variant famine. The laws of supply and demand imply that payment would decline sharply. There is some evidence for this, from a survey by Save the Children Fund into commercial sex worker livelihoods in Binga, Zimbabwe, in March 2002 (SCF 2002). During the survey, a group of well-established sex workers in their thirties identified a new group of sex workers: 'These are women and girls as young as 15 who come from rural areas in bad times such as drought years to earn money from commercial sex work. The interviewees said that there had been a definite increase in the number of such women coming to Binga since 2001 when food security in rural areas began to deteriorate, and they estimated that there are approximately 200 women engaged in commercial sex work' (p. 2). The CSWs further reported that these younger girls were more ready to engage in sex without a condom, both because the price was higher, and because they were less aware of the risks.

Most of the market for fall-back income generating activities lies in urban areas or small towns. It is a reasonable prediction that the food crisis will witness considerable migration to towns and cities, and that relatively little of this will be reversed should the rains return. This not only threatens long-term destitution for the distress migrants, but also impoverishes the lower strata of the urban poor, who have to compete with the incomers for the lowest level of jobs.

The next questionable (but still provisionally intact) assumption is that adults in households threatened by famine have the skill and experience to implement coping strategies. The fact that famine victims are very poor does not mean that they are ignorant. On the contrary, survival skills are sophisticated. We may fear loss of these skills. Three examples will suffice. One: collecting wild foods is a very common strategy. Knowledge of wild foods and how to prepare them is handed down from mother to daughter. If this knowledge is lost, an important coping strategy will vanish. Two: many strategies involve migration, which in turn requires knowledge of economic geography. Young people may not know where they can earn an income. Three: an effective coping strategy requires planning a household budget over a period of twelve months or more, and conserving key resources such as seeds for the critical period when they will be needed for planting. This is an activity best carried out by skilled and experienced adults. Presently, we have no information on whether these skills are being lost.

A final assumption that underpins effective coping is the subjective expectation of returning to a viable livelihood at the conclusion of the drought. This is the most difficult to assess, but possibly the most significant of all. The prospect of an economically viable and socially acceptable way of life is the basic motivation for a household to undergo the hardships entailed by a successful response to drought. A cultural archive of historical famine is an important resource in effectively responding to famine. If a community can recall, directly or through historical memory, past disasters, how they were overcome, and how things returned to normal afterwards, this can help frame their responses to current threats (de Waal 1989, Davies 1995). If that archive is lost, or is considered irrelevant because there is no anticipation of returning to 'normality', let alone an upward trajectory, then the motivation for 'coping' may itself be lost. Currently, there is no research into this element. We cannot say if this assumption is justified or should be jettisoned.

What does this mean for recovery? For the AIDS-poor, recovery will be extremely difficult if not impossible. For poor communities, the losses of the famine will be harder to recoup. Livelihood coping strategies will not have worked, and 'coping' is in fact a misnomer (qua Rugalema 2000).

Challenged assumption number 10: 'coping strategies' mean households can 'cope'

For national economies, a new category of destitutes will continue to expand, and HIV/AIDS will increase its drag on economic growth. New variant famine threatens to be a phenomenon with only a modest and temporary recovery. The hunger of the AIDS-poor will continue after the proximate causes of the famine, such as drought, have gone.

Challenged assumption number 11: famines are time-bound events followed by a 'bounce back' to normality

Morbidity and Mortality

Morbidity and mortality in an AIDS-related famine is likely to be different from that in a traditional drought famine. In the absence of any epidemiology and demography from a new variant famine—because none has yet occurred—this section will have to construct plausible hypotheses.

Famine mortality is driven by two factors. One is under-nutrition, especially among young children. The second is 'health crises' defined as migration-induced outbreaks of infectious diseases, congregation of people in displaced camps with inadequate shelter, water and hygiene, and the breakdown of sanitation systems. These health crises and the associated increase in disease prevalence are an important reason for increased malnutrition and mortality during famine (de Waal 1989). Health crises put all at risk, the well-nourished as well as the malnourished, and they can also cause higher death rates in towns. 'Frank' starvation, that is individuals dying simply from lack of food without the presence of an infectious disease, is exceptionally rare.

The concurrent presence of a generalised AIDS epidemic, widespread malnutrition and health crises is likely to cause new patterns and higher levels of morbidity and mortality. At the individual level, there is a vicious interaction between malnutrition and HIV/AIDS. Undernourished individuals are more susceptible to being infected with HIV, and nutritional status is also an important determinant of risks in mother-to-child transmission of HIV (Coutsoudis et al. 1999). This, however, will not rapidly translate into morbidity and mortality. Rather it will exacerbate the AIDS epidemic itself, alongside wider socio-economic factors including the resort to commercial sex work, distress migration and the breakdown of social cohesion.

Most types of nutritional deficiencies suppress the immune system, and thus make infections—including HIV—more virulent. HIV replicates more rapidly in malnourished individuals, hastening the progression from HIV to AIDS (ACC/SCN

1998, Semba and Tang 1999). People living with HIV and AIDS have both increased nutritional needs (to fight the infection) and lower absorption of nutrients. Protein needs are commonly estimated at 30–50% more and energy needs about 15% more. Irregular meals and the consumption of substitute wild foods, which may be hard to digest and cause digestive problems, can only make matters worse. Therefore, at an aggregate population level, widespread malnutrition threatens to accelerate the progression from HIV to AIDS for millions of infected individuals. Will this mean mass mortality of people living with HIV and AIDS during the famine period? Will it mean protracted higher death rates for some years to come? We simply do not know. It is immaterial whether the deaths of these individuals will be diagnosed as starvation, AIDS, or another infectious disease.

The sickness and possible death of these individuals also has knock-on effects for their families and especially their children. These households will face the costs of care and treatment at precisely the moment when they can least afford them. There is already evidence that indicates that children in households where an adult is sick with AIDS, and children orphaned by AIDS, are more likely to be malnourished or sick, and are more likely to die. These effects can only be worsened by a concurrent food crisis.

Famine-related health crises will also be worsened, both by the accelerated collapse of livelihoods and coping strategies, and also by the lower baseline health status of the affected population. Famines typically reduce the general health of the population for an extended period. With widespread immunosuppression due to HIV, susceptibility to infectious diseases can only increase. The chain-reaction in terms of other epidemics such as waterborne infections may extend the period of heightened mortality further into the post-famine period (if such occurs) and increase the demographic categories at risk (more adults may die).

Challenged assumption number 12: increases in mortality will follow the 'traditional' pattern of being time-bound and concentrated among young children

---

However, one piece of good news is that levels of immunisation against key childhood diseases have remained high throughout southern Africa. This high level of childhood immunisation protects a vulnerable population from what have historically been some of the main killers during famine. This also goes some way towards explaining the low levels of child malnutrition recorded until the end of 2002.

More disturbing are the implications of the food crisis and 'coping' strategies for HIV transmission. The combination of factors associated with the crisis, including malnutrition, generally lower health, increased commercial sex work, greater migration and social disruption, and increasing inequality, all create an environment highly favourable for increased HIV transmission. It will also be more difficult to maintain prevention and treatment under these circumstances.

The emergence of AIDS-related food crises has important implications for demographic projections, and indeed other models of the future trajectory of the epidemic and its wider impacts. As hinted at the outset, the secondary impacts of HIV/AIDS, notably famine, may be just as serious as the primary impacts. Famines of all variants tend to kill people, especially young children. A protracted famine

Table 4.3: Immunization, measles and DPT (% of children under 12 months)

	Measles		DPT	
Countries	1990	1999	1990	1999
Botswana	87	86	91	90
Lesotho	80	77	76	85
Malawi	80	83	87	84
Mozambique	59	57	46	61
Namibia	41	66	53	72
Swaziland	85	82	89	99
Zambia	90	90	91	84
Zimbabwe	87	79	88	81

Source: Health, Nutrition, and Population (HNP statistics – the World Bank),
http://devdata.worldbank.org/hnpstats/ accessed on 4 November 2002

afflicting a large population could cause additional excess mortality in the hundreds of thousands, or more. It would probably depress fertility levels as well, due to malnutrition, famine amenorrhea and higher levels of HIV and AIDS. While traditional famines kill more men than women (Macintyre 2002), it is possible that this will change in an AIDS-related famine, which strikes a population with higher HIV rates among women than men. Such a famine would undoubtedly cause increased rural-urban migration as more rural livelihoods collapse and the rural economy cannot sustain the poorest, and increased outmigration of skilled young adults who see better life chances for them and their children elsewhere. It might in turn contribute to political instability, which would have its own implications.

These implications are not reassuring. We are only at the beginning of the principal demographic impacts of HIV/AIDS in southern Africa. If a secondary impact such as the current food crisis can be unleashed by the comparatively modest dependency disjunctures and immiseration processes set in train thus far, what scale of impacts can we anticipate in ten years or so? Neither existing models for famine demography, nor projections for the demographic impact of HIV/AIDS, take into account the interaction between the two. Famine demography anticipates a rapid end to the period of excess mortality, followed by a fertility rebound and a resumption of the former stable trajectory of the population. In the worst case, one famine may create vulnerability to a successor—the so-called 'bang bang famines' (Dyson 2002)—but famines were historically remarkable for the transience of their demographic impacts (Watkins and Menken 1985). Meanwhile, demographic models for the impact of the HIV/AIDS epidemic assume a 'stabilisation' of some kind in ten years or so. They do not factor in secondary effects such as famine. If the current food crisis proves an augur of what is to come, any 'stabilisation' may be much further in the future. It is probable that southern Africa will experience significant demographic instability for the foreseeable future.

Challenged assumption number 13: we have reliable models for the future demography of southern Africa

Conclusion

The evidence summarised in this chapter points to the existence of new patterns of famine vulnerability, new causal factors in the causation of mass hunger, and new trajectories for coping (or rather, failing to cope) with famine, all of them related to HIV/AIDS. This is what we are calling 'new variant famine.' This does not supplant other causative elements in famine vulnerability in Africa, notably extreme poverty, but augments them. However, the scale of the HIV/AIDS pandemic is such that it may be the most important factor determining vulnerability to starvation within famine.

The evidence in favour of the new variant famine hypothesis is considerable. But the hypothesis remains to be tested rigorously, against data sets generated specifically to examine its predictions. In the meantime, it is more in the way of an organising framework for ideas, helping to guide thinking, research and hopefully responses. However, the record of development practitioners absorbing the lessons of research into HIV/AIDS is discouraging. More than a decade after the ODA-sponsored research by Tony Barnett and Piers Blaikie was completed (Barnett and Blaikie 1992), Britain's official aid department had yet to incorporate its findings into its programming. As Barnett and Whiteside point out, 'Anecdotal evidence may be less conclusive but it is sometimes a long way ahead of the "scientific" evidence that moves politicians, donors and multilateral organisations. Experience with AIDS and agriculture leads us to think that the time lag between significant anecdote and quantitative "evidence" may be as long as 20 years' (2002: 237).

Challenged assumption number 14: research findings translate into action

Analysis of possible responses to new variant famine lies outside the scope of this chapter. However, it is clear that it will be less amenable to the kinds of intervention that have been mobilised for traditional drought famines. Targeting the most vulnerable will be much more difficult. New kinds of long-term welfare assistance will be required. Adults will need to be catered for as well as children. Women must be the priority. Some of the relief responses will be improvements on existing best practices, such as the need to focus on food insecure people within food systems, as well as food systems themselves (cf. Davies 1995: 5, Webb and Paquette 2000). Others, such as novel ways for supporting those who care for children orphaned by AIDS, may have to be entirely new.

Challenged assumption number 15: existing modalities for emergency response will do

One of the most disturbing aspects of the new variant famine hypothesis, repeatedly hinted at in this chapter, is its implications for HIV transmission. The vicious cycle of interaction between malnutrition and HIV operates at the individual level, and a similar interaction appears at the social and economic levels. Assumptions about the future trajectories of the AIDS pandemic are thus called into question. There is a real possibility of a new chronic condition in which a substantial category of people, massively impoverished by AIDS and its impacts, require long-term welfare assistance. The prognosis is not good.

References

ACC/SCN (Administrative Committee on Coordination/Subcommittee on Nutrition of the United Nations), 1998, 'Overview to the feature: Nutrition and HIV/AIDS,' *SCN News*, 17, 3– 4.

Baier, E., 1997, 'The Impact of HIV/AIDS on Rural Household/Communities and the Need for Multisectoral Prevention and Mitigation Strategies to Combat the Epidemic in Rural Areas,' FAO, Rome.

Barnett, Tony and Piers Blaikie, 1992, *AIDS in Africa: Its Present and Future Impact*, London, John Wiley.

Barnett, Tony and Alan Whiteside, 2002, *AIDS in the Twenty First Century: Disease and Globalization*, London, Macmillan Palgrave.

Baylies, Carolyn, 2002, 'The Impact of AIDS on Rural Households in Africa: A Shock Like Any Other?' *Development and Change*, 33, 611– 32.

Caldwell, J.C., 1977, 'Demographic Aspects of Drought: An Examination of the African Drought of 1970– 74,' in D. Dalby, R. Harrison-Church and F. Bezzaz (eds.) *Drought in Africa 2*, London, International African Institute.

Coutsoudis, A., K. Pillay, E. Spooner, L., Kuhn, and H. Coovadia, 1999, 'Influence of infant feeding patterns on early mother-to-child transmission of HIV-1 in Durban, South Africa: A prospective cohort study,' *The Lancet*, 354, 471–6.

Davies, Susanna, 1995, *Adaptable Livelihoods: Coping with Food Insecurity in the Malian Sahel*, London, Macmillan Palgrave.

de Waal, Alex, 1989, *Famine that Kills: Darfur, Sudan, 1984–1985*, Oxford, Clarendon Press.

de Waal, Alex, 1990, 'A Re-assessment of Entitlement Theory in the Light of the Recent Famines in Africa,' *Development and Change*, 21.3, 469–90.

de Waal, Alex, and Alan Whiteside, 2003, 'New Variant Famine: AIDS and Food Crisis', *The Lancet*, 362, 1234.

Devereux, Stephen, 2002, 'The Malawi Famine of 2002,' in Stephen Devereux (ed.) *The New Famines*, Sussex, IDS Bulletin, 33.4, October.

Dyson, Tim, 2002, 'Famine in Berar, 1896–7 and 1899–1900: Echoes and Chain Reactions,' in Tim Dyson and Cormac Ó Gráda (eds.) *Famine Demography: Perspectives from the Past and Present*, Oxford, Oxford University Press.

Eldridge, Chris, 2002 'Why was there no famine following the 1992 Southern African drought? The contributions and consequences of household responses,' *IDS Bulletin*, 33.4: 79– 87.

FAO, 2002, 'The Impact of HIV/AIDS on Food Security in Africa,' Paper for the 22nd Regional Conference for Africa, 'HIV/AIDS, Agriculture and Food Security in Mainland and Small Island Countries of Africa,' Cairo, Egypt, 4– 8 February.

Food Economy Group, 2002, 'Household Food Economy and HIV/AIDS: Exploring the Linkages', Food Economy Group.

Government of Malawi/World Bank, 1998, *Malawi AIDS Assessment Study*. Report No. 17740 MAI (place/publisher not cited).

Haddad, Lawrence, and Stuart Gillespie, 2001, 'Effective Food and Nutrition Policy Responses to HIV/AIDS: What We Know and What We Need to Know,' Washington DC, International Food Policy Research Institute, Food Consumption and Nutrition Division, Discussion Paper No. 112.

Husain, Ishrat and Peter Badcock-Walters, 2001, 'Economics of HIV/AIDS Impact Mitigation: Responding to Problems of Systemic Dysfunction and Sectoral Capacity,' Washington DC, USAID and Durban, HEARD, Paper for Barcelona HIV/AIDS Conference.

Illiffe, John, 1987, *The African Poor: A History*, Cambridge, Cambridge University Press.

Kwaramba, P, 1998, 'The Socio-economic Impact of HIV/AIDS on Communal Agricultural Production Systems in Zimbabwe,' Working Paper 19, Economic Advisory Project, Friedrich Ebert Stiftung, Harare.

Macintyre, Kate, 2002, 'Famine and the female mortality advantage,' in Tim Dyson and Cormac Ó Gráda (eds.) *Famine Demography: Perspectives from the Past and Present*, Oxford, Oxford University Press.

Mortimore, Michael, 1989, *Adapting to Drought: Farmers, Famines and Desertification in West Africa*, Cambridge, Cambridge University Press.

Rosen, Sydney, and Jonathan Simon, 2002, 'Shifting the Burden of HIV/AIDS,' Boston University, Center for International Health, February.

Rugalema, Gabriel, 1999, 'Adult Mortality as Entitlement Failure: AIDS and the Crisis of Livelihoods in a Tanzanian Village,' The Hague, PhD Thesis, Institute of Social Studies.

Rugalema, Gabriel, 2002, 'Coping or Struggling? A Journey into the Impact of HIV/AIDS in Southern Africa,' *Review of African Political Economy*, 26.86, 537– 45.

Save the Children Fund, 2002, 'The Livelihoods of Commercial Sex Workers in Binga,' Harare, SCF, March.

Semba, R. D., and A. M. Tang, 1999, 'Micronutrients and the pathogenesis of human immunodeficiency virus infection,' *British Journal of Nutrition*, 81, pp. 181– 189.

Sen, Amartya, 1981, *Poverty and Famines: An Essay on Entitlement and Deprivation*, Oxford, Clarendon Press.

Swift, Jeremy, (ed.) 1993, 'New Approaches to Famine,' *IDS Bulletin*, 24.4.

Topouzis, D., 1998, 'The Implications of HIV/AIDS For Rural Development Policy and Programming: Focus on Sub-Saharan Africa,' FAO, Sustainable Development Dept., and UNDP, HIV and Development Programme.

Watkins, Susan C., and Jane Menken, 1985, 'Famines in Historical Perspective,' *Population and Development Review*, 11, 647– 76.

Webb, D., and Mutangadura, G., 1999, *The Socio-economic Impact of Adult Morbidity and Mortality in Households in Kafue District Zambia*, SAfAIDS.

Webb, D., and Paquette, S., 2000, 'The Potential Role of Food Aid in Mitigating the Impacts of HIV/AIDS: The Case of Zambia,' *Development in Practice*, 10.5, 694– 700.

World Development Movement, 2002, *Structural Damage: The Causes and Consequences of Malawi's Food Crisis*, London, WDM.

Chapter 5

Cultural Hazards Facing Young People in the Era of HIV/AIDS: Specificity and Change

Carolyn Baylies

HIV/AIDS is not one but a multiplicity of epidemics, each with its specific characteristics, imprinting itself on existing structures and practices. As Kreniske (1997) has noted, disease is invariably a social event, which expresses the central realities of the society in which it occurs. While influenced by the very structure of the social and economic environment it enters, AIDS has in turn been characterised as revealing the frailties and divisions of the societies where it gains a grip. Van de Vliet (1996: 78) refers in this vein to AIDS travelling along societies' fault lines and exposing instability, while Santana (1997) likens AIDS to an x-ray which highlights societal flaws and weak points of society.

These comments, if imprecise, are highly evocative, underlying the need to examine the social context in which the epidemic insinuates itself. 'Fault lines' describing global inequalities, and reflected in limited state capacity to secure public health and mitigate the ravages of AIDS on households and larger economic units, contribute to differential levels of prevalence and impact across nations and regions. Within countries, fault lines, flaws and weak points describe patterns of inequality and political and social marginality of the sort referred to by Ramasubban in respect of India:

> AIDS, as no other disease before it, holds up a mirror to Indian society, compelling both policy makers and members of the civil society to bring on centre-stage policies, social processes, social groups and behaviour that had hitherto been relegated to the margins (Ramasubban, R 1999: 358).

Marginality in this sense refers to groups that are subject to social discrimination, whose members lack access to services, or who may be criminalised by virtue of their activities (commercial sex workers, drug users and sometimes those engaging in homosexual activities). They may be refugees, internally displaced persons or those otherwise subject to political and social dislocation. They may be individuals whose impairments cause them to be treated as less deserving or less human and make them particularly subject to sexual abuse. They may be individuals living in extreme poverty or suffering a deficit of human rights.

In some settings there has been an increasing concentration of AIDS among marginal groups across the course of the epidemic. Indeed Mann and Tarantola (1996: 464) suggest that whatever the specific history of the epidemic in a given

71

region or country, 'those people who were marginalized, stigmatised and discriminated against – before HIV/AIDS arrived – have become over time those at highest risk of HIV infection'. However, while this may describe the course of the epidemic in the United States, Brazil or many west European countries, in other cases there has been movement from the sort of marginal groups referred to by Ramasubban, and still identified in India as groups at risk, to the broader population. Whether within marginal groups or the wider population, however, power relations determine patterns of relative risk. Those with lesser capability to enforce their own agency and ensure protection are disproportionately in danger.

Cultural Contexts

Ability to ensure agency and thereby secure protection is partly a consequence of social location, but also of how social location articulates with cultural belief systems and cultural practice. As Daniel and Parker note:

> The epidemic will develop among us according to our specific cultural characteristics – our sexual culture, our material and symbolic resources for dealing with health and disease, and our prejudices and capacity to exercise solidarity (Daniel and Parker, 1993).

In the face of AIDS, some cultural practices and the power relations that enforce them can become harmful. UNAIDS's Technical Update of 1998 puts special stress in this regard on the way 'gender-related norms' can become barriers to protection against HIV and calls for these to be challenged (1998: 7). Such norms are necessarily bound up in broader gender ideologies – ideologies of masculinity and femininity – that are specific to cultural context. As Hamblin and Reid (1991: n.p) put the point more generally – 'culturally created norms of masculinity place men at high risk of becoming infected through accepted male lifestyles. Culturally created norms of femininity place women and children at high risk of becoming infected through the same male lifestyles'.

It is not that all aspects of masculinity, or a particular masculine ideology, are inherently harmful. But those aspects that posit men as legitimately exercising control over women, and thereby condoning gender inequality and inequitable power relations, are problematic. It is in reference to this that Hamblin and Reid state emphatically that 'cultural ideals of masculinity and femininity in themselves have become responsible for a devastating toll of lives, especially women's lives' (1991, n.p.).

Cultural norms and practices are never static and are subject to external influences as well as internal pressures. Indeed HIV is part of those external forces that constitute the fabric of change. In some cases where prevalence is high, HIV may be highly influential in changing behaviours. In others it remains less acknowledged and more hidden, a silent factor that even so alters the socio-cultural-health environment in ways that produce increased 'hazards'.

Youth at the Crossroads

HIV is indeed a disease of society, with transmission following relations of vulnerability and inequitable power relations, emanating in part from the particular political economy that characterises a given social formation. In view of the fact that HIV is also mediated by specific cultural factors, including patterns of sexual practice and sexuality, there have been calls in India for more detailed analysis of the contexts and sequences of sexual behaviour (Pelto, 1999: 562) and of the social and cultural constraints that inform patterns of sexual activity, perceptions of sexual relations and sexual responsibility (Jejeebhoy, 1998: 1287–8). As Kelly and Parker (2000: 38) affirm with reference to southern Africa, 'there is a great deal more work that needs to be done in this area, around issues such as how people select partners, the workings of power in youth sexual relationships, the role of emotional intimacy in sexual relationships, the levels of discussion between partners and so on'. Not least, an understanding of these factors is crucial for any intervention to be effective. As Ashana and Oostvogels (2001: 708) put it:

> ...if appropriate and effective HIV interventions are to be developed, more attention should be paid to the specific cultural context of sexuality and to the ways in which cultural diversity relates to sexual risk behaviour.

With these points in mind, this paper is concerned with exploring the specificity characterising the epidemic in particular locales, alongside elements of broader commonality, by looking across two regions – Africa and South Asia. The focus of the paper is on the situation of young people. This is partly because of their vulnerability, given that adolescence is a time of exploring sexual identities, and partly due to their position at the interface between 'traditional values' and 'new' forms of behaviour transmitted via an increasingly global media. However, this focus also follows from concern about the gaps in knowledge characterising young people in regard to the mode of HIV transmission and means of protection. Surveys from 40 countries have indicated that more than 60% of those aged 15 to 24 have misconceptions about modes of transmission of the virus (UNAIDS, 2002). The majority do not use condoms during their first sexual experience, with the proportion of people failing to use condoms the greater, the lower the age of sexual initiation (Blanc and Way 1998). Younger people also have less access to sexual health services or to condoms and all too often encounter 'unfriendly' attitudes when attempting to access services (Rivers and Aggleton, 1999; Webb, 1997). Yet the crucial position of this group, as initially free from HIV, means that it potentially provides a window of opportunity for stemming the course of the epidemic.

This paper will thus explore the way in which changing cultural practices and prescriptions provide the context in which HIV is transmitted, creating a specific pattern of risk or set of risk factors. It will give particular attention to the articulation of cultural influences – both 'traditional' and 'external' – especially in relation to sexual behaviour. The paper will examine the way in which certain 'cultural practices' may become harmful in the context of AIDS and especially the way in which an evolving articulation of cultural beliefs and practices in respect of sexual initiation, courtship and casual sex may create particular hazards.

Gender relations are necessarily in the foreground of such an exploration. A strong assumption is that hazards apply differently to young men and young women. While both may be at risk, male dominance in sexual relations, exercised in some cases through coercion and violence, means that young women can face particular danger in negotiating their way through adolescence and early adulthood. Their susceptibility to HIV is further exacerbated by biological factors, ideologies of femininity that discourage their acquisition of sexual knowledge, and incidence in some locales in both southern Africa and India of beliefs that sex with a female virgin can 'cure' AIDS.

Specificity and Commonalities across India and Africa

The rate of adult prevalence of HIV in India is much lower than in most African countries, and certainly so than in those African countries most severely affected. Among young people aged 15 to 24 at the end of 1999, estimated prevalence among females was as high as 26% in Zimbabwe and 36% in Botswana, as against just 0.8% in India (*Population Reports*, 2001: 4). In the early stages of AIDS, India was characterised by a set of very different epidemics in different parts of the country, variously linked to injecting drug use, commercial sex and the transport sector. Patterns continue to vary across regions and states in India. However, the apparently inexorable movement of HIV across bridge groups to the general population is a matter of considerable concern (interview UNAIDS India, April 2002).

Even a low prevalence translates into large numbers affected, with India thought to be second only to South Africa as the country with the largest number of cases. Yet low prevalence also means that the impact of HIV/AIDS is less visible and its effects less obvious, and less pressing on individual and collective consciousness. Thus an AIDS NGO working in rural Karnataka encountered the complaint 'why are you telling us about AIDS when we have so many other problems?' (Verma et al, 1999: 409). As HIV travels through the population, however, the effect of pre-existing cultural practices carrying new dangers and transitional behaviours posing even greater risk are as significant in India as in Africa.

Among cultural practices identified in some African settings as hazardous in the face of AIDS are the use of agents to tighten and dry the vagina, widow inheritance, property grabbing and sexual cleansing on the death of a husband. It is arguable that in the case of India, arranged marriages may prove problematic for women where men are likely to have considerably higher levels of pre-marital sexual experience than women. Even these few examples underline how gender relations in respect of sexual encounters within and outside marriage and in respect of customs relating to the acquisition or loss of a marital partner are particularly pertinent in sketching out patterns of vulnerability.

As our primary concern here is with the particular hazards faced by adolescents, it may be useful to provide a brief overview of (changing) patterns relating to choice of marital partners, sexual initiation, and use of contraception in the two regions.

While parents or kin may have arranged marriages of children in the relatively recent past and conventions continue to apply in some settings about the 'inheritance' of widows by a husband's brother, marriage is generally negotiated by individuals across much of Africa. Although economic considerations apply, the ideal of marriage as based on love and affection has gained increasing credence. This means that new patterns of courtship have emerged, based on past practices, but also representing a mediation between past and present, drawing on external influences, not least the global media. In India, in contrast to much of sub-Saharan Africa, arranged marriage continues to be the norm, with parents driven by a strong sense of responsibility to ensure a match providing a secure future for their children, economically and otherwise. While parental approval is still important, however, some of those who are more highly urbanised and more highly educated are beginning to subvert former practices. In the process, they, too, are charting new ground, often without guidance and with limited protection.

Norms proscribing sexual activity prior to marriage remain strong in both regions. The majority of adolescents across both do not engage in sexual relations, or if they do, cannot be said to be promiscuous. Yet as marriage has been delayed, sometimes in consequence of girls remaining longer in school, instances of pre-marital sex are far from absent. In Ghana the difference between the percentage of women aged 20 to 24 who had sex by age 18 and the percentage who had married by this age was 28.4 as against a figure of 19.3 for their mothers' generation. In the case of Uganda the respective figures were 16.2 and 10.5 (Blanc and Way, 1998). In many African settings there is increasing acknowledgement that pre-marital sex occurs and perhaps a greater tolerance of it than applied in the past. There is considerable variation across Africa in median age of sexual initiation and median age of marriage, but while both have edged upward, this is true to a lesser degree for sexual initiation, so that in some areas there is an increasing gap. It has been suggested (UNAIDS, 2000) that there may be a correlation between the length of this gap between age of sexual debut and age of marriage and the prevalence of HIV. Whether valid or not, this presents a time of potential danger for adolescents, particularly when access to means of protection or norms discouraging such protection may apply.

The median age at first sex in India is about 21 years for men compared with 18 years for women, typically higher for both sexes than in Africa (NACO 2002). Across much of India, cultural assumptions that sex must be confined to marriage remain strong and have contributed in some quarters to the belief that the prospect of an AIDS epidemic is low. Jejeebhoy (1998: 1277), however, regards it as a serious misperception that 'adolescents and unmarried individuals rarely engaged in sexual relations, that sexual activity occurs overwhelmingly within the context of marriage, and is not a matter of concern'. Patterns vary considerably between men and women. While much less is known about young women's sexual experience than about young men's (Jejeebhoy, 1998: 1279), most research in India indicates very low or even negligible levels of pre-marital sexual relations among women. A study of 1230 anglophone college students in Mumbai from well educated backgrounds whose modal ages were 17 and 16, for example, found only 8% of males and 1% of females claiming to have had any sexual experience (Mathai et al, 1997). In many places close surveillance of girls by their families remains the norm. Research on the sexual activities of unmarried adolescent males indicate much greater variability, which may reflect real differences across region, class and level of education (Jejeebhoy, 1998). However, a number of studies have found that between 20% and

25% of young men have engaged in sexual relations, often with older women (Jejeebhoy, 1998), but in some cases with their female peers. Studies in an industrial area of Gujarat, whose workforce was drawn from a number of surrounding villages (Lakhani et al, 2001), and in rural South Gujarat (Joshi and Dhapola, 1998, cited in Pelto, 1999) found that the typical partners of single men were unmarried village girls, although some liaisons were also with sex workers or older women. In the rural study, many of the relationships with village girls were conceptualised by the young men in terms of 'love' and were often long-term, in some cases even persisting after arranged marriages to others. These findings confirm that pre-marital sex is far from unknown, even if less common that in many African settings.

The use of contraception is partly associated with its availability. While more accessible in India than in many African countries (although also highly variable across Africa), in both regions contraceptives are far more available for those who are married than for unmarried people. Given the stronger taboos against pre-marital sex in India than in much of Africa moreover, Indian adolescents face particular difficulties in securing protection, whether against pregnancy or sexually transmitted infections, Although other forms of protection are not altogether inaccessible in India, abortion continues to be the main means of 'contraception' for unmarried women. While emphasising the health risks that many face thereby, this also underlines a continuing lack of protection against HIV.

Recent studies in India indicate increasing recognition of the need for protection in casual sexual encounters (NACO, 2002). In spite of this figures of consistent use remain low, perhaps not least because the condom is so little used either as a contraceptive or as a protective measure. Indeed this remains a problematic feature of India's national prevention campaign against HIV. However, there are some positive signs of increased condom use within the general population in recent years in casual encounters (NACO, 2002). Moreover, a study of college students in Mumbai, while revealing low levels of sexual experience, also indicated that of those claiming such, 47% reported having used condoms and in general expressed positive attitudes about their use (Mathai et al, 1997). Condom use is increasing in Africa, especially among young, unmarried people. Yet problems of access often remain acute and gender relations across both regions make for differential potential to secure protection as between young men and young women.

Closer Analysis of Points of Danger

With this general context in mind, specific illustrations of the dilemmas faced by young people in the context of AIDS will be looked at more closely. Common features across Africa and South Asia include the influence of imagery from a global – yet highly westernised – media on the courtship behaviours of young people, the combining of old customs with new notions of sexual freedom and sexual experimentation in ways which can present new hazards, especially for young women, and the reluctance of a parental generation to come to terms with both adolescent sexual behaviours and the dangers posed by AIDS. Precisely how these are played out varies in accord with the specificity of place and its changing cultural configurations and position within a global economy. Drawing on published work relating to Uganda, Zambia and South Africa, as well as studies conducted at various sites in India, the particular way in which these themes apply are explored.

Lusaka, Zambia: Young People caught between a Mixture of Beliefs

Zambia has a higher rate of urbanisation than many African countries, partly in consequence of the historical importance of its copper industry and the towns and cities that emerged in association with it, but also in consequence of the deterioration of rural economies and resultant aspirations of better prospects in the urban areas. All too frequently such hopes are dashed by the mire of urban poverty. Yet this general flight to the towns means that many of the country's urban areas are cosmopolitan in the sense of increasingly comprised of those from a range of different ethnic groups. This is particularly true of Lusaka, which is populated by people from all parts of Zambia as well as from neighbouring countries, rendering it a melting pot of traditional cultures. Adolescents in the city find themselves at the hub of changing ideas and sexual behaviours, having to fashion their relationships among their peers, constrained by both widespread and deep poverty and a high level of HIV prevalence. They draw on a range of 'traditions' as well as the science of health education messages, but they are also strongly influenced by ideas penetrating from external sources, via music, film and the like.

Focus group discussions among young people in Lusaka carried out in the mid-nineties (Baylies et al, 2000) reflected a mixture of confusion, fatalism, and a desire for more information, alongside much rationalising when accounting for behaviours that all too frequently placed them at risk. Participants expressed a diversity of views about how HIV was contracted. Some said it was a result of sexual transgressions, for example having sex with a woman who had had an abortion or a miscarriage. More commonly, however, they linked susceptibility more straightforwardly to unprotected sexual intercourse. Even so, responses reflected a view that being infected could well be a consequence of being bewitched; hence stress was often placed on seeking advice not just from hospitals but also from traditional healers.

Young men debated the extent to which sex was essential for their well being. Young women debated the extent to which they could resist the overtures of both older men and their male peers. Nevertheless there was also some appreciation that both men and women shared responsibility for the transmission of HIV. As one young man said:

> It takes two people to have sex. If one of them refuses, then nothing can happen. If there were no men who patronise the pubs and go for prostitutes, we would not have had women being called prostitutes. I think everyone is primarily responsible for the spread of HIV/AIDS (Focus group, 26 April 96).

Young women admitted that some among their peers succumbed to the advances of men offering material incentives for sex. They might 'go' with married men because, as one said:

> They admire what their wives wear and so they want to have the same..... Young ladies do not even worry about AIDS as long as they had the clothes to wear. (Focus group, 26 April 1996).

But they also worried about the difficulty of avoiding sexual relations, given the persistence and aggression of men:

> For some men, it is as if their work is just to admire young girls and go after them. They just can't see a girl and forget (Focus group, April 1996).

Moreover, many young women felt that means of protection were minimal. In their view condoms were no solution since most of their partners refused to use them and even when they did, they could subvert their effectiveness:

> Some men would cut off the tip of a condom deliberately.... Some boys refuse to use a condom. They say that I cannot be wearing a rain-coat while taking a shower.... All they say is 'why have a girlfriend if I am going to be using a condom?' They prefer skin to skin' (Focus group, April 1996).

The discussions of young people in this case revealed uncertainty, personal anguish and defiance. Although they reflected diversity of opinion and a wide mixture of influences, they also revealed misconceptions and gaps in knowledge. Most worryingly they revealed that in negotiating sexual experience in the era of AIDS, both young men and women are continuing to place themselves in positions of risk, with young women able to claim relatively little agency.

Uganda: Evolving Courtship Practices Defying Danger

Nyanzi et al (2000) describe the patterns of courting that apply among adolescents in south-western Uganda. What is striking about this study is the extent of unsafe, indeed reckless, behaviour that seems to characterise these young people, even more worrying for the fact that they have grown up in the era of AIDS and live in a country regarded as a model for having turned the course of the epidemic and achieved a declining level of HIV prevalence. The authors describe the situation as one where ideas about what constitutes sophisticated sex derived in part from an international media. As elsewhere, individuals drew on celluloid and word images from film and popular song, some imported from the west, and combined them with customary practice to construct behaviours that are hazardous in the context of AIDS. Thus girls sought as partners those boys who had reputations for multiple sexual conquests. 'The boy with many lovers is a star because everyone wonders what they like about him. So some girls accept him, to find out what is so special about him' (2000: 91). Girls also gained prestige from having many partners. The emphasis on multiple liaisons, however, was not accompanied by the practice of safe sex, not least because, as in Zambia, young men eschewed the use of condoms, which they believed would compromise their pleasure and undermine their masculinity.

Material exchange also figured in adolescent relationships, underlining the way in which economic context establishes both constraints and opportunities. In poor communities there is little cash about, but what families have to 'spare' tends to be distributed more readily to young men than to young women, sometimes to be used as a means of attracting girlfriends. Adolescent males frequently resorted to the assistance of 'dealers' (other young men skilled in mediation) to 'soften' a girl so that she might be more ready to engage in sex. The dealer's main tool of persuasion turned on the potential benefit the girl might derive from the boy's money or material possessions. Such dealing is itself presented as a modern version of mediation between prospective partners formerly carried out by a boy's or adult man's paternal aunt. Focusing on material factors while perpetuating male control over courtship, these dealings seem to overlook the new threat that HIV poses.

The exchange of gifts which figures so strongly not just in courtship rituals but also in liaisons with older men allows girls to access goods and currency circulated within their communities. In the area studied by Nyanzi et al (2000), young women have evolved a practice dubbed 'detoothing', whereby they attempted to extract as much as possible from would-be suitors, but then removed themselves from the relationship before sexual submission. The very terminology of 'detoothing' would seem to indicate subversion and manipulation of the gender relations that inform courtship to the material advantage of the girls, indicating calculated agency. Yet ultimately gender relations, underpinned by potential violence, prevail, in that if found out and subjected to coercive sex, the girls regarded this as legitimate 'punishment' for their subversive enterprise.

In the situation described by Nyanzi et al (2000) a high level of risk of both violence and HIV infection attends patterns of sexual networking among adolescents. If they are aware of the threat they face, they would seem to flaunt it in an attempt to construct some normalcy in the midst of contradictory and ultimately frightening pressures. As the authors comment, 'attitudes and forms of behaviour that are risky are part of an adolescent ideal of modernity and sophistication' (2000: 97). There is a huge irony however, in the fact that the images gleaned from a global media which they attempt to emulate are largely fanciful. While levels of protection in the West are far from universal, there is in practice much higher use of condoms for protection there than in countries such as Uganda, where the threat of AIDS, even if reduced, remains far higher and a clear threat to survival, not just of individuals but of entire communities.

South Africa: Variable Futures and Levels of Risk; New Technology Preventing Pregnancy but not HIV

Kelly and Parker's (2000) study across several locations in South Africa demonstrates the adoption of variable levels of protection by young people. As many as 80% reported having used a condom during their most recent intercourse in one site, as against just 20% in another. The authors identify a number of possible factors that may account for such variation. While one of the most important is the availability of condoms, perhaps of particular importance is the extent to which young people can envisage a positive future. 'Those with a sense of the future and who are actively planning their careers and educational futures tend to be less actively defiant and fatalistic, and more actively involved in avoiding risk' (2000: 23). Socio-economic circumstances were clearly significant in influencing responses to AIDS. Those in more privileged circumstances not only had a vision of a viable personal future, they also had greater knowledge of means of protections, more extensive prevention options and greater access to services. At the same time hazardous behaviours characterised the sites with the more impoverished environments where there was a higher incidence of coercive sex and of gift exchange in courtship. Higher levels of sexual activity also tended to characterise those sites with greater evidence of breakdown or dissolution in parental authority and less communication between parents and children.

The concerns of mothers about their daughters in some cases seemed to have been absolved by resort to modern contraceptive technology, through taking them to the clinic for injections at the first suggestion that they might be sexually active. Their daughters, for their part, have found themselves in the midst of a confusing as well as dangerous situation. They are increasingly subject to courtship involving material exchanges for sex, bereft of information about potential dangers, and with access only to services that, while potentially preventing pregnancy, offer little protection against HIV.

Kelly and Parker (2000: 29) note that young people in South Africa are subject to significant changes in sexual behaviours. They describe the 'rapidly changing sexual environment' (29), as involving earlier sexual debut, larger age differentials between partners, lesser gaps between the initiation of a relationship and the beginning of sexual activity, higher levels of casual sex and higher levels of material transactions in the context of sexual relations. They detect increasingly greater initiative being taken by women, but at the same time high levels of pressure on young women to find partners quickly. As in Uganda there was a strong sense that many of these changes have been intensified in consequence of exposure to the media, music videos and soap operas that appear to condone casual sex.

In one of the sites studied there was also evidence of a change or transformation in childhood sexual games toward involving more 'serious' (penetrative) sex than ever applied in the past. Hence old customs continue to be drawn upon, but their content has shifted, posing new hazards to those whose very youth serves as a hindrance to understanding and access to information, let alone protection. Other changes are also problematic. While men traditionally had their own rooms after initiation (with both younger males and females having rooms inside a house), it is increasingly common not just for younger men but also younger girls to have their own rooms, giving space and opportunity for sexual liaisons. A decline in the force of proscriptions that young men and women should not talk in public has also permitted more possibilities for relationships to develop (Kelly and Parker, 2000).

India: Emerging Risks, Especially for Young Women, in the Context of Changing Practice

As in other regions of the world, the threat posed by HIV in India has permitted, indeed necessitated, much closer examination of sexual behaviour and sexuality than occurred previously, opening up areas of deep taboo to scrutiny. Studies carried out have often been small and limited in their generalisability, but collectively they have begun to reveal diversity across the country, as well as the extent of extra- and pre-marital sexual relations and of the practice of men having sex with men. Both men and women put themselves at risk in such relationships, all the more as they remain largely hidden from view and formally unacknowledged. As Ramasubban (1999: 362) argues, the fact that partner change among adolescents (and others) occurs 'within the context of universal marriage and within a framework of gross ignorance about STDs and how these may be prevented, suggests a plethora of channels of HIV transmission into the general population'.

In general, across much of India, it is assumed that girls up to around the age of 14 should be closely supervised and kept separate from males and from male contact. Indeed to some extent such high levels of family surveillance may serve as a form of protection against HIV. Jejeebhoy (1998: 1279) refers to a study of poorly educated and low-income adolescents in a slum in Bombay which suggested that 'girls are so closely watched that pre-marital sexual activity is virtually impossible'. Customary separation of the sexes during adolescence, however, has as its corollary young men frequently having their first sexual experiences with commercial sex workers or older female relatives, but also through encounters with their male peers. These practices, hidden yet highly routinised, can become a source of danger to them in the era of AIDS. To the extent to which young men typically have more sexual experience than women on marriage, dangers are extended to women, with the rubric of arranged marriage reducing the capacity of women to ensure safety, by virtue of limiting their prior knowledge and personal choice of sexual partner.

Where girls succeed in subverting controls exerted by their families over their sexual behaviour – or when they move out of the family home in the process of pursuing further education – they may find themselves in situations where old norms no longer apply but their substitutes remain unclear or potentially dangerous. Thus Sohdi (quoted in Pelto, 1999: 573) notes that continuing assumptions about tight control over girls by families, coupled with the influence of contemporary film, often leaves girls confused, but also subject to coercion: 'In a culture where boys and girls have few opportunities to practise heterosexual conversations, the currently popular movies provide some of the scripts'. However, the romantic view garnered by young girls from film is often naïve and the boundaries between what constitute friendship, love and coercion can vary between young men and young women. In such situations young women may find themselves out of their depth, sometimes forced to have sex with more than one boy and often victimised. Across studies in various sites, girls were found to have few sources of information and were ill-prepared to negotiate relationships with males. As Sodhi et al comment, 'the controlling family structures and values while seeking to protect adolescents may paradoxically increase their vulnerability' (Sodhi et al quoted in Pelto, 1999: 579). Sodhi et al's findings of high levels of sexual activity, STIs and pregnancies confirm the very real present danger faced by young women in the midst of changing norms.

It is in the nexus between gender relations, family practices and new influences, both from Indian film and a global media, that young people find themselves facing new risks of HIV. As Ambati et al (1997: 328) comment, 'the growing influence of Western news media which has produced an atmosphere conducive to casual sex and drug use could not have come at a worse time'. Frequently, however, young people have little understanding of these risks. For young girls, this is partly in consequence of their remaining bound by traditional patterns of socialisation prescribing ideals of sexual purity based on ignorance regarding sex. This leaves them unable to negotiate sex and with limited means of communicating with their partners (Sethi, 1999).

Specific risk configurations, however, vary among young people depending on their social location, as defined by gender, cultural context, class position, education, and other factors. Some positive signs of increased use of condoms in sexual encounters by more highly educated young people (Mathai, 1997) may be suggestive of emergent patterns in South Africa, whereby greater knowledge, access to protection and, in particular, belief in a viable personal future may lead some to take preventive action. As Jejeebhoy affirms (1998: 1284), 'those in the forefront of changing attitudes are boys, and urban and educated adolescents'. Still, within these categories, young men and young women face the epidemic and the dangers it poses in different ways. Hazards of cultural practice in the midst of change remain severe.

Sethi (1999) thus remains highly critical of approaches to AIDS prevention that have taken little account of the specific situations in which those at risk find themselves. Too little attention has been given to the socio-cultural context of the epidemic, the concepts of sexuality that apply among different groups and the values and customs that inform social relationships. The national AIDS programme in India is thus characterised, especially in its first decade, as having 'tried to overcome the barriers imposed by cultural double standards and subterfuges by drawing attention to their existence, rather than understanding them and working within the situation they represented' (Sethi, 1999: 390). In the process young people in particular have been left without the support and information they need, caught up in destructive experimentation that puts them at risk.

Conclusion

Accounts of the dilemmas experienced by young people in the face of AIDS throw up a number of recurrent themes, albeit differently articulated in different situations. Among these are the extent to which adolescence remains a period of experimentation and the way in which gender relations often operate to put both young men and young women, but especially young women, at risk. Young people are constantly constructing and reconstructing patterns of courtship, drawing on custom, but also on images and perceived norms from local and foreign media. As some stay longer in education, they also move away from parental control into a hazy, undefined arena of new modes of behaviour. Quite how these materialise in practice depends on the mixture of old and new, the economic and social context, levels of knowledge about new dangers and access to protection. Each situation is uniquely configured. But the flux itself, the subversion of authority and the inability of the older generation to grapple with the situation and ensure that new, appropriate forms of protection are made available, puts many in danger.

Greater attention has been directed at the dangers which AIDS poses to young people in Africa, especially where the estimated prevalence of HIV/AIDS is devastatingly high, than to those in South Asia. In India there remains a tendency to focus on marginalised groups regarded as at particular risk of HIV – commercial sex workers, lorry drivers, injecting drug users and male migrant workers in urban centres. Yet HIV is a threat to the lives of young people within the general population of India as well as to such targeted sub-populations, no less than in Africa. An understanding of the specific ways in which new patterns of courtship behaviour articulate with customary practice so as to pose dangers and dilemmas for young people is thus a matter of urgency in both regions, if appropriate means of protection against AIDS are to be secured.

References

Ambati, B., Ambati, J. and Rao, M., 1997, 'Dynamic of knowledge and attitudes about AIDS among the educated in southern India' *AIDS Care* 9(3): 319–30.

Ashana, S. and Oostvogels, R. 2001 'The social construction of male "homosexuality" in India: implications for HIV transmission and prevention' *Social Science and Medicine* 52: 707–21.

Baylies, C., Chabala, T. and Mkandawire, F., 2000, 'AIDS in Kanyama: contested sexual practice and the gendered dynamics of community interventions' in C. Baylies and J. Bujra, with the Gender and AIDS Group, *AIDS, Sexuality and Gender in Africa, collective strategies and struggles in Tanzania and Zambia:* 95–112.

Blanc, A. and Way, A. 1998. 'Sexual behaviour and contraceptive knowledge and use among adolescents in developing countries'. *Studies in Family Planning* 29/2: 106–16.

Daniel, H. and Parker, R. (1993) *Sexuality, politics, and AIDS in Brazil: in another world?* London : Falmer Press.

Demographic and Health Surveys, http://www.meausredhs.com/data/indicators

Hamblin, J. and Reid, E. 1991, 'Women and the HIV epidemic and human rights: a tragic imperative' HIV and Development Programme, Issues Paper #8, UNDP, http://www.undp.org/hiv/issues.htm

Jejeebhoy, S 1998 'Adolescent sexual and reproductive behavior: a review of the evidence from India' *Social Science and Medicine*, 46(10): 1275–90.

Kelly, K. and Parker W. 2000. *Communities of Practice, contextual mediators of youth response to HIV/AIDS Sentinel Site Monitoring and Evaluation Project, Stage Two Report, South Africa.*

Kreniske, J. 1997, 'AIDS in the Dominican Republic: Anthropological Reflections on the Social Nature of Disease,' in G Bond, et al, eds., *AIDS in Africa and the Caribbean*, Boulder Colorado, Westview Press.

Lakhani, A. 2000, *Male Semen Loss Concerns*, Deepak Charitable Trust, Deepak Medical Foundation.

Lakhani, A, Gandhi, K. and Collumbien, M. 2001, 'Addressing Semen Loss Concerns: towards culturally appropriate HIV/AIDS interventions in Gujarat, India' *Reproductive Health Matters*, 9(18): 49–59.

Mann, J. and Tarantola, D., eds., 1996, *AIDS in the World II, Global Dimensions, Social Roots and Responses*, Oxford, Oxford University Press.

Mathai, R. Ross, W. and Hira S., 1997, 'Concomitants of HIV/STD risk behaviours and intention to engage in risk behaviours in adolescents in India' *AIDS Care*, 9(5): 563–70.

NACO 2002– Executive Summaries – Indian Scanario – General Population, http://naco.nic.in/venaco/indianscene/executive3.htm Female Sex Workers and their Clients; http://naco.nic.in/venaco/indianscene/executive1.htm MSM and IDUs http://naco.nic.in/venaco/indianscene/executive2.htm

Nyanzi. S., Pool, R. and Kinsman, J., 2000, 'The negotiation of sexual relationships among school pupils in south-western Uganda', *AIDS Care* 13(1): 83–98.

Pelto, P., 1999, 'Sexuality and sexual behaviour: the current discourse' in Pachauri, S ed.; Subramanian, S. technical ed. (1999) *Implementing a Reproductive Health Agenda in India: the Beginning*, New Delhi, Population Council: 539–86.

Population Reports 2001, Series L, Number 12, The Johns Hopkins University Bloomberg School of Public Health.

Ramasubban, R, 1999, 'HIV/AIDS in India: gulf between rhetoric and reality' in Pachauri, S ed.; Subramanian, S. technical ed., *Implementing a Reproductive Health Agenda in India: the Beginning*, New Delhi, Population Council: 349–375. Published earlier in *Economic and Political Weekly*, 7 November 1998.

Rivers, K. and Aggleton, P. 1999. *Adolescent Sexuality, Gender and the HIV Epidemic*, HIV and Development Programme, Gender and the HIV Epidemic, UNDP.: http://www.undp.org/hiv/genderlist.htm

Santana, S. 1997, 'AIDS Prevention, Treatment and Care in Cuba,' in G Bond, et al, eds., *AIDS in Africa and the Caribbean*, Westview Press, Boulder Colorado.

Sethi, G, 1999, 'Government response to HIV/AIDS' in Pachauri, S ed.; Subramanian, S. technical ed. (1999) *Implementing a Reproductive Health Agenda in India: the Beginning*, New Delhi, Population Council: 377–402.

UNAIDS, 1998, *Gender and AIDS*, UNAIDS Technical Update. http://www.unaids.org

UNAIDS, 2000. Report on the Global Epidemic, June 2000:
   http://www.unaids.org/epidemic_update/report_Epi_report_chap_devastation.htm

UNAIDS, 2002,
   http://www.unaids.org/barcelona/presskit/youngpeople/YoungpeopleHIVAIDS_en.pdf

UNICEF, with UNAIDS and WHO, 2002, Young People and HIV/AIDS, Opportunity in Crisis, http://www.unaids.org/barcelona/presskit/youngpeople/YoungpeopleHIVAIDS_en.pdf

Van de Vliet, V. 1996: *The Politics of AIDS*, London: Bowerdean.

Verma, R. Bhende, A, and Mane, P. 'NGO response to HIV/AIDS: a focus on women' in Pachauri, S ed.; Subramanian, S. technical ed (1999) *Implementing a Reproductive Health Agenda in India: the Beginning*, New Delhi, Population Council: 403–21.

Webb, D. (Central Board of Health [Zambia]/Unicef) 1997. *Adolescence, Sex and Fear, reproductive health services and young people in urban Zambia*, Lusaka.

Interview, UNAIDS India, D Pradeep, Strategic Planning Officer, 4 April 2002.

Chapter 6

HIV/AIDS: The Nigerian Response

Morenike Folayan

HIV/AIDS has been increasing steadily in Nigeria since 1987. Poor education and awareness about the disease as well as high levels of stigmatisation and discrimination have all contributed to the growing crisis in the country. According to the latest statistics, there is a new infection every minute with the most prevalent route of transmission being heterosexual sex. The emergence of a democratic government in 1999 has prioritized the struggle to curb the growth of the pandemic. The following chapter will review the emerging governance structure in Nigeria, with specific focus on governmental strategies.

Magnitude of the HIV/AIDS Problem in Nigeria

The seroprevalence rate in 2001 was 5.8 percent, an increase from 1.8 percent in 1992. In real terms, this increase represented 10 percent of the total figure on the continent and 8 percent of the 42.1 million people who are currently thought to be living with HIV/AIDS, globally. Across the country, prevalence varies with different zones and states. The worst affected zone is Southern Nigeria, with an average prevalence of 7.7 percent, while the lowest area is the North West with a 3.3 percent prevalence. Twelve out of the 36 states of the federation have a prevalence of 7 percent and above, with one as high as 13.5 percent, whilst there is just 1 state with a prevalence under 3 percent. Despite the variations of prevalence, there has been a steady increase recorded in the incidence rate in most states over the years. A good example is the Southern state of Cross Rivers, where HIV prevalence has increased from 0.0 percent in 1991 to 8.0 percent in 2001. This represents about an 800 percent increase in the incidence of the infection. Not only is the prevalence figure skewed in relation to states but also in terms of age and gender distribution. The most severely affected are adults in the sexually reproductive and economically active years, where twice as many women as men are infected. In the reproductive age group, 53.8 percent of the infected are females. Young women also attain high HIV infection level at a notably younger age than young men. (See Figure 6.1 and 6.2 courtesy of the Federal Ministry of Health, Nigeria, 2001.)

The Political Economy of AIDS in Africa

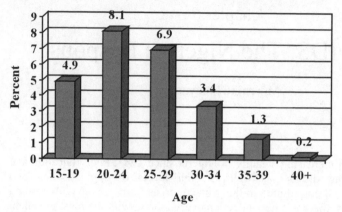

Figure 6.1: HIV prevalence by age group: national average 1999

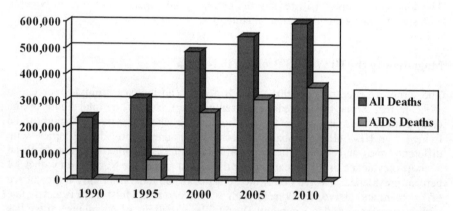

Figure 6.2: AIDS deaths versus all deaths among the age group of 15–49 years

In June 2001, the number of reported AIDS cases stood at 60,564. This was more than twice the reported figure just two years earlier when it stood at 26,276. An actual estimate of the cumulative number of deaths due to AIDS in 2001 was put at 1.2 million. The result of AIDS related death is the growing number of children orphaned by AIDS. For Nigeria, the 1990 estimates showed that 8 0 percent of the child population were orphans, 1.7 percent of whom lost their parents through AIDS. By 1995, the estimated percentage of orphans was put at 8.4 percent of which 7.2 percent were from AIDS. The year 2000 estimate is much more gloomy; 8.6 percent of the population below the age of 15 years have been orphaned of which 27.0 percent is AIDS related. For 2002, the reported number of AIDS orphan is 847,000. By the year 2010, it is estimated that AIDS will have claimed the lives of 49.8 percent of all parents of the orphaned population.

The impact of the epidemic has been enormous. Just like what happens in neighbouring sub-Saharan nations, the growing epidemic has exponentially increased Nigeria's national and state health care costs, the requirement to train and retrain health professionals in addition to the associated problems of HIV/AIDS on hospital management. Costs which have been passed on to the infected themselves resulting in a reduced amount of discretionary income for individuals and families to fund education, health and to improve their standard of living has resulted in a drastically unsettling medical, emotional and social costs on people living with HIV/AIDS (PLWHA).

Contributing Factors

The determinants of the HIV/AIDS epidemic are similar to those witnessed throughout the sub-Saharan region. These include:

Social Determinants

Poverty is a big national issue in Nigeria as it is for most African countries. Nationally, close to 35 percent of the national population is considered to be poor, while up to 13 percent is extremely poor. Approximately 16 percent of this extremely poor populace are found in the rural area where 64 percent of the national population reside. This affects individuals and the states both socially and economically as it plays an important role in the spread of HIV infection. The significance of this relationship is known to exist as an equivalent is illustrated in the nexus between poverty and illiteracy. The adult literacy level is put at 51 percent, which is low when compared to that of developing nations. Although about 11 percent of Nigeria's national budget is spent on education, the actual amount is usually insufficient in comparison to the actual needs of the nation. This is made even worse by poor implementation of such projects and the reluctance of the government to release the funds for the educational schemes. As a result the level of literacy remains low, as many families do not have the financial capability to provide a good standard of education for their children, when the need for it is appreciated. Thus, a vicious cycle of low literacy level and poverty is established. The result of this is often multiple.

As a result of the low literacy level, job opportunities are often limited to low and at best, middle cadre jobs. Income is thus low, as reflected by the per capita statistics, of 1997, when the per annum figure was $270. At the microeconomic level, individuals have to find ways of supplementing their incomes. One of the easiest ways of achieving this is to resort to the commercial use of sexual activities, most commonly by the female members of the family. This may entail migration from (the rural) home to the nearest urban and commercial settlement, where they are not personally known and income generation is better. This may entailing selling sex for favours, a phenomenon which is not limited to the cities and is often seen within the rural community. This mode of income generation for the family that was once frowned upon by society is gradually becoming acceptable in the face of increasing poverty especially in the Edo and Delta States of Nigeria. The issue of

sex workers being important in the HIV/AIDS epidemic in Africa is highlighted by
the high seroprevalence of HIV infection found amongst them (Figure 6.3).

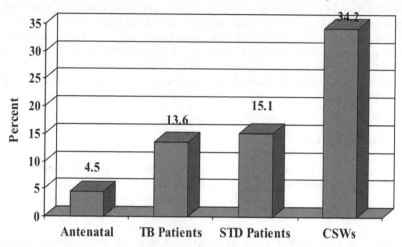

Courtesy: Federal Ministry of Health, Nigeria, 2000

**Figure 6.3: HIV prevalence among specific population groups (national
average in 1996)**

Commercial sex activities further thrive in Nigeria because of the high rural-urban
migration which is also linked to the level of poverty in the country. Although 64
percent of the population live in the rural area, the distribution of social
infrastructure, industrial and commercial activities are lopsided to the advantage of
urban centres. Men thus migrate to urban centres to find better paying jobs, which
are often associated with improved standards of living. However, due to the high
cost of living in the urban centre, families are left behind in the rural areas. The
result is that these men often patronise sex workers where more often, they pay
higher to have sex without condoms despite the hazards involved. Sex without a
condom is preferred as the condom is perceived to be a barrier, reducing sexual
pleasure., Since commercial sex activities are more often done for financial gains,
the sex workers agree to the demands of their customers despite their being aware of
the dangers involved.

Male urban migration creates an additional sexual externality; as it produces an
opportunity for women to get involved in extramarital relationships. The
understanding that their husbands are miles away in town, spending their hard
earned money on girlfriends and sex workers gives some of the women further
leeway for such practices.

Compared to the WHO's stipulation of 5 percent, as little as 2 percent of the
average African budget is allocated to health, Nigeria inclusive. This represents a
poor prioritisation of their budget. The result of this is the poor development of
health infrastructures and limited availability, either in terms of distance or cost. The

ratio of trained health personnel to the population to be served is drastically too low. Worse still, the rural populations are often underserved because many health care professionals prefer to practice in the urban areas. A large number of patients are forced to resort to untrained traditional healers and spiritualists. The outcome is a high level of morbidity/mortality in the country, with under-5 mortality being as high as 159/1,000 and infant mortality being as high as 105/1,000.

Cultural Determinants

There is also the culturally dictated subjugation and subordination of women which enhances the spread of HIV infection. One such example is a practice that encourages multiple sexual partnership by men. This is in the form of polygamy, wife inheritance and the encouragement of middle aged men, who are sexually experienced, to seek younger sexual partners and wives. For Africans, Nigerians inclusive, male infidelity is seen as being consistent with the extension of the familial line. Also, the societal sanctioning of husband infidelity is not disassociated with the traditional postpartum female abstinence which is linked with the need for uninterrupted breastfeeding and enhanced child survival and spacing. This may last as long as three years in some communities. This culture thrives because sex for women is an instrument of procreation and not pleasure.

Other forms of encouragement of multiple sexual partnership in the various cultural practices include cleansing rituals for widows. There is also the practice of wife hospitality whereby women sexually entertain their husband's close guests. This practice is widespread in Benue State which presently has the highest seroprevalence percent in the country. Nigerian social values also place a prime value on marriage and motherhood in that the woman produces the children needed to farm the land which often is the main source of income for the family. The woman thus has both reproduction and production values. For many, the need for a continued lineage identity in the form of a son makes motherhood an essential issue as it is their only source of identity in the matrimonial home. The value placed on childbirth makes the women often resort to help from traditional and spiritual healers in cases of primary and secondary infertility and when there is a need for a particular sex. The ritual with traditional healers may entail having sex with them and thus exposing females to multiple sex partners.

The importance placed on traditional healers and traditional birth attendants as health care providers for the majority of people dwelling in the rural area is not without its problems. They take 60 to 80 percent of deliveries with health care also provided by them. However, most of them are untrained and do not have the facilities for sterilisation of the instruments they use thus encouraging HIV transmission.

Furthermore, sexuality education is often referred to as a taboo subject, leaving many youths uneducated and uninformed about sex and sexuality. As a result they often become wrongly informed by their peers and through self education. Many learn from experimenting with sex in a search for adventure, self actualisation, exploration and formation of relationships. This often results in youths having multiple sexual partners due to frequent changes in partners. With Nigerian youths engaging in sex as early as 10 years old, and using condoms inconsistently and infrequently (with only 25 percent using condoms consistently), there is a tendency for HIV infection to occur at a very high rate amongst them. This is reflected in the national age distribution of those affected by the infection.

The issue of bride pricing, which is prevalent in the Eastern part of Nigeria, also holds attendant consequences. As a result of the rising cost of living and the economic value of women in terms of the bride price being paid in many communities, adolescent marriages are now being arranged with increasing frequency. This on the one hand helps the family to raise income to look after the other children. On the other hand, the financial responsibility of the daughter is now passed on to the bridegroom. Such arranged marriages usually involved older men who are financially capable but, most often, already have older wives. A consequence of the high bride price is that it forces young men to wait several years prior to marriage in order to save, and in the mean time they usually have multiple sex partners. Others may opt to have a live-in wife whom they are not committed to.

There is also the issue of women's dependency on men. Women lack economic empowerment and assertiveness skills with which to enforce their will and desire, even in sexual issues. It is difficult for the women to assert her rights and wishes in sexual issues even when she thinks her husband is unfaithful or probably infected. This is made worse by the fact that, most often, women are in polygamous relationships in a society that frowns on the use of contraceptives by couples. A problematic off shoot of this is that the rights and autonomy of the wife are strongly tied to their husband's status and person. When the husband dies, they tend to lose all except where the child or children have some entitlement. These cultural values allow for practices such as widow inheritance to thrive otherwise the woman is left with nothing, more so when she has little or no skill with which to fend for herself and her children. Finally, there is presently no specific legislation on HIV/AIDS that protects the rights of those infected, especially in the face of discrimination and stigmatisation. In some areas of HIV/AIDS control and mitigation, policies exist but they remain weak due to the non-existence of guidelines, strategies or funding to aid the implementation and/or coordination of such activities.

Behavioural Determinants

Due to the high level of mortality in the country, with life expectancy having dropped to 52 years, there was an initial apathy developed to the message of HIV as a killer disease. It was seen as one of the many other diseases that were around to kill and thus there was nothing special about it. This attitude was reinforced, as there was open denial of the infection due to the associated stigmatisation and discrimination. The message was taken as western propaganda resulting in the continuous spread of the disease unabated. Late diagnosis was also a contributory factor as the symptoms of HIV infection was similar to that of many other common placed infections in the community. Over the counter symptomatic treatment of diseases is common, due to the high cost of management in the hospitals. Even in the hospitals, costs limit doctors' requests for the minimum required tests needed for the management of diseases. Thus, an HIV test is often one of the last tests requested, especially in view of the associated consequences of stigma the patient may have to deal with.

Biological Determinants

The level of sexually transmitted disease is high in the country. This is a major route for HIV infection transmission. This level remains high despite the various programmes designed by the Federal Ministry of Health to address the problem. Identified limitations to the successes of these programmes include the centralisation of the programme implementation with Government health institutions being the main implementers. Unfortunately, most of the populace visit traditional healers and receive over the counter treatments for their symptoms which will often become chronic and persistent. There is also the continuous transfusion of unsafe blood. This accounts for as high as 40 percent of infections in the country presently, although this may not be unconnected to poor implementations of national policies and protocol regulating blood transfusion in the country.

National Response to the Epidemic

The Government of Nigeria established an AIDS/STDs control programme (NASCP) with assistance for its first medium term plan (MTPI) from the WHO Global Programme on AIDS, as early as 1987. In 1991, the then Military Head of State, General Ibrahim Babangida, launched the War against AIDS campaign. He made a donation of 20 million Naira and promised that AIDS issues were going to be of national priority. As a part of this initiative he directed all states and local governments to commit an annual sum of 1 million and 500,000 Naira respectively, to fight the disease. All state owned media were also directed to transmit all HIV related promotional broadcasts free, and the Ministry of Education should see to the inclusion of HIV/AIDS into the educational curriculum. These promises were never fulfilled and neither were the proposed programmes.

By 1992, under the largely ineffective MTPII, the NASCP had disbursed only $428,000 of funds, over a five year period. This doomed scheme was followed by the development, in 1997 of a Nigerian National policy on HIV/AIDS/STIs, which was to enhance the implementation of these plans. However, in 1992 substantial efforts in the fight to prevent and control HIV/AIDS began with $4.6 million of USAIDS funds which were distributed over a 5 year period by AIDSCAP. This led to the development of a network of 13 NGOs with the capacity to implement community based HIV/AIDS prevention activities.

These plans, actions and policies had little or no impact in controlling and mitigating the HIV epidemic in the country due to the presence of an unstable political climate, portrayed and perpetuated by successive military coups. As with most regimes of this type there was a lack of political will, commitment and involvement. The government gave the impression that there were more pressing competing priorities and developmental needs. Consequently, neither were enlightenment campaigns nor care for PLWHA considered national health priorities as the country's prevalence rate rose progressively from under 1 percent in 1990 to 5.4 percent within a decade. Instead, misconceptions about the disease gained grounds. Those infected or affected did not get any help and faced severe social discrimination for disclosing their status. Poor government commitment also led to poor resource allocation for HIV/AIDS intervention programmes, as did the lack of a coordinated multisectoral approach in planning and implementation of programmes as well as an overcentralisation of intervention programmes. Hitherto, HIV/AIDS has been dealt with as a health issue; the focal point being primary health care, which contributed to the failure of the plans.

However, with the emergence of democratic governance in 1999, political will to face the reality of HIV/AIDS in Nigeria and combat the disease has been demonstrated. This new national and regional commitment was illustrated by the government hosting a summit of all African Head of States in April 2001 to discuss the HIV epidemic in the region. A follow-up summit followed in the Nigerian capital, Abuja, in November 2001.

Nationally, a lot of changes have been made and programmes have been strategically developed to help control and mitigate the impact of the epidemic. Of particular significance has been the establishment of the National and Presidential Action Committees on AIDS (NACA and PACA, respectively), the latter was formed in 1999, with the office coming under the jurisdiction of the Presidency and the president himself as the chair of an inter-ministerial committee. Its specific purpose was to provide an advocacy role, to mobilise resources and formulate policy. These innovations facilitated the establishment of the coordinated use of multisectoral and multidisciplinary organisations, combining the efforts of the private sector, PLWHA, NGOs as well as the public sector, which are all represented on the National Action Committee. The principal responsibilities of NACA is advocating the government's proactive response whilst coordinating all sectors involved in controlling the epidemic through resource mobilisation, supervising, monitoring and evaluating programmes as well as ensuring there is a capacity to build necessary coalitions for controlling the epidemic.

As one of its response, NACA, with the support of the government and its developmental partners, has facilitated an extensive process of programme formulation whose elements include a Situation Analysis, the development of the HIV/AIDS Emergency Action Plan (HEAP) as well as a review of the 1997 HIV/AIDS/STIs National Policy. The Federal Ministry of Health in conjunction with NACA published the Situation Analysis Report in March 2000. The objective of the analysis was to identify the most important areas to be developed in the strategic plan and budgeted plan of action. These studies enabled the identification of the groups most vulnerable to HIV/AIDS/STIs in the country, the factors that impeded the successful implementation of MTPI and MTPII and the opportunities that are available for expanding the response of the country to the epidemic. The 58 page document, which involved representatives from all stakeholders in the control and mitigation of HIV/AIDS/STIs, had identified and collected information on 11 priority areas. This included information on safe sex practices, STI/HIV/AIDS prevention in women and youths as well as on care and support for PLWHA. In addition, information was collected on 7 cross cutting issues including funding and community involvement in HIV/AIDS control.

Development of HEAP

Based on the Situation Analysis done for the country, the HEAP was developed between July 2000 and February 2001 and published for circulation in April 2002. This plan was built around two strategic components: namely, the creation of an environment, enabling control of HIV/AIDS and the development of specific intervention programmes. In creating an enabling environment, 4 strategies were identified:

1. The removal of socio-cultural barriers through advocacy initiatives. This would entail sensitising the general public and ensuring the development of legislation and policies centred on human rights of PLWHA and women.
2. Removal of information barriers through the development of information bases at all national and state levels. It is expected that NACA and its partners will address the need to develop a reliable and timely flow of information to decision makers and programme organisers, as well as working with key ministries to establish an overall framework for HIV/AIDS research.
3. Removal of systemic barriers through the development of organisational capacities in national, state and local government. This involves capacity development of NACA, and specifically its state (SACA) and local government (LACA) arms, in order to ensure implementation of concrete activities of HEAP programmes.

The catalysing effects of community based responses is achieved through the decentralisation of the nation's political environment and the mobilisation of local communities. The mobilisation of the local community would be achieved through the design and implementation of community based action plans with technical support given by LACA and funding of these programmes through SACA. Specific programmes emphasising prevention should targeted identified groups with high risk behaviours, namely; youths, women, the military, sex workers, prisons, the immigration borders and transport workers. Some programmes would be targeted at the general population, with the aim of providing syndromic management of STIs, development and implementation of policies and regulations with reference to a safe blood supply and provision of affordable voluntary counselling and confidential testing. For the infected and affected care and support programmes are being planned.

Review of the National Policy

The Nigerian Government had committed $40 million, while the World Bank, through its International Development Association (IDA) credit, committed $90.3 million to facilitate the implementation of the HEAP in the area of HIV prevention, treatment and care for the affected, particularly orphans. However, to enhance its implementation, there is the need for a comprehensive policy package: the existing 1997 HIV/AIDS/STIs policy had a lot of deficits and weaknesses in it and so, cannot enhance the execution of the emergency plan in its present form. This policy did not address the issue of the client's access to anti-retroviral drugs (ARV) and was silent in respect of international patents and trade agreements for HIV/AIDS drugs.

Despite the importance placed on the regional HIV candidate vaccine development to control the epidemic, Nigeria does not have any policy in place with regard to this, neither are there national policies in relation to voluntary counselling and confidential testing (VCCT). Gaps also exist in the specific policies targeting the control of the epidemic in the prisons, where studies have reported the practice of high risk behaviours. Of particular concern is the high prevalence of men having sex with men without protection, an activity which 35 percent of the inmate population has experienced during their prison term. In some areas of HIV/AIDS control and mitigation, policies exist but they remain weak due to non-existent guidelines, strategies or funding to complete the implementation and/or coordination of activities. These identified areas are in relation to removal of the information barrier, community mobilisation, care and support of PLWHA, blood safety and inclusion of HIV/AIDS education in school curriculum.

In 2001, implementation guidelines and protocols were developed and finalised on drug use to reduce the incidence of mother-to-child transmission (MTCT). The protocols for clinical trials for access to anti-retroviral drugs, as well as its implementation guidelines were also developed. In August 2001, NACA along with Policy Project, an international partner, undertook and developed the first draft of a more comprehensive national HIV/AIDS/STIs policy. The draft has been sent out to all relevant stakeholders for review and input. An open discussion among all stakeholders on various themes relevant to NACA's plan, policies and implementation strategy development went on for six months on the Nigerian AIDS forum, the inclusion of all ensures a maximum input by all in the final draft of the comprehensive National HIV/AIDS/STIs policy. The project was supported by NACA as well as Policy Project, a donor agency.

Access to Drugs

In January 2002, the planned anti-retroviral treatment programme under which 10,000 adults and 5,000 children will each receive the required cocktail of drugs for less than US $1 daily started in 25 centres around the country despite a myriad of problems. On the other hand, a pilot study using Nevirapine, a drug used to prevent mother-to-child transmission of the virus, kicked off in June 2002 in eight pilot project centres across the country. The HIV positive mothers enrolled in the programme will receive the treatment free of charge. On delivery the mothers from the PMTCT programme will graduate to the adult ARV scheme, while the children who turn out to be HIV positive will be enrolled in the paediatric ARV scheme.

The drugs produced by the India-based pharmaceutical company, Cipla Ltd, are generic versions of more expensive anti-retroviral drugs produced by Western drug companies. The Nigerian government, through negotiations with the company, is buying the drugs for US $350 a year per person. The government is heavily subsidising the programme, paying up to 80 percent of the cost, leaving the patients to pay the rest, which amounts to no more than eight dollars a month. The Federal Government plans to continue with the provision of subsidised anti-retroviral drugs for these 15,000 throughout their lifetime. It is expected that this figure will increase by thousands over the next two years.

The new treatment programme is novel on the continent. Nigeria is an early beneficiary of the decision, early this year, by leading Western pharmaceuticals to drop their law suit against the South African government which insisted it had a right to produce or buy cheaper generic versions of their anti-HIV/AIDS drugs. According to details of the treatment regime revealed by Nigeria's Ministry of Health, 60 percent of the beneficiaries will receive two pills, three times daily, while the remaining 40 percent will receive two pills twice daily. Over time the effectiveness of the treatment will be evaluated at two laboratories, one in the capital, Abuja, and another in Lagos. The US Ford Foundation has pledged to pay for the laboratory evaluations.

NGO Involvement as Partners in HIV/AIDS Control in Nigeria

The NGOs primarily involved in HIV/AIDS prevention and control in the country mainly draw upon resources from international donor agencies, and especially did so during the military era. Very little support from the government, in terms of finance and positively enhancing policy implementation, meant that the often uncoordinated activities had a limited impact in the country in relation to the amount of funds committed to them. There was replication of efforts with donor driven activities only increasing a confused and disorganised system. This messy situation existed in the absence of a national action plan, which could guide interested donor agencies. Many of the problems have been overcome through the creation of a coordinating national body, and the formation of a clearly defined mandate for the network of NGOs involved in HIV/AIDS activities. These activities have become more directional and focused and thus have resulted in a greater regional impact than was viable under the previous 'system'.

NGOs as well as a number of Federal Government agencies are involved in prevention programmes through production and distribution of IEC materials and advertising campaigns on radio and television which focus on ways of avoiding infection, specifically highlighting the importance of condoms. On the other hand, care and support activities for the infected and the affected are solely undertaken in the country by NGOs. Coordination of activities between the government and the NGOs in the area of HIV/AIDS impact mitigation is just in its infancy with NACA and CISGHAN, a coalition body for NGOs involved in HIV/AIDS activities, interacting so as to ensure efficient and effective dissemination of information, and coordinated HIV mitigation-related activities around the country.

Involvement of Multinationals in HIV/AIDS Control in Nigeria

Presently, the Johns Hopkins University Centre for communication programmes has a hotline service in Lagos state. It offers information services on HIV/AIDS to the general public. Also, DFID, the World Bank, UNICEF and USAIDS have contributed to supporting pilot initiatives in community mobilisation. The Ford

Foundation, the MacArthur Foundation, DFID, USAIDS, UNICEF, ILO and UNIFEM have substantially funded NGOs in the area of care and support. FHI, Pathfinders, British Council and Engender Health (USAIDS) have been in the forefront of training counsellors for the country with the Ford Foundation supporting the establishment of an HIV/AIDS research and testing laboratory in the country. The Federal Ministry of Health is presently conducting pilot studies in six states on prevention of mother-to-child transmission with financial support from UNICEF, DFID and FHI. The Bill and Melinda Gates foundation also contributes to this area through the provision of a grant to Harvard University for use of two states in the federation. WHO, DFID, USAIDS, UNAIDS, Centre for Disease Control, Coca-Cola Company and Policy Project have significantly supported the government in the area of research and sentinel surveillance conducted on an average of 3 years since 1991. The Japanese International Cooperation Agency is also committed to supporting research activities through competitive grants to selected research institutions. Key players in the area of institutional capacity building are UNICEF, UNAIDS, DFID, USAIDS, UNDP, the Ford Foundation and the MacArthur Foundation. International AIDS Alliance is one of the newest of the interested donor agencies involved in training civil based organisations involved in the provision of home based care in the country having started with pilot studies in South Western Nigeria in July 2001. It has presently expanded its scope to providing support for NGOs involved in community response to HIV epidemic.

Challenges

The major challenges being faced in controlling the epidemic in the county range from political, to resource mobilisation, through capacity building issues. In view of the developed plans and policies, there is the need to sustain political commitment at the three tiers of governance. The Federal Government is providing so much political and financial commitment towards the implementation of a multisectoral and decentralised national response to the epidemic. Although the presidency has given its support, there has been no sign of commitment to controlling the epidemic by all the political parties present in the country. There has been a slow response by the other two tiers of government in implementation of the national plans and policies, which would entail their financial and political will and commitments. Hitches are met where these governments do not make HIV/AIDS agenda a priority in their programmes. This slows down the implementation of programmes. Decentralisation would thus not only entail the formulation of functional and effective political guidelines and administrative framework but also a legal framework which would address these issues.

Another challenge to be faced is the establishment of a financial management and accounting system which would help to ensure prudent management of funds while ensuring they flow to all sectors for the implementation of programmes. Systems would also have to be developed to ensure effective coordination, monitoring and evaluation of all the multisectoral activities going on in relation to HIV/AIDS. To this end, The UN Expanded Theme Group was set up to assist with the coordination of activities of the international partners. This would compliment the efforts of NACA in coordination, monitoring and evaluation activities.

Past studies have also shown that more than programmes, effort should be directed at effecting behavioural changes as this often mitigates against objective analyses of successfully implemented programmes. Behavioural changes are needed for successful prevention and care programmes. This would require participation of all stakeholders in ensuring participatory policy evolution, so as to raise the awareness of the communities and institutions at all relevant levels, as well as gaining the acceptance for the policies in the attendant community, and achieving the institutional implementation responsibilities. Although there are a large number of NGOs, CBOs, faith based organisations and other stakeholders involved in HIV/ AIDS prevention and control programmes in the country, their non-involvement in HIV/AIDS policy formulation and implementation process would clog the process during the vital stage of implementations. There is thus the need to develop tools, mechanisms, technology and processes to ensure their continuous scrupulous involvement in the ongoing analysis and review of existing plans, policies and strategies of implementations to make them continuously relevant to the community needs. Communication with them is also important as they are important in translating information necessary for behavioural change to the grassroots and thus, help bridge the gap between government and the people.

Impact and Constraints

The geographical scope of Nigeria coupled with years of neglect under successive military regimes have made the contributions made by the federal government to date seem insignificant. Thus though political support for the process is high, considerable work still needs to be done. The present prevalence is relatively low when compared with the most severely affected African countries. Local health officials and their international partners realised that the spread of the disease had approached the threshold of exponential growth. The next years would thus witness an increase in the country's HIV/AIDS prevalence due to the 'harvesting' phenomenon, wherein past infections would only become diagnosed if there were to be a stop in the acquisition of new infections. The result of these present meticulously planned programmes would therefore take years to become reflected in statistically appreciable figures.

The late response to the gradually growing HIV epidemic in the country poses its own threats. In view of the need to implement an emergency plan to ensure prompt and adequate intervention for the control of the country's epidemic, the inadequacy in human resource capacity needed to play key roles in the implementation of these programmes would be a limiting fator. Human capacity takes time to build. Finances needed for training is also limited, as the Federal Government cannot turn all its attention to HIV/AIDS alone despite making it a priory agenda. It also has to contend with other issues that affects the daily lives of people which all together act to worsen the epidemic in the African continent. Although the goodwill demonstrated by multinationals to the present democratic government would significantly help to cushion the huge financial needs for curbing the epidemic, the pace for human capacity building may not meet up with that needed to all together produce an effective response to the rapidly growing epidemic. These are issues to be discussed in the yet to be defined national strategy for effectively implementing the various outlined plans and policies.

Institutional capacity required to tackle the epidemic is also deficient. Although the Ford Foundation supported the establishment of the only reference laboratory for Basic, Applied and Operational Research on HIV/AIDS present in the country, this is far short of that required in a country with a wide geographical area and still at the preliminary stage of HIV/AIDS management. Although with the present laboratory, clinical samples, which hitherto would have been sent to laboratories outside the country, can now be handled, costs for the use and maintenance of this facility may be a hindrance in the maximum utilisation of the facility. Although a number of organisations have contributed to institutional capacity building through the training of personnel through workshops, seminars and have provided vital equipment, with the provision of vehicles, computers and the giving of technical support, it all appears to be somewhat insignificant in view of the magnitude of the problem as well as the large area of the country. There have also been HIV/AIDS research collaborations in the area of identifying the specific Nigerian HIV strain, to isolate the subtype and commence developing the appropriate candidate vaccine at various institutions across the globe, such as the Institution of Human Virology, Baltimore, the Robert Koch Institute in Germany and the University of Alabama, USA. This collaboration has often been achieved in conjunction with the National Institute of Pharmaceutical Research and Development and the University of Jos, both in Nigeria, and The Federal Ministry of Health, which can often encompass some form of capacity development. This has however, been very little and insignificant in view of the present magnitude of the Nigerian HIV problem. The lack of implementation of the existing policies to guide and ensure capacity building in the past has been a major obstacle in the way of fast and efficient capacity development.

One other identified problem in the area of institutional capacity building need is in the area of expanding existing health care facilities in terms of structures and personnel. Presently, 1–2% of teaching hospital beds are occupied by PLWHA. The annual cost of scaling up health care related HIV/AIDS programmes is estimated to be between US$229 million and US$329 million. This is approximately US$2–3 per capita or approximately 0.8% of GDP. One of the many reasons for people making use of traditional healers is their proximity to the people when compared with that of health care facilities. Documented experiences of other developing nations, like Nigeria, that have had to contend with this type of problem complain about the overburdening of their health care systems. Although the national plan intends to increase the skills of personnel in the area of patient management, with care being hinged on home base care, there seem to be no plans to expand hospital capacity in view of the impending increase need for hospital care for PLWHA. This prospective medium term project may create a flaw in the success of the Nigerian strategy if not taken care of.

Other identified constraints in effective implementation of the Nigerian plan for HIV/AIDS control include the constant civil unrest and disruptions of ethnic clashes and religious upheavals that sporadically occur in the country. This may significantly affect programme implementations as well act as a mode for HIV infection spread especially when they develop into protracted strife.

Cultural views and beliefs that long helped in promulgating the spread of the infection may be difficult to change. Strategies have to be developed in the long term to address the issues of women's empowerment, wherein relations between men and women are transformed. Women must be enabled to have a full say in decisions affecting their lives that would enable them to protect themselves and their children against HIV. Yet this must be done without interfering with or disrupting the traditional setup, on the strength of which care and support for the infected and affected presently depends.

Africans have been identified as strongly religious and thus religious institutions are one of the many stakeholders that are involved in HIV/AIDS control in the country. However, their actions and policies are presently not helping in the prevention and care programme. One such action is their stance against the inclusion of sexuality education in the school curriculum. A national consensus to include sexuality education in the curricula of secondary and tertiary educational institutions was only passed in August 2000. The present strong stance against open media adverts on the use of condoms has led to a significant decrease in the airing of a very successful and persuasive route for public information, which in this instance highlighted condom use and aided HIV/AIDS prevention. They advocate messages on abstinence only in primary and secondary schools. One of the present policies in the Anglican Church generating much controversy is that of compulsory HIV testing for intending couples before marriage. This is against the currently accepted principle of voluntary counselling and testing which is to help with the care of the infected and to prevent infection of the uninfected.

The rise of false claims of a possible cure, enhanced by the high level of stigmatisation and discrimination as well as the inadequacy in facilities available for care and support in the country, have also acted as a mitigating factor for significant progress to be made in HIV/AIDS control and care. The infected and affected have thus had to try out these claims rather than sit, watch and wait for death. Most times these offered treatment only worsen the financial plights of PLWHA as they procure treatment at exorbitant costs with little or no results. Worse still, the legal system in the country often offers little or no recourse for this as the Nigerian constitution only protects civil and political rights and not social and economic rights. Legal fees are often out of reach, while many do not want to get entangled in the complex intrigues involved in seeking a legal recourse for injustice.

In view of the problem the government has to deal with traditional healers and their many false claims of being able to cure HIV/AIDS/STIs. There is the need to look into the feasibility of integrating them into the health care delivery system. It would entail educating them and authenticating the numerous claims of healing and then developing a health system whereby western and traditional medicine complement one another in the delivery of health care services to the people. This has been successfully done in Senegal but it took years of planning with their system being established prior to the HIV epidemic. The two systems of care complement one another and have thus helped in ensuring community mobilisation for the care and support of PLWHA, while enhancing prevention through effectively reaching the people as the traditional healers are often community leaders as well. Senegal has thus been able to stabilise its HIV prevalence rate at less than 2 percent of the population. Efforts have been made by the NACA at this but with limited success.

These constraints may also be better addressed through pursuing law reform programmes on HIV/AIDS. Unfortunately, there is no legislation which specifically deals with PLWHA. Neither is there any judicial authority on the issue. While great attention has been paid on prevention and control of the epidemic, little effect has been achieved in protecting the rights of people already infected. The poor attention being given to the welfare of PLWHA is further reflected in the non-inclusion of HIV/AIDS management in the newly launched National Health Insurance Scheme in the country. This all helps to encourage discrimination and stigmatization thereby worsening the crisis. Also, the fact that the costs for care and support are extensively left to be borne by the infected may act as a constraint to the proposed target of reducing the high rate of early AIDS related deaths. The national plan has only made available significant technical support for the care and support of a few. More often than not, the cost of drugs is presently too high for the average Nigerian to bear. Analyses show that close to 80 percent of income is expended on food and the remaining 20 percent has to be shared on other necessities. The high and increasing cost of drugs needed for the management of the many opportunistic infections the infected would have to bear, is an issue that may mitigate against decreasing the number of AIDS related deaths if not addressed in policy and strategy development. Strategies thus have to be developed to improve the pricing and affordability of HIV related drugs. This could possibly meet the year 2003 target set by the United Nations.

Even the present anti-retroviral therapy scheme operated by the Government has its loopholes. Despite this effort on the part of the government to provide for the teeming number of PLWHA, many find the programme inaccessible because the cost of baseline investigation which has to be borne by the clients (about $400) is still out of the reach of the majority of Nigerians. Thus it is the rich PLWHA who can afford to purchase the drugs at the market prices that benefit from the subsidized treatment programme. There may be a need to look into ways to re-evaluate the effectiveness of this programme if its objective would be met.

It is thus apparent in view of these constraints, that the effective curbing of the epidemic would be limited in the short run. The NACA target of stabilizing the national HIV prevalence rate to 3.5 percent, increasing condom use from 30 percent to 80 percent, increasing community involvement in prevention care and support to 30 percent from zero percent at the end of the 3 year HEAP project, might be a difficult objective to achieve. Also the possibility of meeting the United Nations target of reducing the prevalence amongst the 15–24 year-olds by 25 percent in the year 2005 in the country is poor. However, concerted efforts may ensure the achievement of the UN target and timetable of ensuring that by 2005, 90 percent of 15–24 year-olds have access to information and services needed to reduce vulnerability, reducing the proportion of infants infected by HIV by 20 percent and implementing national strategies to provide a supportive environment for orphans and children infected and affected by HIV/AIDS.

Conclusion

With the high level of political will that presently exists, international partnership, moral and financial support, the nation has all that it takes to implement an emergency plan, although it must be realized that poverty, a high recurring decimal, has to be effectively tackled alongside as resources are also an important part of prevention and care plans. Although the government, in an effort to increase the spending ability of the people, increased the basic salary of civil servants by 300 percent in January 2000, it must also increase the non taxable income as well as put in place favourable policies that would increase foreign investments in the country. Another positive step is the National Poverty Alleviation Programme, which operates in all the States, wherein registered unemployed persons are helped to acquire skills that would enhance self employment. These efforts are all still in their infancy and have presently not yet, all together, addressed the issue of poverty.

The implementation of the present emergency plan, which is a fall out of lessons learnt from past unsuccessful programmes, could at best help in the development of a more comprehensive plan, in view of its limitations on reducing the present infection rate significantly. However, concerted efforts by all relevant stakeholders, including the international community following the call made at the United Nations Special Session on HIV/AIDS in June 2001, would help put in place structures and programmes that would help in the reduction of the present prevalence rate in the country.

Acknowledgement

I would like to acknowledge the contributions of Dr AO Fatusi and Mrs O Irinoye with the editing of this manuscript. I would also like to thank Mr Omololu Falobi whose organisation's well managed website provided a lot of information.

References

Akanni O. Open electronic conference on HIV/AIDS in Nigeria: the polity and policies -3. Nigeria-AIDS e-forum. August 13th 2001.

Akanni O. Open electronic conference on HIV/AIDS in Nigeria: the polity and policies -13. Nigeria-AIDS e-forum. August 23th 2001.

Akinsete I. Open electronic conference on HIV/AIDS in Nigeria: the polity and policies -2. Nigeria-AIDS e-forum. August 13th 2001.

Ankrah EM, Mhloyi MM, Manguyu F, Nduah R. 'Women and children and AIDS.' In: *AIDS in Africa*. New York: Raven Press. 1994:533–546.

Caldwell JC, Caldwell P. 'The role of marital sexual abstinence in determining fertility: a study of the Yoruba in Nigeria.' Population Studies, 1977;31(1): 193–216.

Caldwell JC, Caldwell P and Quiggin P. 'The social context of AIDS in Sub-Saharan Africa.' *Population Development Review*. 1989;15:185–234.

Durojaiye E. 'Ethical, legal and human rights issues surrounding HIV/AIDS'. Presentation at a workshop for Media Gate Keepers organized by Journalists Against AIDS (JAAIDS) Nigeria. July 24–26, 2002.

Falobi O. 'Back to the roots'. *POZ in Africa*. July 1999:58–62.

Federal Ministry of Health, Nigeria. *The Technical Report on 2001 national HIV/syphilis sentinel survey report*. 2001.

Federal Ministry of Health/National Action Committee on AIDS. *Situation analysis report on STD/HIV/AIDS in Nigeria*. March 2000.

Federal office of Statistics/UNICEF, Nigeria. *Multiple indicator cluster survey 1999*. June 2000.

Folayan MO, Fakande I, Ogunbodede EO. 'Caring for people living with HIV/AIDS and AIDS orphans in Osun state: a rapid survey report'. *Nigerian Journal of Medicine* 2001; 10(4):177–181.

Hunter S and Williamson J. *Children on the brink. Executive summary*. United States Agency for International development. 2000.

Kafaru EO. 'Socio-economic challenges to PLWAS – a traditional healer's experience'. Paper presented during the International workshop on Socio-economic Impact of HIV/ AIDS in Africa. Ile-Ife, Nigeria. July, 1998.

Kolo SA. Open electronic conference on HIV/AIDS in Nigeria: the polity and policies -9. Nigeria-AIDS eforum. August 19th 2001.

Mafeni J. Open electronic conference on HIV/AIDS in Nigeria: the polity and policies 7. Nigeria-AIDS e-forum. August 20th 2001.

National Action Committee on Aids, *HIV/AIDS in Nigeria. An overview of the epidemic*. March 2002.

National Action Committee on AIDS. *Project implementation plan for Nigeria IAP on HIV/ AIDS prevention and impact mitigation*. June 2000.

National Action Committee on AIDS. *The HIV/AIDS Emergency Action Plan (HEAP)*. February 2001.

National Population Commission, Nigeria. *Child survival protection and development in Nigeria. Key social statistic*. April 1998.

Nigeria-AIDS e-forum. August 27th 2001.

Nigeria-AIDS e-forum. NIGERIA: focus on HIV/AIDS treatment programme. August 27th 2001.

Okonofua FF. 'Need to address adolescent reproductive health in Nigeria'. *Women's Health Forum*. 1997; 2(2):1–2.

Olayinka BA and Osho AA. 'Changes in attitude, sexual behaviour and the risk of HIV/AIDS transmission in Southwest Nigeria'. *East African Journal of Medicine* 1997;74(9):554–560.

Omorodion FI. 'Sexual networking of market women in Benin City, Edo State, Nigeria.' *Health Care Women International*. 1993;14(6):561–671.

Orubuloye IO, Caldwell JC and Caldwell P. 'African women's control over their sexuality in an era of AIDS: a study of the Yoruba of Nigeria.' *Social Science and Medicine*. 1993;37(7):859–872.

Page HJ, Lesthaeghe R. *Child spacing in Tropical Africa: tradition and change*. New York: Academic Press, 1981.

Population Information Program, 'Meeting the needs of young adults', *Population Report* Vol. XXIII, 3, October 1995, The Johns Hopkins School of Public Health, Baltimore.

Sunanda R. 'A family stuck with consequences of a value system.' *Reproductive Health Matters* 2000;8(15):113–114.

Topouzi D and Hemrich G. 'The socio-economic impact of HIV and AIDS on rural families in Uganda: An emphasis on youths. HIV and development programme'. UNDP, New York. Oct. 1995.

Tusabec C, Kalisa K, Nduwala K, Kihinda M, Nabawanuka M. 'The spiritual concept in relation to the spread of HIV'. IX International Conference of AIDS and STDs in Africa. December, 1995 (Abstract TUD187).

UNAIDS and World Bank. *Costs of scaling HIV programmes to a national level in Sub-Saharan Africa*. Draft Report. April 2000.

UNICEF. *State of the world's children*. 2001.

United Nations Special Session on HIV/AIDS. Global Crisis and Action. New York. 25–27th June 2001.

US Agency for International Development, *HIV infection and AIDS. A report of Congress on the USAIDS program for prevention and control*. U.S. Agency for International Development. Washington DC 20523. July 1990:pp12.

Wilson D, Sibanda B, Mboyi L, Msimonga B, Duke G. 'A pilot study for an HIV prevention programme among commercial sex workers in Bulawayo, Zimbabwe.' Social Science and Medicine. 1990;31(5):609–618.

Chapter 7

Between State Security and State Collapse: HIV/AIDS and South Africa's National Security

Robert L. Ostergard, Jr. and Matthew R. Tubin

Introduction

Since the early 1980s, the social science and international relations research agendas associated with the Human Immunodeficiency Virus (HIV) and Acquired Immunodeficiency Syndrome (AIDS) have been dominated by matters concerned with the human tragedy that the pandemic has wrought in the developing world. The strong emphasis on the human tragedy component, while certainly important and with merit, has left neglected other consequences of the pandemic in parts of the developing world. While the post-Cold War period unleashed ethnic strife, refugee problems, civil unrest and other forms of security issues for many states, the HIV/ AIDS pandemic unexpectedly has contributed to the security threat that many countries face in the turbulent international environment.

From a theoretical perspective, the type of threat that the HIV/AIDS pandemic poses to state security is contingent upon time and scope. From a short-term perspective, the pandemic poses the greatest threat to political and military institutions; from a long-term perspective, the pandemic's threat is centred on entire populations and state economic performance. Equally important is that the pandemic has pitted the security interests of developed states directly against those of developing states. Multilateral agreements governing the protection of intellectual property rights (IPR) to protect pharmaceutical patents have made vital pharmaceutical patents expensive for developing countries that need the medicines to stem the HIV/AIDS pandemic. The IPR issue has evolved into a major dispute between developed and developing countries that has placed the economic security interests of the major powers on a collision course with the political, military and economic security threats posed by the HIV/AIDS pandemic.

For South Africa, the security impact of the HIV/AIDS pandemic is already showing. From the civil service to the economy, South Africa's political and economic security has been compromised from the strain that the pandemic has placed on resources and manpower. The loss of manpower will mean that South Africa's capacity to maintain a regional hegemonic role will diminish in the short term, while in the long-term, the impact on South Africa will amount to a human catastrophe unseen in South African history. The long- and short- term political and economic stability of the entire southern African region will be jeopardized, as South Africa becomes less capable of coping with the fallout of the pandemic.

HIV/AIDS and National Security

While most conceptualizations of security focus on threats from groups or states, HIV/AIDS poses a challenge to this traditional conceptualization of a security threat because it is a virus. Another troubling characteristic of the pandemic is that its impact varies geographically. Despite all of this, HIV/AIDS does have an impact on security, but to what extent? While the HIV/AIDS pandemic poses a threat to individuals, the state and the international system, the impact on each of the levels and even the direction of the impact on each of the levels varies temporally and in intensity and scope. In part this is due to the nature of the virus' pattern of spread and the affected individuals. The HIV-1 strain of the virus is dominant in the United States and Western Europe, with the primary groups affected being homosexuals and intravenous drug users (Pattern I spread characteristics). The HIV-1 strain is also dominant in Africa, but its pattern of spread has been primarily among heterosexuals (Pattern II spread characteristics). A second strain, HIV-2, has been found predominantly in west Africa with the primary affected groups being heterosexuals as well (Whiteside 1993: 4–5). On the surface, this may seem to be just another characteristic of the virus, but the emergence of the two strains and whom they affected had significant consequences for how policymakers would respond to virus.

When news of the virus emerged in the 1980s, how the international community and national leaders perceived the virus had a dramatic impact on the response to the ensuing pandemic. In the West, and particularly in the United States, the virus became primarily associated with two groups: homosexuals and Haitian immigrants. As for the latter, the entire country of Haiti was stigmatized by the association. For the former group, the disease became known primarily as a 'gay' disease. The labelling could not have come at a worse time. With the American political climate turning distinctly towards a conservative agenda that emphasized family values and religion as necessary components of society's foundation, the media in the United States helped to brand the gay community with the stigma of the HIV/AIDS pandemic. It was only when 'average Americans,' women, children and blood recipients, were touched by the disease, that the media turned its attention away from the strict HIV/AIDS association with the gay community. However, in doing so, the media at the same time created a two-tier structure of victims – the 'innocent victims' consisting of those who contracted the disease through non-sexual contact and 'guilty' victims consisting of those who contracted the disease through homosexual activity and (later) through intravenous drug usage (Bastos 1999: 24–25). The two-tier public perception of the disease promoted, at first, a lack of urgency in coping with it. The early association of HIV/AIDS with the politically unpopular gay community caused early calls for policy action to be approached with indifference at best.

At the international level, the same two-tier structure emerged when it became clear that the pandemic was sweeping through Africa. As reports emerged from

Africa about the spread of 'slim disease,' the international community turned a blind eye to the problem. This was just another problem, another travesty that had struck an impoverished continent. The virus also hit Africa at the worst possible time internationally. The disappearance of the Soviet 'threat' in Africa after the Cold War also marked the beginning of the United States' diplomatic departure. Within three years of the fall of the Berlin Wall, the State Department's Bureau of African Affairs lost seventy positions, and consulates in Kenya, Cameroon and Nigeria were scheduled to be closed. The United States Agency for International Development's Africa desk lost between thirty and forty officers out of a total of a normal staff size of 130 (Michaels 1992: 96–98). The end of the global ideological tug-of-war between the United States and the former Soviet Union marginalized Africa in United States foreign policy and in the international community and consequently marginalized Africa's social problems, not the least of which was the growing HIV/ AIDS pandemic. The spread of the HIV/AIDS pandemic in Africa was not a *direct* security threat to the West in any sense of the word. This was not the case for African states, however, as the virus posed a direct threat to their security. Comparative data illustrate this point clearly for both Africa and South Africa particularly.

The Nature of the Pandemic

As Table 7.1 (Appendix) shows, more than 28 million people in sub-Saharan Africa are infected with the HIV/AIDS virus as of the end of 2001. But that number alone does not establish the severity of the problem as the following data illustrate. These data are sorted by the percentage of adults infected, which range from 38.8 per cent in Botswana to less than 1 per cent for several countries. In twelve countries, more than 10 per cent of the population of adults between the ages 15–49 (the most economically productive demographic group for a country) are infected. Additionally, 11 million children in Africa have been orphaned (losing the mother or both parents to the virus) by the pandemic. In total, about 9 per cent of sub-Saharan Africa's population is infected with the HIV/AIDS virus.

In shear numbers, the magnitude of the pandemic in Africa is staggering. However, these data only present part of the problem. In order to see why sub-Saharan Africa's pandemic has a greater sense of urgency, comparative data are useful. Table 7.2 (Appendix) presents those data. Compared to other regions, sub-Saharan Africa possesses 71 per cent of the infected people in the world and 78 per cent of those children orphaned by the virus, exceeding the percentages of all other areas combined. On the whole, the data reveal that Africa has been hit hardest by the virus compared to other regions of the world.

South Africa

South Africa's position in these data is also a stark example of the extent of the problem. The first two AIDS cases in South Africa were reported in 1982. Since then, South Africa's HIV/AIDS pandemic has become one of the worst in the world.

The most recent UNAIDS/World Health Organization (WHO) report placed the estimate of HIV infection at approximately 4.2 million South Africans, the largest population of HIV infected people among all countries in sub-Saharan Africa. As a percentage of the total population, approximately 20 per cent of South Africa's population is infected, ranking it seventh behind Botswana, Zimbabwe, Swaziland, Lesotho, Namibia, and Zambia. Additionally, the UNAIDS/WHO report estimated that South Africa's residual orphan problem now affected 660,000 children. Within South Africa, some provinces are experiencing pandemics that are worse than the national average. According to government data released by the Ministry of Health, prevalence rates for some provinces exceeded the 30 per cent level or higher (see Appendix Table 7.3).

The subsequent problems associated with AIDS have begun to appear in full force. Opportunistic infections associated with HIV positive status, such as tuberculosis, have increased since the onslaught of the HIV/AIDS pandemic. Tuberculosis (TB) infections and mortality rates increased dramatically as AIDS patients became more susceptible to infection and disease with the weakening of their immune system. From 1994 to 1995, for example, TB mortality rates rose from 38 to 53 per 100,000 males and from 15 to 23 per 100,000 females, with the highest incidents of death being recorded in provinces that have the highest incidents of HIV prevalence among women (Kwazulu-Natal and North West) (Kleinschmidt 1999). Overall, the pandemic in South Africa presents one of the greatest humanitarian crises ever faced by the government.

What both Table 7.1 and Table 7.2 reveal is a humanitarian crisis that will have short-term (indirect) and long-term (direct) effects on African countries' ability to manage their political and economic affairs. For African states, including South Africa, the long-term effects are in the loss of human life. People may be able to live years with the virus before AIDS develops and takes their lives. With inadequate health care and the lack of access to life-extending drugs, there appears to be little that can be done for those already infected in Africa; government efforts now focus on AIDS prevention (the reactive policy element) to curb the pandemic in Africa. The human catastrophe in Africa is extensive and poses a long-term threat to one of the base elements of the nation-state – population. In traditional security terms, however, the threat appears in the short-term in the form of indirect effects that the virus has on the political and military security of African countries. However, while much research has focused on the catastrophic humanitarian crisis of the pandemic, scholars and policymakers have conducted little research and analysis on the pandemic's impact on issues affecting South Africa's long- and short- term security with respect to the HIV/AIDS pandemic.

Domestic Security: States, Institutions and Bureaucracy

After the struggle against apartheid, the African National Congress (ANC) took power through free and democratic elections in 1994. The issue of how the ANC would rule quickly blossomed as South African society transformed from decades of racist oppression to a new period of democratic reforms. While the change in government went smoothly, the change in society lagged, partly because of the strength of the ANC itself and the resulting over-centralization of the national government. The ANC was not only able to garner significant national electoral strength, but it was also able to capture control of the nine provincial governments. The ANC became the dominant national party, similar to the circumstances of other parties such as the Kuomintang in Taiwan, the Institutional Revolutionary Party in Mexico and the United Malays National Organization in Malaysia (Giliomee 1998).

Based on the final constitution of 1996, a weak form of federalism emerged, which helped the ANC to consolidate power and the national decision-making process. The strength of its national appeal allowed the ANC to centralize much of the decision-making process without significant input from provincial leadership. While this may have been a strong political move for the ANC in the short term, it may ultimately be a political liability in the long term. When the ANC took control of the national government, local and provincial governments barely stayed afloat as their ability to deliver services declined and their authority within their territories eroded. According to Giliomee, '...of the approximately seven hundred local governments, about a third can manage, another third are salvageable, and the remaining third are collapsing to one degree or another' (Giliomee 1998: 139-140).

Provincial and local institutional decay and the decline in public confidence in those institutions have significant political affects. The inability of provincial and local institutions to provide services to citizens may place additional strain on national services as the national government attempts to fill the services gap at these levels. An important sign of public confidence in the national government will be in how well the government is able to provide needed services to its people. To this effect, the ANC has not met this challenge. One sign of this has been the role of non-governmental organizations in the transformation of South African society.

Prior to the collapse of apartheid, non-governmental organizations (NGOs) played a significant role in the delivery of services to local communities in South Africa. While many NGOs existed solely for the anti-apartheid struggle, since the end of apartheid, many have lost their purpose. NGOs involved in other activities outside of the apartheid struggle curtailed their involvement in South Africa, assuming that the new national government would be able to provide services as part of its state functions (James and Caliguire 1996). However, this has not been the case. The ANC has concentrated power at the national level in the areas of policing, education, and health, leaving provincial and local leaders impotent in providing necessary local services and functions (Giliomee 1998: 138). In some cases, domestic and foreign corporations or local companies have stepped in to provide some of these basic services to their own employees. But still, the over-concentration of power in the central government has been particularly noticeable in the health sector, and with AIDS policy in particular.

In early 1999, South Africa's Health Minister Nkosazana Zuma removed state funding for a program to distribute the anti-viral drug Zidovudine (AZT) to pregnant HIV infected women, arguing that the scarce resources may be better allocated in prevention programs (Baleta 1999: 908). The political fallout reached international levels, with boycotts of the July 2000 World AIDS Conference in Durban, South Africa. Domestically, the Western Cape province broke with national policy, supplying the drug as needed to pregnant women. Zuma later accused the Western Cape's New National Party of using AZT to buy votes in elections (Baleta 1999: 908).

More recently, a chasm has opened between national and provincial government policy over the distribution of Nevirapine to pregnant women. While the national government has refused to sanction the use of Nevirapine in curtailing mother-child transmission, provincial governments have begun to defect from the policy. In two of nine provinces where the national governing African National Congress is in local coalitions, its partners have announced a break from the national government's Nevirapine policy. Provinces and local doctors have defied the government by issuing Nevirapine doses to patients beyond those that were accepted into a pilot study on the drug. In effect provincial and local leaders have broken with national policy, recognizing that the national government's policies may not provide the care and services needed to their constituents. The relationship between national institutions and provincial institutions has eroded as provincial leaders distance themselves from unpopular, over-centralized national HIV health policies.

The pandemic's potential impact on government services is significant, but extends far beyond the national political configurations that evolved from the post-apartheid transition. The essence of government services, the bureaucracy, is jeopardized by the onslaught of the HIV/AIDS pandemic. The pandemic is affecting civil servants, which could further cripple the national government's ability to deliver services that maintain civil order and promote public confidence in political institutions. The problem is likely to affect provincial and local governmental institutions first, given locally high prevalence and infection rates (see Appendix Table 7.3). In South Africa, it has been estimated that as many as one in seven civil workers (150,000 or more) are HIV positive (ICG 2001; Canadian Development Agency) with educators, health care workers, and the police most affected. South Africa has been able to cope with the problem for now, but the long term situation may provide a greater challenge.

All forms of services are affected by the HIV/AIDS pandemic, but some are burdened more than others. Two service areas affected most in the long term by the pandemic are health care and police services. Strains on the health care system are obvious in that the health care system in South Africa will be pressured to deal with the pandemic as it progresses. However, the health care system may not be able to cope with potentially the most drastic fallout of the pandemic. The number of orphans in South Africa is increasing with the spread of the pandemic. Sadly, the increase in orphans may result in an increased propensity toward what could best be termed 'extended suicide'. One ethnographic study of inner-city Detroit residents clinically diagnosed with AIDS and their families revealed a horrific trend toward 'survivor terror' (Tourigny 1998). Children of parents diagnosed with AIDS may adopt self-destructive rationales deeply rooted in the conditions they face, such as poverty, crime, fear, depression and hopelessness, and seek intentionally to expose themselves to the HIV virus. Such behaviour may be an extreme reaction, but it can hardly be ruled out as a potential outcome of the desperate conditions created by the pandemic. The manifestation of this form of behaviour would serve to extend the pandemic in South Africa while creating additional stress on medical and psychiatric services that would be needed to deter orphaned children from pursuing such a drastic course of action.

Another area that has had little attention paid to it has been the impact on crime. Schönteich (1999) draws attention to the long term impact that the HIV/AIDS pandemic may have on South Africa's violent crime rates. Because of the increasing orphan population and the breakdown of the family structure, which occurs when parents die from the virus, orphans may resort to crime to survive under conditions of poor supervision and upbringing. Of course, sex crimes (prostitution) may increase as a way for orphans to survive while sex victimization (rape) may also increase because of the social vulnerability of the orphan population. Though these issues focus on individuals, the implications for provincial and national security are significant. Schönteich's work, though by no means conclusive, opens up a new avenue of concern for the security of South Africa.

Having to contend with this issue are South Africa's police forces. Following the transition from apartheid, crime rates in South Africa skyrocketed, with 2000 having the highest crime rates on record. According to Schönteich and Louw (2001), between 1994 and 2000, violent crime increased 34 per cent and property crime increased by 23 per cent. In 2000, 825,000 violent crimes were reported, up from 618,000 in 1994. In short, South Africa's police forces confront conditions that currently make South Africa as dangerous as a war zone. If Schönteich (1999) is correct the potential exists for South Africa to experience an even larger jump in crime rates than what has occurred already in the post-apartheid era. The crime problem in South Africa has extended beyond the capacity of the police forces to control it. In 1996, a white paper on National Defence for the Republic of South Africa concluded that while policing of crime is predominantly a responsibility of the South African Police Service (SAPS), there is a clear need for assistance from the South African National Defence Forces (SANDF) – i.e. the military.

AIDS and the Domestic-National Security Nexus

Constitutionally, the SANDF shares an auxiliary law enforcement role with the SAPS, an unusual role for the military in a democracy. While there is tremendous reluctance to involve the SANDF in policing affairs, the extensive crime problems have necessitated it (Winkates 2000; National Defence for the Republic of South Africa 1996). The lack of an overt external threat to South Africa means that the domestic policing role may increase for the SANDF. However, they are not allowed to conduct normal police functions, investigations, suspect arrests or actual involvement in the criminal justice system. Despite these restrictions, the deployment of the SANDF in cases of 'serious crime' has been done. These crimes include armed attacks on farms, stock theft, arms trafficking, and car hijackings. The SANDF and SAPS have shared scarce equipment, supplies, and services, but forces also share the same problem: the HIV/AIDS pandemic.

In the general literature the overall impact of HIV/AIDS on the military has been dichotomized into the two spheres: the impact of HIV/AIDS on the military and the impact of the military on the spread of HIV/AIDS. The former is a security issue while the latter is a behavioural issue, though separating the two is a difficult proposition as behaviour ultimately affects security in some form. The more obvious security problem is with the military and the impact that the HIV/AIDS virus has on the military's capacity to carry out its duties. This issue appears at a critical time in Africa's history when Africa has been freed from external influences to manage its own affairs. The post-Cold War period has placed responsibility for Africa's problems in Africans hands, almost by default. Given the lack of interest the international community has in Africa, the options for maintaining peace have narrowed, perhaps for the better in terms of the managing of Africa's affairs by Africans. In one sense, the idea of Africans handling their own crises has tremendous appeal, particularly given that the will of others was the determining factor in settling Africa's crises during the Cold War. But the additional responsibility being taken up by African governments puts a strain on already scarce resources. Much of those resources have been devoted to expanding military operations in conflict areas.

After the United States' disastrous peacekeeping efforts in Somalia in 1992, regional and sub-regional organisations have acted to maintain peace in Africa, most prominently in southern Africa, the Southern African Development Community (SADC). SADC has officially committed itself to the expansion of peacekeeping operations in the southern African region; however, resource and power issues may hinder it from becoming active in this area. The only country capable of carrying out any significant foreign military peacekeeping is South Africa, but it has little ambition to take an active stance in any conflicts. The doomed Lesotho intervention of 1998 was the only exception (Danish Defence Ministry 2001). Despite the initial reluctance and even opposition from Zimbabwe (which fears South African regional hegemonic status), it is clear that South Africa will need to take a leading role in peacekeeping operations in southern Africa if the idea of 'Africans solving African problems' is to materialize. Should South Africa take a more prominent role in this capacity, they will need to contend with the threats posed by the HIV/AIDS virus, as other countries have had to do.

In the short-run, the virus has the potential to compromise military performance because of the chance for opportunistic infections to appear as a result of soldiers' weakened immune systems. In the long-run, fewer capable people will be able to join military forces as the number of suitable recruits, particularly among young people, declines from increasing death rates. At the same time, troops incapacitated by the virus and the decrease in suitable recruits will also have an impact on the available corps of experienced military leaders. The decrease in available, experienced military leadership may contribute to a decline in military performance and even a further breakdown in military discipline, particularly in war-prone areas. Domestically, the same problem confronts political leaders as additional questions have been raised concerning the capacity of the military to maintain stability under conditions of high HIV infection rates (Copson 2001). The weakness of the military can also promote the opportunity for invasion if other countries perceive a major weakness in the military. In battle, the soldiers' compromised immune systems also make them more vulnerable to chemical and biological attacks, even on a small scale.[1] Hence, HIV infection of military personnel poses serious challenges for security and stability.

Data are scarce and contested, but estimates of HIV infection among the SAPS and the SANDF show a blossoming crisis that will affect South Africa's domestic and international security. For the SAPS, reports by the South African Health Department have placed HIV infection among the police at between 20 per cent and 25 per cent, though that figure is strongly contested by the SAPS (*The Star* 1998;

South African Press Association 1998). According to the Department, the highest infection rates were among those police serving in the Caprivi Strip in Namibia or in exile. Infection rate estimates among members of the SANDF have also been controversial. While some have estimated that as much as 40 per cent of the SANDF are HIV positive, the SANDF itself has acknowledged an infection rate of approximately 17 per cent (Magardie 1999; Beresford 2001). The latter figure is based on a survey of military personnel in three of South Africa's provinces, though the army says that infection rates most likely resemble overall provincial infection rates throughout South Africa (Beresford 2001).

The levels of HIV infection within the military create special circumstances that warrant attention to the behaviour of military personnel both in and out of conflict zones. From a behavioural perspective, the general conduct of military personnel has been linked to behaviour that is conducive to the transmission of the HIV virus (Carballo, Mansfield and Prokop 2000; UNAIDS 1998; United States Institute of Peace 2001; Heinecken 2001; Goyer 2001). The majority of soldiers tend to be young, sexually active men between the ages of 18-25. They are usually single and often discouraged from marrying while serving in the armed forces. Peer pressure and the general military culture that favours 'macho' behaviour often view sexual activity as a social necessity or reward. When the military demographics are combined with the social pressures of the military, the conditions for behaviour conducive to viral spread emerge.

South Africa had to confront the problem of soldier rape in its 1998 peacekeeping operations in Lesotho. Massive public demonstrations against the presence of SANDF appeared in Maseru after allegations that SANDF soldiers had raped three young girls at Ha Leqele village near Makoanyane Barracks. In another incident accusations were levied against seven SANDF soldiers who allegedly raped a married woman at gun point in front of her husband.

One of South Africa's greatest foreign policy challenges in the post apartheid era may come with the addition of South African troops to a peacekeeping operation in the war torn region of the Democratic Republic of the Congo. South Africa has offered to take a prominent role in peacekeeping operations in the region should a cease-fire emerge from the warring parties. From a foreign policy perspective, this may heighten South Africa's regional stature; from an AIDS policy perspective, this may be a move toward disaster. War-torn regions promote an indiscriminate sexual culture among military. The presence of the military attracts sex trade workers that promote the spread of the virus to soldiers who may return home to their families. Of course, their families back home are then at risk.

War-torn regions can also promote the spread of the virus through terror. In Sierra Leone, violence against women has been used as a weapon of terror and torture by revolutionaries fighting the government army and peacekeeping forces. Rape and sexual slavery have been systematic and indiscriminate. From the very young to the very old, women have been raped and tortured by revolutionary soldiers, further spreading the HIV virus. The ongoing war in the Democratic Republic of Congo involves seven countries whose armies are reported to be from 50 per cent to 80 per cent HIV-infected. Reports of soldiers raping civilians in the Democratic Republic of the Congo's ongoing civil war have become commonplace. But perhaps most disconcerting has been the reaction of government officials who look upon such behaviour in war regions as 'boys being boys.' South Africa will need to contend with the behaviour of its own SANDF soldiers along with these other possible issues should a solid role for them emerge in the DRC.

HIV/AIDS and South Africa's Economic Security

Researchers and scholars have examined the long-run economic impact of the HIV/ AIDS pandemic in a number of studies that indicate the pandemic will have tremendous consequences for Africa (Barnett and Whiteside 2000; Cross and Whiteside 1993; Nevin 1998; Over 1992; Tbaijuka 1997; Topouzis 1998). South Africa's current economic condition reflects these basic conclusions. Since the transition from the apartheid government in 1994, South Africa's general economic conditions have declined. Unemployment in South Africa jumped dramatically between 1994–2000, with current unemployment hovering between twenty-five per cent and thirty per cent. The unemployment problem has been compounded by a lack of incentive for domestic investment. Inflation in South Africa's economy is running at close to forty per cent annually, while the central bank has increased interest rates to between fourteen and eighteen per cent in order to control the high levels of inflation. Annual economic growth has stagnated at under two per cent, while per capita gross domestic product has declined in recent years.

Economic problems associated with an increase in HIV/AIDS in countries include lost productivity, decreased investment, worker illness, increasing government expenditures, higher insurance costs, and the loss of trained workers, which all translates into a decline in gross domestic product over the long term. Most prominent among the economic problems is the increased government expenditures needed to combat the pandemic. Increased expenses arise in two areas, government prevention programs and government health care expenses for those already infected. Government prevention programs become a fundamental necessity in trying to stem the pandemic from doing further population damage. Government health care expenses increase through two factors: the number of people infected (more people needing assistance) and the basic costs of assisting those people (drugs and other medical supplies).

While these increased costs are necessitated by the nature of the pandemic, the expected increase in health related expenditures by the central government has not fully materialized. In fact, from 1993–1998, health expenditures per capita have actually declined more than six per cent. This fact alone calls into question a number of studies that have projected the impact of the HIV/AIDS pandemic on increased government expenditures for health care. For instance, Quattek (2000) has estimated that government health care expenditures per capita would remain constant, with the number of AIDS patients rising, indicating that overall government expenditures would quadruple by 2010. However, even this brief time series indicates that declining economic conditions could actually *decrease* health expenditures per patient, drastically hindering the government's effort in stemming the HIV/AIDS pandemic. South Africa's recent economic downturn has hindered its battle against the pandemic.

South Africa's domestic economy presents a distinct problem in combating the pandemic: how to maintain economic growth which is needed to fight the pandemic while maintaining a healthy work force which will drive the economy? To answer this question, the South African government must pay attention to two aspects: cutting the incident of HIV/AIDS transmission while at the same time decreasing the overall death rate due to the pandemic. The former is a matter of education (and possibly vaccination, though this approach seems unlikely in the near future); the latter is a matter of politics and economics. The issue manifests itself in the inability to produce pharmaceuticals that could extend peoples' lives, which originates in the global intellectual property rights regime that prevents South Africa from manufacturing patented pharmaceuticals. South Africa's adherence to the global intellectual property rights regime constitutes a direct threat to its long term national security.

In 1994, the Marrakesh Agreement establishing the World Trade Organization was signed by over one hundred states. In that agreement, a global trade regime for the protection of intellectual property rights (IPR) was included as a result of a strong lobbying effort by the United States and private corporations (Sell 2000; Ryan 1998). The Trade Related Intellectual Property Rights (TRIPS) agreement binds *all* signatory nations to implementing a full Western-style intellectual property (IP) regime within sixteen years of the agreement's national ratification.[2] The agreement itself was the final product of a long process that brought the IPR issue from an obscure, esoteric legal field to a critical political and economic issue that has brought states to the brink of trade wars.

The TRIPS agreement provides national treatment for intellectual property across a range of property rights areas (copyrights, patents, and trademarks being the primary ones).[3] Covered under patents in particular are pharmaceuticals. Under the agreement, foreign pharmaceutical companies can apply for patents on pharmaceuticals in individual countries and receive exclusive rights to produce the pharmaceutical product in that country. In essence, intellectual property rights provide a limited monopoly to the pharmaceutical producer; in the case of the TRIPS agreement, the time limit is twenty years. Because the producer has a monopoly on the market, price is not dictated by open market conditions (supply and demand); the producer has more control in establishing the price for the product. This issue has become the source of international disputes, particularly between developed and developing countries, and major ethical dilemmas in international trade policy that pit the economic security of the major market powers against the national security of developing countries.[4]

The impact of the TRIPS agreement generally can be seen in the cost of antiretroviral therapy drugs in Africa. Though the drugs could have an important impact on curbing the death rate in these countries, the cost for them is prohibitive. The cost of providing the drugs to eleven African countries has been calculated to exceed 28 per cent of the GNPs of these countries (Rao 2000: 124). In countries where the drugs are generally less expensive (Brazil and India for example), the governments do not abide by the TRIPS restriction for the production of pharmaceuticals. However, attempts by South Africa to bypass the TRIPS agreement have been met with threats of bilateral trade retaliation from the United States.

In an attempt to curb the skyrocketing costs of pharmaceuticals, the South African government submitted to Parliament the Medicines and Related Substances Control Amendment Act in August 1997. The bill sought to amend the 1965 Medicines and Related Substances Act by establishing a drug pricing committee, regulating wholesalers, providing procedures for expediting essential medicines, allowing physicians to make generic substitutions, and providing measures supplying more affordable drugs under certain circumstances. It was the last two measures that provided the most controversy both nationally and internationally. Section 15(c) of the bill gave the Health Minister the ability to abrogate patent rights to pharmaceuticals issued under South Africa's Patents Act of 1978 and to import identical pharmaceutical compounds from manufactures other than the registered owner. The bill also allowed for generic substitutions, a common practice in many countries (National Assembly of South Africa 1997).

The United States State Department instructed US Ambassador James Joseph to express strong opposition to the pending changes in South Africa's pharmaceutical statutes. Despite testimony by United States officials in Parliamentary hearings, the bill passed in November 1997, but its implementation was delayed due to a constitutional challenge by the South African Pharmaceuticals Industry (supported by European and American industry representatives). During the challenge period, the Ministry of Health introduced a bill that repealed the contentious elements of section 15(c), however, it later reintroduced the provisions of section 15(c) after public hearings were completed. In December 1998, President Mandela signed the bill into law. The law was met with fierce condemnation by the South African Pharmaceutical Manufacturers Association and the Pharmaceutical Research and Manufacturers of America (PhRMA). Shortly after the bill was signed into law, the PhrMa filed suit in South African courts to block its implementation.

In the United States, the PhRMA contended that South Africa's action posed a challenge to the TRIPS agreement. As such, the PhRMA sought the assistance of the United States government under Section 301 of the Trade Act of 1974 in confronting South Africa's government. In 1998 and 1999, the USTR placed South Africa on the Special 301 Watch List, based partly on the new revisions to South Africa's pharmaceuticals law.[5] In making its decision, the USTR complained that the Medicine's Act granted to the Health Minister 'ill defined authority to issue compulsory licenses, authorize parallel imports and potentially otherwise abrogate patent rights' (United States Trade Representative 1999: 22). The USTR agreed with the PhRMA and viewed the law as being symptomatic of South Africa's leadership in the World Health Organization in trying to reduce the level of protection for pharmaceuticals under the TRIPS agreement. United States Trade Representative Charlene Barshefsky stated that she intended to continue to address the intellectual property rights issue with the South African government and to begin a full investigation in September 1999.

By 2000, public pressure was mounting in industrialized countries over the HIV/AIDS issue in Africa. Before the USTR could fully investigate the South African government's new pharmaceuticals law, President Bill Clinton signed Executive Order 13155 (May 10, 2000), which forbade the USTR and other US government agencies from pursuing intellectual property rights violation cases against any sub-Saharan African country provided that the country was still in compliance with the

TRIPS agreement. What this meant in practical terms was that sub-Saharan African countries could relax any patent restrictions that would prevent them from utilizing generic substitutes and other mechanisms for lowering pharmaceutical prices. Clinton's executive order was followed by dramatic changes in the policies of the pharmaceutical industry.

In March 2001, the lawsuit filed by the industry went to court; however, the case turned immediately into a public relations disaster for the thirty-nine companies that had filed the suit. In a quick turnaround, the companies began a radical price cutting program on their HIV/AIDS drugs for African countries. Before the court case could proceed, the pharmaceutical industry reached a tentative agreement with the South African government that would allow the new patent law to stand, but the government would only buy or make generic drugs within compliance with TRIPS. The PhRMA unconditionally withdrew their lawsuit and agreed to pay all costs associated with the case.

Conclusion

While the pharmaceutical industry's challenge to South Africa's patent law changes were eventually set aside, the issue is still salient because the pandemic shows no sign of dissipating, even beyond the 2006 deadline for full TRIPS compliance by developing countries. Hence, the overall threat to South Africa's stability should not be perceived as being at its end. Rather, the threat to South Africa's political and economic stability is in its infancy. As the pandemic winds its way through South African society, the government's capacity to cope with the pandemic's extent and impact will diminish, with the effects appearing in three forms.

First, at the domestic level, the government's ability to provide needed services (i.e. health care) will dwindle in the face of an overwhelming demand for resources. The division between the central government and the provisional governments will continue to grow, challenging the central government, and further illustrating the inability of the government to cope with the impending crisis.

Second, South Africa's ability to be the bedrock of regional stability will continue to diminish as resources and manpower are drained from the foreign policy and military institutions needed to carry out such expectations. While South Africa has managed to keep out of severe conflict, its desire to enter the DRC conflict may prove to be a catastrophic foreign policy decision based on its inability to sustain a long-term peacekeeping operation. The failed operation in the tiny country of Lesotho is only a precursor to the disaster that may await South Africa in the DRC if it is unable to dedicate appropriate resources to peacekeeping efforts.

Finally, South Africa's economic stability is compromised by long term exposure to the pandemic's impact. From macroeconomic problems to microeconomic incapacity the South African economy may falter under the long term impact of the pandemic. Corporations will need to close the gap where the government will be unable to provide services, which provides a serious problem for state security and for the political development of South Africa. The drain on corporate performance and long term corporate profits will generate detrimental macroeconomic problems such as chronic unemployment and possibly forms of hyperinflation as costs increase and are passed to the consumer.

However, the impact on corporations runs much deeper than the economic implications. In general, international trade and competitiveness policies have overtaken traditional state security concerns in the foreign policy arena which means that multinational corporations have an impact on the security agenda of states, both as agents of security (in the case of developed countries where corporations are perceived as vital to national economic security) and as threats to security (in the case of developing countries where corporations are perceived as having an inordinate amount of bargaining power).[6] In developing countries, both foreign and domestic corporations have become agents of political and economic stability by filling the gap between people's expectations regarding state benefits and services and what the state can actually provide. South Africa is no exception to this dilemma as its problems in dealing with the HIV/AIDS epidemic illustrates.

These three areas pose the greatest short-term and long-term threats to South Africa's security. Without adequate attention to the consequences of the HIV/AIDS pandemic in South Africa, the very existence of the state itself is certainly in doubt.

Notes

1   While this may sound implausible, the use of biological weaponry does not require a sophisticated delivery system. For instance, smallpox infested blankets and handkerchiefs were used to 'reduce' Native American populations during the French and Indian War (1754–1767). See Christopher et al. (1997) for additional examples of low technology biological warfare. More recently, the use of anthrax tainted letters by bio-terrorists in the United States illustrates the low-tech nature that can characterize biological terrorism.

2   An introduction to the TRIPS agreement and its associated issues can be found at the World Trade Organization web site http://www.wto.org/english/tratop_e/trips_e/trips_e.htm.

3   National treatment refers to treating domestic and foreign intellectual property equally under national laws.

4   For a discussion of the theoretical issues in the ethics of intellectual property rights see Hettinger 1989; Ostergard 1999.

5   Section 301, through its subcategory provision 'Special 301', requires the United States Trade Representative (USTR) to determine if the actions of foreign countries deny sufficient protection of intellectual property rights or fair and equitable market access for people who rely on intellectual property protection. With the help of public input and information from interested parties such as industries, individual corporations and trade associations, the USTR creates a list of countries with inadequate intellectual property rights protection. The USTR is then required to categorize these countries into three lists: the priority countries list, the priority watch countries list and the watch countries list. Priority countries must meet two criteria to be placed on the list:
    1.   They have egregious policies or practices that have actual or potential impact on U.S. products.
    2.   The have not engaged in good faith negotiations or made significant progress in negotiations to address the IPR problem (United States Trade Representative 1999).
    If a country is designated a priority, the USTR decides whether to begin an investigation into the practices that were the foundation for the country's designation. Countries that

are found to engage in unfair intellectual property rights practices are subject to sanctions based on the USTR investigation findings and the decision of the Section 301 Committee. The final decision to impose sanctions rests with the president.

Priority watch list countries are those that the USTR has identified as having intellectual property rights inadequacies, but are making efforts unilaterally or in conjunction with international organizations or the United States to improve the situation. The United States may also be pursuing dispute resolution measures against these countries with international organizations such as the World Trade Organization.

Watch countries are those that are implementing commitments with regard to intellectual property rights protection or have been initially cited with new developments that effect their intellectual property rights protection. In this sense, the list acts as a way for the United States to monitor other countries' progress in complying with intellectual property rights obligations.

6 For a greater discussion on the security issues surrounding the new international environment, see Ostergard 2002.

References

Baleta, Adele. 1999 'South African Government faces furious Zidovudine debate (News).' *The Lancet* 353, no. 9156: 908.

Barnett, Tony, and Alan Whiteside. 2000. 'The Social and Economic Impact of HIV/AIDS in Poor Countries: a review of studies and lessons.' UNAIDS.

Bastos, Cristiana. 1999. *Global Responses to AIDS : Science in Emergency*. Bloomington: Indiana University Press.

Beresford, Belinda. August 3, 2001. 'Army Survey Shows Decline in AIDS Cases'. *Mail & Guardian (Johannesburg)*. http://www.aegis.com/news/dmg/2001/MG010802.html. Accessed February 19, 2002.

Canadian International Development Agency. 'Overview: HIV/AIDS in South Africa.' http://www.acdi-cida.gc.ca/cida_ind.nsf/360fc575bb8b152185256778004fa91f/ cb8a9c4d6d8a87bb8525683a006678b9?OpenDocument. Accessed February 19, 2002.

Carballo, Manuel, Carolyn Mansfield and Michaela Prokop. 2000. 'Demobilization and Its Implications for HIV/AIDS.' Background Paper. Geneva: International Centre for Migration and Health.

Centers for Disease Control. 1998. 'CDC Update: Human Immunodeficiency Virus Type 2.'

Christopher, George W., Theodore J. Cieslak, et. al. 1997. 'Biological Warfare: A Historical Perspective.' *Journal of the American Medical Association*. Vol. 278, No. 5: pp. 412–417.

Copley, Gregory R. 1999. 'National Security in a Pandemic Situation.' *Defence & Foreign Affairs Strategic Policy* :7.

Copson, Raymond W. 2001. 'AIDS in Africa.' Washington DC: Congressional Research Service.

Cross, Sholto, and Alan Whiteside. 1993. *Facing Up to AIDS : the Socio-Economic Impact in Southern Africa*. New York: St. Martin's Press.

Danish Ministry of Foreign Affairs. 2001. 'Conflict Prevention and Peace-building in Africa: Report from the Maputo Conference 28-29 June 2001.' http:// www.um.dk January 18, 2002.

Giliomee, Hermann. 1998. 'South Africa's Emerging Dominant-Party Regime.' *Journal of Democracy*. Vol. 9 No. 4: 128-142.

Goyer, KC. 2001. 'HIV and Political Instability in sub-Saharan Africa.' *AIDS Analysis Africa*. Vol. 12. No.1: 13, 16.

Hazlett, Thomas W. 1977. 'The Road from Serfdom–Forseeing the Fall: F.A. Hayek interviewed by Thomas W. Hazlett.' : Reason Online.

Heinecken, Lyndy. 2001. 'Strategic Implications of HIV/AIDS in South Africa.' *The Conflict, Security and Development Group Bulletin*. Issue 7: 110-115.

— 2000. 'AIDS: the New Security Frontier.' *Conflict Trends*. No. 4. Accord Online.

Hettinger, Edwin C. 1989. 'Justifying Intellectual Property.' *Philosophy and Public Affairs* 18:31–52.

'HIV/AIDS: KwaZulu-Natal To Provide Nevirapine Despite Federal Policy [South Africa]'. Jan. 2002 *UN Wire*: 23.

International Crisis Group (ICG). 2001. 'HIV/AIDS as a Security Issue.' Washington DC: http: //www.intl-crisis-group.org/projects/reports.cfm?keyid=24. Accessed February 1, 2002.

James, Wilmot and Daria Caliguier. 1996. 'Renewing Civil Society.' *Journal of Democracy*. Vol. 7 No. 1: 56–66.

Kleinschmidt, I. 1999. 'South African Tuberculosis Mortality Data – Showing the First Signs of the AIDS Epidemic?' *South African Medical Journal* 89, no. 3: 269-273.

Magardie, Khadija. October 18, 1999. 'HIV Soldiers to Fend for Themselves.' *Johannesburg Mail and Guardian*. http:// www.fedword.gov. Accessed January 20, 2002.

Michaels, Marguerite. 1992. 'Retreat from Africa.' *Foreign Affairs* 72:93–109. 'Police Reject Claims that 33000 Members Suffer from AIDS.' October 9, 1998. *Global News Wire*. South African Press Association.

National Assembly of South Africa. 1997. *Medicines and Related Substances Control Amendment Act*, No. 90.

Nevin, Tom. 1998. 'Will AIDS Kill Africa's Economy?' *African Business* :16–19.

Ostergard, Robert L. 1999. 'Intellectual Property Rights: A Universal Human Right?' *Human Rights Quarterly* 21:156–178.

— 2002. 'Politics in the Hot Zone: AIDS and the Threat to Africa's Security' *Third World Quarterly* Vol. 23 No. 2: 333–350.

Over, Mead. 1992. 'The Macroeconomic Impact of AIDS in sub-Saharan Africa.' Population and Human Resources Department, the World Bank.

'Quarter of Police Force Said HIV Positive.' December 1, 1998. *The Star*: 1.

Quattek, Kristina. 2000. 'Economic Impact of AIDS in South Africa.' ING Barings Johannesburg. Obtained from the Author.

Rao, V. Bhargavi. 2000. 'HIV in the Developing World – Meeting the Challenge of the Growing Dichotomy.'*McGill Journal of Medicine*. 5: 121–126.

Rothschild, Emma. 1995. 'What is Security?' *Daedalus* 124:53–98.

Ryan, Michael. 1998. *Knowledge Diplomacy: Global Competition and the Politics of Intellectual Property*. Washington DC: Brookings Institution Press.

Schönteich, Martin and Antoinette Louw. 2001. 'A Profile of Crime in South Africa: Its Perpetrators and Victims, and Where It is Committed.' Annual Congress of the South African Sociological Association, Pretoria, South Africa: July 2. http://www.iss.co.za/Projects/CrimeAndJustice/ConferencePapers/SocAso01.html Accessed February 21, 2002.

Schönteich, Martin. 1999. 'Age and AIDS: South Africa's Crime Time Bomb?' African Security Review. Vol. 8 No. 4: http:// www.iss.co.za/Publications/Asrindex.html. Accessed February 21, 2002.

Schoofs, Mark. May 7, 2001. 'Mining Firm Combats AIDS via Drug Plan.' *Wall Street Journal*: A3.

Sell, Susan. 2000. 'Structures agents and institutions: private corporate power and the globalisation of intellectual property rights' in Richard A. Higgott, Geoffrey R. D. Underhill and Andreas Bieler (eds) *Non-State Actors and Authority in the Global System*. London: Routledge.

Shisana, Olive. 'New Medicines Bill Will Benefit Consumers. Statement by Dr. Olive Shisana, Director General of Health.' Department of Health, 1997.

South African Government. 1996. 'Defence in a Democracy White Paper on National Defence for the Republic of South Africa.' May. http://www.mil.za/Articles&Papers/Papers/WhitePaperonDef/white.htm Accessed January 15, 2002.

Strange, Susan. 1996. *The Retreat of the State : the Diffusion of Power in the World Economy*. Cambridge UK ; New York: Cambridge University Press.

Stopford, John M., Susan Strange, and John S. Henley. 1991. *Rival States, Rival Firms: Competition for World Market Shares*. Cambridge; New York: Cambridge University Press.

Tbaijuka, Anna Kajumulo. 1997. 'AIDS and Economic Welfare in Peasant Agriculture: Case Studies from Kagabiro Village, Kagera Region, Tanzania.' *World Development* 25:963–975.

Topouzis, Daphne. 1998. 'The Implications of HIV/AIDS for Rural Development Policy and Programming: Focus on Sub-Saharan Africa.' New York: Sustainable Development Department, FAO HIV and Development Programme, UNDP.

Tourigny, Sylvie C. 1998. 'Some New Dying Trick: African American Youths "Choosing" HIV/AIDS.' *Qualitative Health Research*. Vol. 8 No. 2: 149-167.

UNAIDS. 1998. 'AIDS and the Military.' http://www.unaids.org/publications/documents/sectors/military/militarypve.pdf Accessed August 22, 2001.

United States Institute of Peace (USIP). 2001. 'AIDS and Violent Conflict in Africa.' Special Report, October 15.

United States Trade Representative. 1999. '"Special 301" on Intellectual Property Rights and 1996 Title VII Decisions.'

Whiteside, Alan. 1993. 'Introduction' in Sholton Cross and Alan Whiteside (eds) *Facing up to AIDS: The Socio-Economic Impact in Southern Africa*. New York: St. Martin's Press.

Winkates, James. 2000. 'The Transformation of the South African National Defence Force: A Good Beginning.' *Armed Forces and Society: An interdisciplinary journal*. Vol. 26. No. 3: 451–472.

Appendix

Table 7.1: HIV/AIDS infection data for sub-Saharan Africa, end of 2001*

Estimated Number of People infected with HIV/AIDS					
Country	Adults and children	Adults (15–49)	Adult rate (%)	Women (15–49)	Children (0-14)	Orphans cumulative
Botswana	330,000	300,000	38.8	170,000	28,000	69,000
Zimbabwe	2,300,000	2,000,000	33.7	1,200,000	240,000	780,000
Swaziland	170,000	150,000	33.4	89,000	14,000	35,000
Lesotho	360,000	330,000	31	180,000	27,000	73,000
Namibia	230,000	200,000	22.5	110,000	30,000	47,000
Zambia	1,200,000	1,000,000	21.5	590,000	150,000	570,000
South Africa	5,000,000	4,700,000	20.1	2,700,000	250,000	660,000
Kenya	2,500,000	2,300,000	15	1,400,000	220,000	890,000
Malawi	850,000	780,000	15	440,000	65,000	470,000
Mozambique	1,100,000	1,000,000	13	630,000	80,000	420,000
Central African Republic	250,000	220,000	12.9	130,000	25,000	110,000
Cameroon	920,000	860,000	11.8	500,000	69,000	210,000
Cote D'Ivoire	770,000	690,000	9.7	400,000	84,000	420,000
Rwanda	500,000	430,000	8.9	250,000	65,000	260,000
Burundi	390,000	330,000	8.3	190,000	55,000	240,000
Tanzania	1,500,000	1,300,000	7.8	750,000	170,000	810,000
Congo	110,000	99,000	7.2	59,000	15,000	78,000
Sierra Leone	170,000	150,000	7	90,000	16,000	42,000
Burkina Faso	440,000	380,000	6.5	220,000	61,000	270,000
Ethiopia	2,100,000	1,900,000	6.4	1,100,000	230,000	990,000
Togo	150,000	130,000	6	76,000	15,000	63,000
Nigeria	3,500,000	3,200,000	5.8	1,700,000	270,000	1,000,000
Angola	350,000	320,000	5.5	190,000	37,000	100,000
Uganda	600,000	510,000	5	280,000	110,000	880,000
Dem. Republic of Congo	1,300,000	1,100,000	4.9	670,000	170,000	930,000
Benin	120,000	110,000	3.6	67,000	12,000	34,000

Chad	150,000	130,000	3.6	76,000	18,000	72,000
Equatorial Guinea	5,900	5,500	3.4	3,000	420	...
Ghana	360,000	330,000	3	170,000	34,000	200,000
Eritrea	55,000	49,000	2.8	30,000	4,000	24,000
Guinea-Bissau	17,000	16,000	2.8	9,300	1,500	4,300
Mali	110,000	100,000	1.7	54,000	13,000	70,000
Gambia	8,400	7,900	1.6	4,400	460	5,300
Somalia	43,000	43,000	1	...	...	...
Senegal	27,000	24,000	0.5	14,000	2,900	15,000
Madagascar	22,000	21,000	0.3	12,000	1,000	6,300
Mauritius	700	700	0.1	350	<100	...
Comoros **	...	...	...	...	...	...
Djibouti **	...	...	...	...	...	...
Gabon **	...	...	...	...	...	...
Guinea**	...	...	...	...	...	...
Liberia**	...	...	...	...	...	...
Mauritania**	...	...	...	...	...	...
Niger**	...	...	...	...	...	...
Sub-Saharan Africa	28,500,000	26,000,000	9.0	15,000,000	2,000,000	11,000,000

Source: UNAIDS, *Report on the Global HIV/AIDS epidemic, 2002,*
http://www.unaids.org/barcelona/presskit/report.html, accessed March, 2003
*Data are sorted by Adult Rate, reflecting the percentage of the population estimated to be infected with **HIV/AIDS. Data were not available for these countries

Table 7.2: Comparative HIV/AIDS regional data, end of 2001

Estimated Number of People infected with HIV/AIDS					
Region	Adults and children	Adults (15–49)	Adult rate (%)	Women (15–49)	Children (0-14)	Orphans cumulative
Sub-Saharan Africa	28,500,000	26,000,000	9.0	15,000,000	2,000,000	11,000,000
East Asia & Pacific	1,000,000	970,000	.10	230,000	3,000	85,000
Australia & New Zealand	15,000	15,000	0.10	1,000	<200	<1000
South & South-East Asia	5,600,000	5,400,000	0.60	2,000,000	220,000	1,800,000
Eastern Europe & Central Asia	1,000,000	1,000,000	0.50	260,000	15,000	<5000
Western Europe	550,000	540,000	0.30	140,000	5,000	150,000
North Africa & Middle East	500,000	460,000	0.30	250,000	35,000	65,000
North America	950,000	940,000	0.60	190,000	10,000	320,000
Caribbean	420,000	400,000	2.30	210,000	20,00	250,000
Latin America	1,500,000	1,400,000	0.50	430,000	40,000	330,000
Global Total	40,000,000	37,100,000	1.20	18,500,000	3,000,000	14,000,000

Source: UNAIDS, *Report on the Global HIV/AIDS epidemic, 2002,*
        http://www.unaids.org/barcelona/presskit/report.html, accessed March, 2003
Data have been rounded

Table 7.3: Estimated HIV prevalence rates for women aged 15–49 years, 1990–1999

Year	Natn'l	W. Cape	E. Cape	N. Cape	Free State	Kwazulu / Natal	Mpumu - langa	Limpopo	Gauteng	North West
1990	.7	0.06	0.44	0.2	0.59	1.61	0.38	0.26	0.66	1.05
1991	1.7	0.08	0.58	0.12	1.5	2.86	1.21	0.48	1.12	6.54
1992	2.2	0.25	0.96	0.65	2.86	4.5	2.23	1.05	2.53	0.94
1993	4.0	0.56	1.94	1.07	4.12	9.53	2.4	1.79	4.13	2.19
1994	7.6	1.16	4.52	1.81	9.19	14.35	12.16	3.04	6.44	6.71
1995	10.4	1.66	6	5.34	11.03	18.23	16.18	4.89	12.03	8.3
1996	14.2	3.1	8.1	6.47	17.5	19.9	15.8	7.9	15.5	25.1
1997	17.0	6.3	12.6	8.6	19.6	26.9	22.6	8.2	17.1	18.1
1998	22.8	5.2	15.9	9.9	22.8	32.5	30	11.5	22.5	21.3
1999	22.4	7.1	18	10.1	27.9	32.5	27.3	11.4	23.9	23
2000	24.5	8.7	20.2	11.2	27.9	36.2	29.7	13.2	29.4	22.2
2001	24.8	8.6	21.7	15.9	30.1	33.5	29.2	14.5	29.8	25.2

Sources: University of Capetown, Department of Pharmacology
http: //www.uct.ac.za/depts/mmi/jmoodie/anc0.html
Swanevelder, J.P., H.G.V Kustner, and A. Vanmiddelkoop. 'The South African HIV Epidemic, Reflected by Nine Provincial Epidemics, 1990-1996.' *South African Medical Journal* 88, no. 10 (1998): 1320-1325
South African Department of Health, *National HIV and Syphilis Sero-Prevalence Survey in South Africa, 2001*, http://196.36.153.56/doh/aids/index.html, accessed March 2003

Chapter 8

What People Really Believe About HIV/AIDS in Southern Africa

Alan Whiteside, Robert Mattes, Samantha Willan, and Ryann Manning

Is AIDS a catastrophe for sub-Saharan Africa? Many people would have us believe this is the case. UNAIDS has since its inception consistently warned of the implications of this new disease. In the past few years other international agencies have begun to appreciate what AIDS does and might mean for them and their activities. In the USA the National Intelligence Council has released a number of reports warning of the likely effect of AIDS (NIC. 2002). It was the first disease to be debated at the Security Council; the first disease to have a special session at the United Nations General Assembly and so on. Despite this there is still a huge gap in the response of almost every African leadership and government, and the citizens of most African countries do not frame it as a priority for their political leaders.

Apart from international agencies (and until recently only some of them) the global response has been muted. The truth is yes, people are concerned about the epidemic but they are also concerned about trade, terrorism, global warming, and a myriad of other issues. One of the key indicators of the relative importance of AIDS is the allocation of resources rather than rhetoric. There are two estimates of resource needs – the UN General Assembly special session on HIV/AIDS in June 2001 called for the spending of US$9.2 billion on HIV/AIDS prevention and care in low and middle income countries by 2005. The Commission on Macro-economics and Health estimates that $14.5 million will be needed by 2007 (McGreevey, Bertozzi et al. 2002). The new mechanism for channelling resources, the Global Fund for AIDS, TB and Malaria had received just over $2.2 billion in total (not annual) pledges as of 5 November 2002. It is estimated that $3 billion is the minimum needed in 2003 and $4.9 in 2004 (Fund 2002).

Why is there this apparent fracture between what is and will happen in terms of excess morbidity and mortality in the cities, villages and kraals of Africa, and the local and national responses? This chapter suggests there are four reasons:

1. In some settings there is no documented evidence of increased morbidity and mortality – and even where there is it is hard to link this to the abstract concept of 'HIV/AIDS'.
2. People have other priorities, AIDS is a 'long-wave' disaster and other things command immediate attention.
3. Leadership has not responded – partly because they do not know what to do and partly because this is an unattractive issue.

4.   People may not define HIV/AIDS as a political or governmental problem but rather as a community, household or personal problem.

The chapter uses the original and unique data set found in Afrobarometer attitude surveys to try to understand the public and political inaction. As these data are only available for Botswana, Lesotho, Malawi, Namibia, South Africa, Zambia and Zimbabwe we will concentrate on these countries.

Epidemiological Data

In order to understand the HIV/AIDS pandemic, one must proceed from the fact that it is complex, multi-faceted and influenced by many medical, social, economic, and cultural factors. Though it has much in common with other infectious diseases, it also presents a unique challenge, because of the lengthy incubation period between HIV infection and the onset of illness, the factors that impact susceptibility and vulnerability to HIV/AIDS, and the rapidity and extent of the epidemic's spread.

Epidemic Curves

As shown in Figure 8.1, epidemics generally follow an 'S'-shaped curve. They start slowly and gradually. If, however, they reach a critical mass of infection, the growth of new infections accelerates and the epidemic spreads through a population until all those who are exposed and susceptible to infection have been infected. The epidemic then reaches a final phase – where the 'S' flattens off at the top – and the number of those alive and infected passes its peak. In most cases, the curve begins to decline for some combination of two reasons: because people are recovering from the disease, or because the number of deaths has surpassed the number of new cases, thereby decreasing the total number currently infected.

What sets the HIV/AIDS epidemic apart from other epidemics is the presence of two curves. The *HIV Curve* precedes the *AIDS Curve* by about five to eight years, reflecting the incubation period between infection and onset of illness. This is why HIV is such a lethal epidemic compared to, say, cholera. With a disease such as cholera, victims fall ill quickly. This alerts the general population and public health professionals who then take precautions to halt the spread. In the case of HIV, however, the epidemic silently creeps through the population and it is only later – when the HIV pool has risen to a considerable level – that the true impact of the epidemic is felt in terms of AIDS deaths. By then, the epidemic is in full swing and – since there is no known cure – the only way people leave the pool of infections is by dying.

Figure 8.1 illustrates this point. The vertical axis represents the number of cases and the horizontal axis represents time. At T_1, when the level of HIV is at A_1, the number of AIDS cases will be much lower (B_1). AIDS cases will only reach A_2 (i.e. the same level as A_1) at T_2 sometime later. HIV prevalence may rise even higher.

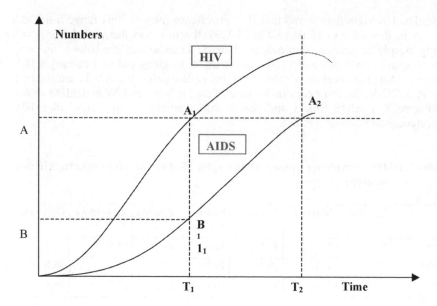

Figure 8.1: The two epidemic curves

One of the major problems is that most of the data available measures the prevalence of HIV infection in just one group – pregnant women attending public sector ante-natal clinics (ANCs). It does not tell about the dynamics of the disease – for that we would need incidence data. It does not tell us about other population groups although we can (and do) make assumptions and use models to show what is happening. The reason for this limited data was that, until recently, the only way to test for HIV was to take a blood sample.

Epidemiological modelling techniques are then used to adjust the raw ANC statistics in order to estimate other population statistics, such as the percentage of all adult men who are infected, or the percentage of children who will be born HIV-positive. These models incorporate information on how we expect HIV infection among ANC attendees to differ from that of other population groups – such as the expected differences in prevalence between ANC attendees and younger and older women, men, and children – as well as known transmission rates between infected mothers and newborn children.

Based on these adjustments to official ANC clinic data, UNAIDS calculates an estimated adult prevalence rate (the percentage of adults between 15– 49 infected) for nearly every country in the world and also disaggregates prevalence by urban and rural distinctions and particular population groups. However, it should be noted there are cross-national inconsistencies created by the fact that each country carries out its own ante-natal surveys with differing sample sizes, weighting procedures, and intervals between surveys.

Table 8.1 lists recent UNAIDS estimates of adult (aged 15–49) prevalence in the seven Southern African countries on which we focus, and Figure 8.2 graphs these data. The UNAIDS data shows that HIV prevalence rates in 2001 range from 38.8 percent in Botswana to 15 percent in Malawi. It also shows that prevalence is still rising steeply in several countries, particularly Lesotho and Zimbabwe, but may have begun to level out in the other countries. A levelling-out of a country's HIV epidemic does not necessarily mean a decline in new cases, but may be caused by a rise in AIDS deaths. Furthermore, because of the lag between HIV and AIDS shown in Figure 8.1, AIDS illness and deaths will continue to rise even after HIV prevalence stabilises or declines.

Table 8.1: HIV prevalence among adults aged 15–49 in seven Southern African countries

	Lesotho	Malawi	Namibia	South Africa	Zambia	Zimbabwe	Botswana
1997	8.4	14.9	19.9	12.9	19.1	25.8	25.1
1999	23.6	16.0	19.5	19.9	20.0	25.1	35.8
2001	31.0	15.0	22.5	20.1	21.5	33.7	38.8

Sources: UNAIDS 1998; UNAIDS 2000; UNAIDS 2002

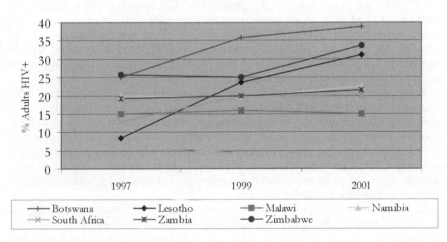

Figure 8.2: Adult prevalence

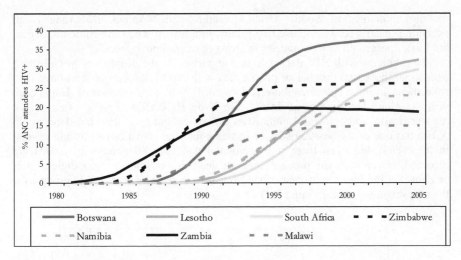

Figure 8.3: National trends in HIV prevalence: projected ANC prevalence, 1980–2005 (Policy Project 2001)

From Figure 8.3, we learn much more about the countries' epidemics. First, these seven countries are at different stages of their epidemics. South Africa's epidemic began in the late 1980s, and Botswana's a few years earlier, but the epidemics in countries to the north began even earlier, in the early 1980s. In addition, the seven countries have differently-shaped epidemics. For instance, the Zambian epidemic rises steadily through the 1980s and early 1990s, while Botswana's epidemic begins later but rises much more rapidly and to a higher overall level. These differences, and not just overall prevalence rate, affect how people experience the epidemic. For instance, in a country with an 'older' epidemic – such as Zimbabwe, Zambia, or Malawi – people have had a longer time to become aware of HIV/AIDS, and to experience the epidemic first-hand. In a country like Lesotho or South Africa, however, where the epidemic began quite recently but has grown very rapidly, people may not yet have developed the same level of awareness around HIV/AIDS even if the overall prevalence rates have matched or even surpassed those of the other countries. This concept of the 'speed' of the epidemic again relates back to Figure 8.1 and the lag between HIV infection and AIDS-related illness and death. If the HIV epidemic curve is very steep, then the apparent gap in severity between visible AIDS illness and invisible HIV prevalence at a given point in time will be very wide. For instance, in Botswana in the mid-1990s, the ANC prevalence had already topped 30 percent, but the level of illness and death was determined by the prevalence 5–8 years earlier, at the beginning of the decade, which was below 5 percent. Such disparities can contribute to ignorance and denial in countries with fast-moving epidemics.

Thus, based on a combination of current prevalence rates and the 'age' of the epidemic in each country, we can distinguish between the 'mature' but less severe epidemics of Zambia, Zimbabwe, and Malawi, and the more recent but very fast-

132   *The Political Economy of AIDS in Africa*

moving epidemics of South Africa, Lesotho, and Namibia. Botswana is an
exception: it falls between these two groups in terms of when the epidemic began,
but has surpassed all other countries in terms of overall prevalence.

The problems with HIV data pale in comparison to the difficulties in collecting
data about the actual number of people sick with AIDS illnesses or who have died
from them. In most countries there is no record of the total number of deaths each
year, let alone the number of deaths caused by HIV/AIDS. People often do not
register deaths and/or central authorities do not collect or collate the data. South
Africa has one of the best registration systems for vital statistics (births and deaths)
in the region, but even there it is estimated that only 80 percent of deaths are
recorded. Even then the precise cause of death is not known. Nonetheless, it is
evident that the number of deaths has been increasing within each age group over
the past seven years (see Figure 8.4).

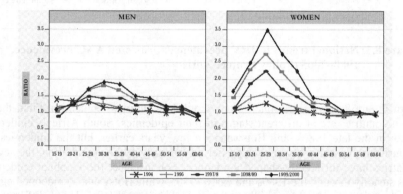

**Figure 8.4: Estimated increase in adult death rates (South African men and
women)**

*Source: Dorrington et al, The Impact of HIV/AIDS on Adult Mortality in South Africa,
Technical Report, Burden of Disease Research Unit (Pretoria: Medical Research
Council of South Africa, September 2001), p. 29. http://www.mrc.ac.za/bod/
index.htm (July 31, 2002)*

The Spectrum AIDS Impact Model from the Spectrum Policy Modelling System
(System 2002) was used to calculate estimates of the number of AIDS cases and
AIDS deaths over time in each of the countries we discuss. These data, used in the
analysis later in the chapter, are listed in Table 8.2.

Table 8.2: AIDS deaths and cases – Spectrum AIDS Impact Model

	Botswana	Lesotho	Malawi	Namibia	S. Africa	Zambia	Zimbabwe
AIDS Deaths							
1998	19491	7681	60930	6713	89985	90509	142426
1999	23220	10847	68480	8871	135997	95047	150099
2000	26466	14538	74842	11205	193599	98431	155034
2001	29061	18600	80088	13558	262037	100710	158263
Current AIDS Cases							
1999	87508	32381	297700	28950	352610	626170	876929
2000	112855	46864	364763	39947	541039	720874	1034091

The Lack of Lived Experience of the Epidemic

The epidemiological data illustrate the extensive spread and severe scope of the HIV/AIDS pandemic in Southern Africa. Given this picture, relevant attitudinal indicators would be expected to produce evidence of widespread contact with the disease (for instance, through individual illness and personal exposure to AIDS-related deaths). Moreover, because Afrobarometer studies are based on nationally representative samples, these responses can be used to corroborate the accuracy of the epidemiological data (given the data's weaknesses as outlined above). Finally, given the picture of the pandemic provided by the epidemiological data, rapidly rising public demands for the region's governments to confront HIV/AIDS might be anticipated.

However there is little evidence of political engagement around the HIV/AIDS issue. The perceptions and experiences of ordinary people are different from what might be expected given the objective data. The relatively long time lag between HIV infection and AIDS-related illness and death, during which the epidemic is largely invisible, is only one of several reasons why citizens may not accurately recognize and appraise the nature and extent of the disease. Even in countries where AIDS-related deaths have reached high and very visible levels, the pattern of death may be sufficiently geographically scattered to mask the national scope of the epidemic. The severity of the epidemic can vary greatly across geographic areas within one country. In addition, social stigma around HIV/AIDS may prevent a full and candid appraisal of the extent and causes of illness and death. Such stigma and community taboos may disrupt the social flow of information about the disease. It is not clear, for instance, whether the ubiquitous reference to local elites and national leaders who 'died after a long illness' sends a coded signal that these were AIDS deaths, or rather serves to confuse people.

Even where people are accurately aware of the increasing death rate, social and religious beliefs may lead them to conceive of or frame the epidemic as a consequence of personal morality or as fate, rather than as a 'public problem' that the government should address. Although people might be expected to clamour for government intervention to slow the spread of HIV and mitigate the impacts of the disease, they may in fact perceive HIV/AIDS as a problem for communities, households, and individuals to address, rather than an area for government involvement.

Perhaps most importantly, the lack of certainty about HIV data and AIDS cases (due to time lags between infection and illness and death, differing national epidemic curves, and problems with obtaining accurate data) has provided hesitant governments and politicians with an excuse for obfuscation, misdirection and inaction. They can question the validity of the HIV data and contest the severity of the epidemic, or they can accept the data but question its usefulness because they contest the link between HIV and AIDS. Probably the best known example of the latter approach is South African president Thabo Mbeki, who personally and repeatedly questioned the link between HIV and AIDS, and whose government often echoed these doubts. South African officials argued there were no observable increases in mortality to 'corroborate' the HIV epidemic, and doubted the results of a study by its own Medical Research Council that found evidence of such an increase (Dorrington 2001).

Contact with AIDS

To what extent have people experienced AIDS personally through the death of someone close to them? The Afrobarometer asks: 'Do you know of a close friend or relative who has died of AIDS?' This is an admittedly imperfect proxy for actual contact with the AIDS epidemic. It is certainly possible that people may have had close friends or relatives die of the disease and not know it, or know of someone who had died of the disease and simply refuse to admit it (two types of 'false negative' responses). It is also possible that respondents may misinterpret the reasons for some deaths: they may falsely assume from the death of someone from tuberculosis, for example, that the person had developed AIDS (a type of 'false positive' response).

In some countries there are high levels of reported contact with and knowledge of AIDS-related mortality. In 1999, roughly two thirds of Zimbabweans (68 percent), Zambians (65 percent) and Malawians (65 percent) said they knew of at least one 'close friend or relative' who had died of AIDS. Namibia (40 percent) and Botswana (31 percent) have lower numbers of people who say they have lost someone close to AIDS. At the other end of the spectrum, relatively low numbers of South Africans (16 percent) and Basotho (11 percent) say they know of someone.

Table 8.3: Awareness of AIDS deaths ('do you know of a close friend or relative who has died of AIDS?')

% respondents who answered:	Botswana	Malawi	Namibia	Zambia	Zimbabwe	Lesotho	South Africa
Yes	31	65	40	65	68	11	16
No	59	33	52	31	25	81	80
Will not say	3	1	4	2	5	1	3
Don't know	4	1	3	2	3	5	2

Stigmatization and Reported Contact

Are people willing to talk openly about HIV/AIDS? The first thing to note is that in every country, at least 95 percent of the respondents offered a response to the question of whether they knew someone who had died of AIDS. While a structured survey is clearly not equivalent to a normal free flowing conversation, we would not expect to find as high levels of reported contact as we did if social stigma made ordinary Africans reluctant to speak about the disease. Only in Zimbabwe did as many as 5 percent refuse to answer the question.

It is particularly fascinating that Zambians and Malawians are so willing to admit personal or family experience with AIDS even though they are the most highly religious countries discussed in this chapter. Eighty-two percent of Zambians and 65 percent of Malawians attend meetings of religious groups (excluding formal church or mosque services), higher than any of the other five countries, and much higher than their attendance of other types of community organizations (Mattes, Davids et al. 2000). If there is any significant pocket of hesitance to speak about the disease, it appears to be amongst older respondents. Almost one in ten Basotho (inhabitants of Lesotho) and Batswana (inhabitants of Botswana) (9 percent) over the age of 65 refused to answer the question as did 18 percent of Zambians, 14 percent of Malawians, and 7 percent of Zimbabweans over the age of 75.

The absolute levels of reported contact, the relatively infrequent rate at which people refused to answer or equivocated in their response, and the lack of any impact of perceived freedom of speech all suggest that social stigmatization of HIV/AIDS may not be as great as believed, or have as strong an impact as expected on people's response to formalized, impersonal questions on HIV/AIDS. One factor that probably facilitated more candid responses was that people were not asked for specific names, but merely whether or not they knew of *some* close friend or relative who had died of AIDS. Regardless, ordinary Southern African citizens seem to be much more willing to acknowledge the presence of AIDS than their leaders. Why then are they not more demanding of a response from their leaders?

AIDS and the Public Agenda

Given the epidemiological data and the nature of the epidemic curves AIDS might be expected (or have been expected) to dominate the national political agenda in almost every country in the region: that mass publics would be clamouring for governments to redirect large proportions of national resources to health care and other anti-AIDS interventions. In order to understand how people understand and politically prioritise AIDS, an open-ended question in the Afrobarometer survey asked people 'What are the most important problems facing this country that government should address?' Interviewers offered respondents no response alternatives; answers were completely spontaneous, and people could provide up to three answers, which interviewers transcribed verbatim. The tables below offer an after-the-fact aggregation of responses into broader categories. These tables provide a concise description of citizens' priorities for government action, or 'the people's agenda.'

   Given the extent of infection, illness, and death illustrated by the epidemiological and survey data, a widespread popular demand for governments to confront HIV/AIDS might be expected. As Table 8.4 shows the data do not bear this out. In fact, 'HIV/AIDS' features prominently on the public agenda of only three Southern African countries. One quarter of Batswana (24 percent) and just over one-in-ten Namibians (14 percent) and South Africans (13 percent) cite this problem as one of the top three facing the country. AIDS was the second most frequently cited problem in Botswana, and the fifth most frequently cited in Namibia and South Africa. In contrast, just one-in-twenty Zimbabweans (4 percent), one-in-fifty Malawians (2 percent), and less than one-in-one-hundred Basotho (<1 percent) mention HIV or AIDS as one of the most pressing problems that government should address. Absolutely *no* Zambians used the words 'HIV' or 'AIDS' to describe the most important national problems. In general, issues such as job creation, the national economy, and crime and security received far higher attention from Afrobarometer respondents than did the HIV/AIDS epidemic.

What are the Most Important Problems Facing this Country that Government Should Address?

Southern Africans simply do not list HIV/AIDS as a political priority for their governments. On its own, this might have been seen to indicate the presence of social stigma, but the evidence rules this out. To further investigate this surprising finding, the possible impact of other factors was considered. First, it could be that people see the responsibility for HIV/AIDS to lie with individuals and communities, rather than governments, perhaps because they do not believe that governments have the ability to deliver in this area, or more worrying because they have no engagement or expectation with and of government. Second, it could be that people's living conditions are already so desperate that government action against AIDS is seen as a lower priority than action to address more immediate needs by creating jobs and holding down prices so that people can live decently. Thus, it simply becomes a question of priorities. There is some support for this argument: as individual levels of poverty increase, people become less likely to cite AIDS as an important problem. Third, these figures may reflect the role of leadership on the part of both elected officials and civil society. In Botswana, for example, public exposure to AIDS deaths is relatively low, yet citizens have placed the epidemic as the second priority for the government. Though Botswana's HIV/AIDS epidemic is relatively young, the government has been open about the epidemic and has in some sense 'claimed' it as an appropriate issue for government intervention; international donor funding is pouring in; and the main private sector employer Debswana Diamond Company has embarked on a comprehensive campaign to address HIV/ AIDS.

Table 8.4: Most important problems (all problems mentioned by at least 10%)

Botswana	Zimbabwe	Zambia	Malawi	Lesotho	Namibia	South Africa
Job Creation (58%) AIDS (24%) Education (20%) Poverty / Destitution (17%) Health (15%) Farming / Agriculture (14%) Crime / Security (12%)	Economy (74%) Job Creation (37%) Health (18%)	Health (41%) Job Creation (32%) Education (31%) Farming / Agriculture (26%) Economy (20%) Transport-ation (18%) Poverty / Destitution (14%)	Economy (48%) Health (29%) Crime / Security (28%) Food (26%) Transport-ation (16%) Water (16%) Farming / Agriculture (13%) Education (12%) Poverty / Destitution (11%) Job Creation (11%) General Services (10%)	Job Creation (63%) Crime / Security (28%) Food (20%)	Job Creation (54%) Education (46%) General Services (21%) Health (18%) AIDS (14%)	Job Creation (76%) Crime / Security (60%) Housing (25%) Education (13%) AIDS (13%) Health (12%) Poverty/ Destitution (11%)

In South Africa, a great deal of time and money has been spent on awareness and prevention campaigns. The prolonged public visibility created by President Thabo Mbeki's controversial remarks about the link between HIV and AIDS may have also, perhaps, paradoxically raised awareness of the epidemic in recent years. An examination of successive nationally representative surveys conducted by IDASA since 1994 demonstrates that public awareness of HIV/AIDS as a key issue has increased steadily, moving from less than 1 percent in 1994. The July-August 2000 survey (conducted just after the XIII International AIDS Conference) in Durban was the first time that more than 10 percent of South Africans nationally cited the problem.

The lack of public emphasis on AIDS as a national problem could reflect the way people 'name and frame' political issues. Table 8.5 shows that 'health' or 'health care' is mentioned by large proportions of respondents in several countries, especially Zambia (41 percent, which made it the most often mentioned problem), Malawi (29 percent), Zimbabwe (18 percent) and Namibia (18 percent). These percentages are much higher than the percentage of respondents who mentioned HIV/AIDS as a problem.

Table 8.5: Spontaneous mention of HIV/AIDS vs. health as an important national problem

% respondents who mentioned	Botswana	Zimbabwe	Zambia	Malawi	Lesotho	Namibia	South Africa
Health	15	18	41	29	8	18	12
HIV/AIDS	24	4	0	2	<1	14	13

Does this emphasis on health actually signify a (silent) prioritization of HIV/AIDS? Are people thinking of HIV/AIDS when they say 'health?' Support for this hypothesis can be found in the strong relationship between the proportion of people who have had contact with an AIDS death and the proportions that cite 'health' as an issue (see Figure 8.5). Similarly, the number of cumulative AIDS deaths in a country is also associated with higher levels of prioritization of 'health' as an area of government attention. This suggests that people conceive of the political consequence of the pandemic as a national health crisis, rather than as an HIV/AIDS crisis *per se*. People seem to say that HIV/AIDS should be addressed primarily as a health problem. If this is a correct interpretation of the citizens' sentiments, it is somewhat unfortunate because it ignores the multi-faceted nature of the pandemic. To simply address AIDS as a health crisis is to neglect all the other aspects such as its impact on households, the economy, employment, gender relations, governance, democracy, poverty, etc.

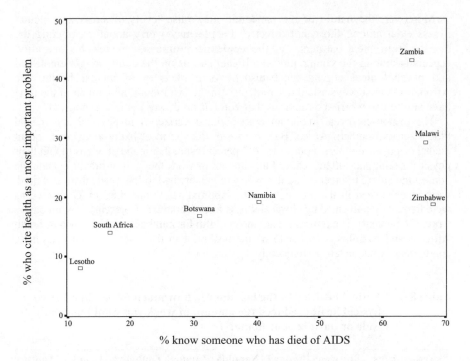

Figure 8.5: Exposure to AIDS deaths and citing health as a national priority

There is evidence of ill health. As a measure of physical health, the Afrobarometer asked respondents: 'In the last month, how much of the time has your physical health reduced the amount of work you would normally do inside or outside your home?' Certainly this measures a whole range of ordinary, non-HIV/AIDS related sicknesses. However, the potential social, economic and political impacts of AIDS on society stem not so much from the peculiar nature of the sickness itself, but from the fact that it makes people very ill (and ultimately kills them). Thus, to the extent that the chief interest is sickness (and subsequent mortality) a simple measure of sickness is useful to track the socio-political impact of the disease.

The extreme physical consequences of the types of disease brought on by immune deficiency not only make a person ill and lead to early death, but are also likely to lead to high levels of anxiety and depression among the sick. In general, levels of stress and anxiety tend to increase when one is ill. However, if people know or suspect they are ill with HIV/AIDS, the resulting stress and depression is likely to be even greater. They may face discrimination in the workplace, at school, in the community, or even at home. They must worry about the possibility of infecting their partner and women face the stress of possibly infecting their newborn children. Eventually, most people face permanent physical disability and the inability to earn an income for themselves or their family; or provide for the future of their spouses and children after their death.

Moreover, the nature of the pandemic may raise levels of stress and mental illness even among those not infected. People may worry about contracting the disease from their partners. As the epidemic progresses, increasing mortality, especially among the young, puts significant strains on the community's emotional and psychological coping mechanisms. As a measure of mental health, the Afrobarometer surveys asked respondents: 'In the last month, how much of the time have you felt so worried or anxious that you felt tired, worn out, or exhausted?'

The responses reveal important cross-national variations in physical and mental illness across Southern Africa. Basotho are by far the most likely to report frequent mental or physical illness. Four in ten (42 percent) said that in the previous month their physical health had 'often' reduced the amount of work they did, inside or outside the home. One half (51 percent) said that worry or anxiety had 'often' made them feel tired, worn or exhausted in the previous month. Approximately one third of Zimbabweans were frequently prevented by physical illness from working (31 percent) or worn out by worry (36 percent). The figures are around one fifth for Zambians and Malawians. South Africans and Namibians appear to be the healthiest in these surveys, but even here, approximately one in ten are frequently ill or anxious.

Table 8.6: **Physical health ('In the last month, how much of the time has your physical health reduced the amount of work you would normally do inside or outside your home?')**

% respondents who answered:	Botswana	Malawi	Namibia	Zambia	Zimbabwe	Lesotho	South Africa
Often	15	16	9	19	31	42	7
Sometimes	29	27	37	38	27	12	25
Rarely	19	21	16	14	18	13	18
Never	36	36	36	28	23	33	49

Table 8.7: **Mental health ('In the last month, how much of the time have you felt so worried or anxious that you have felt tired, worn out, or exhausted?')**

% respondents who answered:	Botswana	Malawi	Namibia	Zambia	Zimbabwe	Lesotho	South Africa
Often	15	20	8	22	36	51	12
Sometimes	34	25	36	42	29	14	32
Rarely	19	25	17	12	17	13	19
Never	32	30	37	22	16	21	37

Confirming the logical connection between physical illness and mental stress, there is a very strong correlation between physical and mental health on the individual level. Of those respondents who said they frequently missed work due to physical problems, 71 percent also said they were frequently stressed or anxious. More than one in ten (13 percent) of *all* respondents interviewed across Southern Africa were *both* frequently sick and frequently depressed. It is this group that is likely to contain the highest proportion of fully developed AIDS cases. The degree to which there is empirical support for this assertion is discussed in the next section.

Corroborating Attitudinal and Epidemiological Data

Given what we think we know about the pandemic, do these responses on contact with AIDS deaths and severe illness make sense? Or, to put it another way, do they corroborate, broadly speaking, the epidemiological data on AIDS prevalence and AIDS deaths? First the data on awareness of AIDS deaths are examined. If both sets of data were valid and reliable reflections of the underlying reality of HIV/AIDS then highest levels of reported contact with AIDS deaths would be expected in those countries that the epidemiological data claim have suffered the most deaths. Figure 8.6 plots the total percentage in each country who say they know someone who has died of AIDS (on the Y, or vertical axis) against epidemiological data estimating the cumulative number of AIDS deaths from the beginning of the epidemic up to one year prior to the date of the survey (on the X or horizontal axis). The AIDS death data is modelled data, based on statistically adjusted extrapolations of the ANC HIV prevalence data. In spite of this limitation, there is a strong relationship between the two types of data. As estimated national level of AIDS deaths rise, the proportions of actual people who have had contact with an AIDS related death rise in predictable ways.

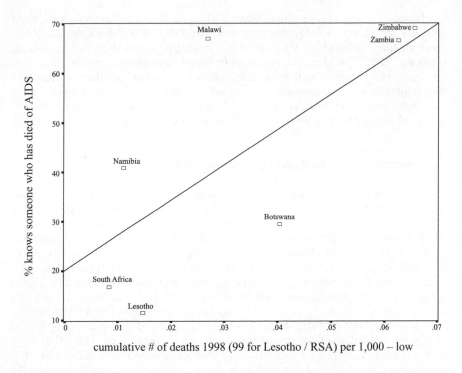

cumulative # of deaths 1998 (99 for Lesotho / RSA) per 1,000 – low

Figure 8.6: Awareness of AIDS deaths by cumulative number of AIDS deaths

In addition to the simple number of cumulative deaths, the extent of popular contact with AIDS deaths also appears to be a function of where each country is on the epidemic curve. As explained earlier, it is important to look not only at absolute levels of HIV prevalence and AIDS deaths, but also at how advanced or recent the epidemic may be in a given country.

An inspection of the regression line drawn through the country points on the graph in Figure 8.6 represents the 'expected' rate of contact with an AIDS death given a specific level of cumulative deaths. Countries with a more 'mature' epidemic are above the line, meaning that they tend to 'over-report' to varying degrees (Zambia, Zimbabwe, and especially Malawi). This could be because where AIDS deaths have become a prominent feature of society there is a tendency for people to assume people have died from AIDS regardless of whether they have. Where AIDS is a more recent phenomenon, people may tend to 'underreport' because people are less likely to realize why people are dying (Botswana, South Africa, and especially Lesotho). Namibia is the only country that does not conform to this pattern: it falls above the line but has a more recent epidemic.

To what extent do the survey responses about physical and mental illness reflect AIDS-related illness? Are people more likely to report levels of severe illness in those countries with the highest levels of current estimated AIDS cases? In order to test this, a composite measure was created of the proportions of people in each country who both often miss work due to illness and suffer from anxiety. This measure was then correlated with the estimated number of current AIDS cases per 1,000 people, as of the year of the Afrobarometer survey (see Table 8.2 and Figure 8.7). The combined illness measure fits very closely with the AIDS case data for five countries (Malawi, Namibia, South Africa, Zambia and Zimbabwe). For these five countries, reported serious illness increases consistently with rising levels of estimated AIDS cases.

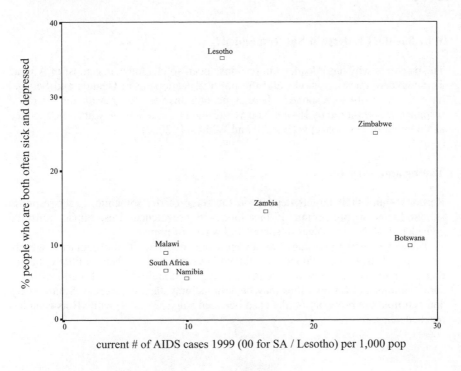

current # of AIDS cases 1999 (00 for SA / Lesotho) per 1,000 pop

Figure 8.7: Severe illness by current AIDS cases

There are two outliers in this graph, however: Botswana and Lesotho. Botswana's position indicates that levels of severe illness in that country are much lower than expected given the estimated number of current AIDS cases. This may be due to the fact that Botswana is a relatively wealthy country (compared to the others) with a good public health system, and the Debswana mining company – the country's largest employer – offers relatively comprehensive and high-quality health coverage to its employees. Lesotho fits even less well than Botswana. Here, there are far greater levels of severe illness than would be expected given its current level of AIDS cases. This suggests that the country's relatively high levels of reported illness reflect many factors other than AIDS including migration, unemployment and poverty.

Taken together, these figures suggest that both the epidemiological HIV/AIDS data (even with all its shortcomings) and relevant attitudinal data from the Afrobarometer independently reflect the common underlying phenomenon of the HIV/AIDS pandemic. Where epidemiological data suggest the disease is most advanced, survey respondents are also most likely to indicate that someone they know has died of AIDS or (with some exceptions) report higher levels of severe illness.

Why has the Leadership Not Responded?

The puzzle is why has a leadership response been so lacking across most of Africa? The converse question is why did the political leadership in Uganda and Senegal have the capacity to respond? There is no one answer. The reason for a lack of response was explored by Barnett and Whiteside in a recent book where they looked at a number of key concepts (Barnett and Whiteside 2002).

Timing and Targeting

Responses and their targets depend on the stage of the epidemic. Early response should focus on prevention. If this fails and prevalence rises, impact must be considered. There are waves of spread and waves of impact.

Table 8.8 shows six stages as an epidemic evolves. In the countries we are reviewing Zimbabwe, Zambia and Malawi have reached 5. There is little evidence that any country has moved beyond that stage although at the sub-national level, some regions and communities may be approaching stage 6. Lesotho, South Africa and Namibia are probably on the cusp between stages 3 and 4, while Botswana has reached stage 4.

Table 8.8: The evolution of the HIV/AIDS epidemic and its consequences

Stage	Epidemiology and prevention	Impact and response
Stage 1: No-one with AIDS identified; some HIV infections	HIV prevalence >0.5 percent in high risk groups, targeted prevention	Planning only required
Stage 2: A few cases of AIDS seen by medical services; more people are infected with HIV	HIV prevalence < 5 percent in high risk groups, targeted prevention	Impact on medical demand and use of facilities: need to plan for this
Stage 3: Medical services see many with AIDS. Some policy-makers aware of HIV infection and AIDS. The incidence of reported TB cases increases	Prevalence > 5 percent in high risk populations. Targeted prevention but general information	Impact still mainly medical but need to begin Human Resource planning and targeted mitigation especially for most vulnerable groups, institutions and sectors
Stage 4: AIDS cases threaten to overwhelm health services. Widespread general population awareness of HIV/AIDS	Prevalence > 5 percent in ANC women. Information available to all, continuing targeting of high risk groups	Impact now broader – need to start looking at education sector and all government activities. Private sector plans for impact
Stage 5: Unusual levels of severe illness and death in the 15–50 age group produce coping problems, large number of orphans, loss of key household and community members. TB is a major killer	Prevalence > 20 percent in ANC clinic attendees and has been so for 5 years. Full battery of prevention according to resources	Impact at all levels. Responses need to be equally diverse. They may include targeted relief or targeted Anti-Retroviral Therapy
Stage 6: Loss of human resources in specialized roles in production and economic and social reproduction decreases the ability of households, communities, enterprises, and districts to govern, manage, and/or provision themselves effectively. Responses range from creative and innovative ways of coping to failure of social and economic entities	Prevalence >15 percent in 15–49 age group and has been so for 5 years. Most cost effective prevention now needs to be focused on key groups and interventions. Efforts to reach those below age 15 and for over 15s emphasis on Voluntary Counselling and Testing	This impact requires massive intervention at all levels. The emphasis should be on children in crisis including orphans. Local programmes need to be scaled up and made sustainable perhaps with donor money

Source: Barnett and Whiteside, 1999

On the basis of this it is hardly surprising that politicians find it hard to address the epidemic and its consequences.

Information, Observation or Instruction

For action to take place individuals must be able to make decisions to protect themselves. Effective impact mitigation requires understanding the effects that the epidemic will have and reacting to them, preferably in advance. There are three ways in which prevention and mitigation responses can be triggered:

- by information;
- through observation;
- via an instruction.

Information-based decisions are grounded on messages and the theory of reasoned action and planned behaviour rather than experience or observation. People learn what is happening or may happen, they process this information and make decisions to change (or not change) their behaviour. An observation-based decision is one where behaviour change is based on what people see or of which they have personal experience. Instruction-based decisions are where people are told to do things and do them. There may be disincentives for not following the instructions (in some countries you will be fined if you do not wear a seatbelt) or incentives for following them (tax cuts for having children). The instruction may come from various sources: religious leaders with moral authority or dictators with powers to coerce. Such instructions may smack of desperation and unreality. In July 2001, in a speech to the Kenyan Pharmaceutical Society, President Daniel Arap Moi said that he was reluctant to spend money on importing condoms to Kenya and that 'As president, I am shy that I am spending millions of shillings importing those things': it was better for Kenyans to refrain from sex 'even for only two years' and that this was the best way to curb the epidemic (Barnett and Whiteside 1999).

In the countries examined in this article responses cannot be based on observation as:

- HIV spreads invisibly and AIDS follows on some years later;
- it is hard to ascertain causality; and
- cases and impact are diffuse.

Indeed the Afrobarometer data shows that people are not seeing and certainly not prioritising the HIV/AIDS epidemic. The relative roles of information, observation and instruction are important for HIV/AIDS prevention programmes, their design and understanding why they have succeeded or failed. For example the gay community in the US based much of its response on information and observation. The first indication something was wrong was when men started falling ill and dying. This lead to demand for knowledge and the process is documented in *And the Band Played On* (Shilts 1987). This community asked: 'What is killing our colleagues, friends and lovers? Where did it come from? What can we do about it?' These questions arose from observation and required information. As this became available so it shaped the response. Once the potential for transmission through sexual intercourse became apparent the bathhouses were closed and safe sex practices encouraged. Behaviour change was proposed and adopted before the HIV epidemic reached its 'natural' peak.

By contrast in much of Southern and Eastern Africa, information about HIV/ AIDS, how it is transmitted and how people may protect themselves, has been around for more than a decade and yet HIV prevalence continues to climb. Knowledge and observation have not translated into action. In South Africa one of the recent anti-AIDS campaigns was called 'Beyond Awareness'. Recent realisation of the scale of the problem in this region is partly due to the dramatic increase in mortality rates and the inescapable personal observations which go with these levels of illness and death. Here behaviour change is observation-based, although information is a prerequisite. It should also be noted that it is by no means certain that the 'right' behaviour change will occur – there may be a feeling of helplessness, disempowerment and fatalism. Among young men in South Africa 'Contracting the HIV/AIDS virus was seen more or less as a new part of growing up, surely not something to be eagerly anticipated, but accepted nonetheless as an almost inevitable consequence of being an adult, a status which presupposes being sexually active' (Leclerc-Madlala 1997). In addition the 'instruction' option does not work unless the authorities have legitimacy and sanction.

Uganda has steered a middle course. Here government, communal and individual response was based on a mixture of information, observation and instruction. However the information and in particular its source was crucial for acceptance of the message and subsequent action. This has been illustrated by Low-Beer and others (Low-Beer, Stoneburner et al. 2000). They compared epidemic patterns in Uganda with Zambia, Malawi and Kenya. The most important behavioural changes in Uganda related to lower percentages of 15–19 year olds having sex, a higher percentage of people delaying sex until after marriage, and fewer non-regular partners. Condom use was similar across countries and condom usage at levels of 40–50 percent with non-regular partners was not in itself sufficient to substantially reduce HIV incidence.

Despite limited options and resources, Ugandans developed personal behavioural strategies which dramatically reduced HIV prevalence. These changes were related to and driven by personal communication networks through which knowledge about AIDS was acquired. The main communication channel was discussions among friends and family. While 90 percent of Ugandans were having these discussions less than 35 percent of South Africans were. In Uganda 82 percent acquired AIDS knowledge through personal networks, in the other four countries the figure was 40–65 percent. In Uganda personal networks have been crucial rather than institutional or mass channels which dominate in other countries. The effective content of AIDS messages is only brought home after being communicated among family and friends.

Analysis of communication networks shows that even limited increases in 'openness', defined as discussing AIDS and AIDS status with 20 percent of close contacts, can result in most people knowing someone with AIDS at an early stage in the epidemic when HIV prevalence is less than 10 percent. In Southern Africa this wave of communication and identification of personal risk may only occur after HIV incidence has peaked. In Uganda AIDS responses have been at family/

friendship level, people developed personal solutions with dramatic impact on the epidemic.

These findings have important implications for prevention programmes, one of which is that the context must be right. A key feature of Uganda's response was leadership. This ensured AIDS was consistently on agendas and people were not stigmatised. It began with President Museveni talking openly and frankly about AIDS as early as 1986 (Kaleeba, Kadowe et al. 2000). Information requires:

- the appropriate medium;
- the ability of the target audience to access it;
- the conceptual framework to understand it and translate it into action;
- legitimacy and a framework for it to be processed.

Poor people in any society have constrained decision horizons and little knowledge of scientific ideas about disease. Knowledge and experience of HIV/AIDS is related to their own cultural-conceptual frameworks and to their material circumstances. Television or newspaper advertisements cannot reach populations who cannot read and who do not have access to electricity. Disease cannot be explained in terms of germ theory in cultures where this concept has no meaning.

Conclusion

Ordinary people in Southern Africa are slowly beginning to see the effect of the AIDS epidemic on their communities. However the nature of the disease is such that they cannot appreciate the long-term consequences – that in every country described here the number of illnesses and deaths will increase in the years ahead. Evidence from other countries suggests as mortality rises people begin to respond, but the hope is that there is a way to short circuit this process. Uganda suggests that the only way to do this is through leadership creating the environment in which society can discuss these issues. There is not much evidence of this happening in most of Southern Africa (Botswana is the possible exception).

An additional problem is that people are increasingly impoverished (see the chapter 'Responding to AIDS in Crisis Situations' by Alan Whiteside in this volume). The peoples' agenda in this chapter shows the priority of ordinary South Africans is employment and the economy. This indicates that they want opportunity to work and earn a living, and perhaps, that they have little faith in governments providing many of the things they need.

What we do not (and cannot) know is how the AIDS epidemic will affect the political processes. Indeed it is possible that at worst there may be disengagement and a sense of anomie. This would ensure that the disease has long term consequences for the region. The converse, leadership and engagement, while it will not prevent excessive morbidity and mortality, could lead to building new societies and redefining the social contract.

References

Barnett, T. and A. Whiteside (1999). *Guidelines for the Preparation and Execution of Studies of the Social and Economic Impact of HIV/AIDS.* Geneva, UNAIDS: Best Practice Collection.

Barnett, T. and A. Whiteside (2002). *AIDS in the Twenty-First Century: Disease and Globalisation.* Basingstoke, Palgrave Macmillan.

Dorrington, R. (2001). *The Impact of HIV/AIDS on Adult Mortality in South Africa, Technical Report.* Pretoria, Medical Research Council of South Africa, Burden of Disease Research Unit.

Fund, G. (2002). www.globalfundatm.org . 'Resource Mobilisation: Status and Forecasts'.

Kaleeba, N., J. N. Kadowe, et al. (2000). *Open Secret: People Facing up to HIV and AIDS in Uganda.* London, Strategies for Hope Series No. 15: ACTIONAID.

Leclerc-Madlala, S. (1997). '"Infect One, Infect All": Zulu Youth Response to the AIDS Epidemic in South Africa'. *Medical Anthropology* **17***(4): 363–80.*

Low-Beer, D., R. Stoneburner, et al. (2000). *Knowledge Diffusion and Personalizing Risk: Key Indicators of Behavior Change in Uganda Compared to Southern Africa.* XIII International AIDS Conference, Durban, South Africa, 7–14 July.

Mattes, R., Y. D. Davids, et al. (2000). *Public Opinion and the Consolidation of Democracy In Southern Africa.* Cape Town / Accra / East Landing, Afrobarometer.

McGreevey, W., S. Bertozzi, et al. (2002). Current and Future Resources for HIV/AIDS, in State of the Art: AIDS and Economics. *The Policy Project.* S. Forsythe. Washington.

NIC (2002). *The Next Wave of HIV/AIDS: Nigeria, Ethiopia, Russia, India and China.* New York, National Intelligence Council (NIC).

Shilts, R. (1987). *And the Band Played On: Politics, People and the AIDS Epidemic.* London, Viking.

System, S. P. M. (2002).
http://www.futuresgroup.com/WhatWeDo.cfm?page=Software&ID= Spectrum.

UNAIDS (1998). *UNAIDS Progress Report: 1996–1997.* Geneva, UNAIDS.

UNAIDS (2000). *Report on the Global HIV/AIDS Epidemic.* Geneva., UNAIDS.

UNAIDS (2002). *Report on the Global HIV/AIDS Epidemic.* Geneva, UNAIDS.

Chapter 9

The HIV/AIDS Pandemic in Botswana: Implications for the 'African Miracle'

Ian Taylor

The war in Botswana rages unabated. While the origins of the conflict remain murky, the appalling devastation is painfully clear. Estimates vary, but more than 100,000 have died as a result of the fighting, and that figure continues to escalate by the day. One in three adults in Botswana have been wounded. At Gaborone's main hospital, up to 80% of the beds in the male ward are filled with wounded who are not expected to survive ... The toll on the beleaguered Botswana military continues to be alarmingly high, with more than one-third of the forces suffering casualties. Such attrition causes loss of continuity at command level and within the ranks, increases costs for the recruitment and training of replacements, and reduces military preparedness, internal stability and external security. The war raging in Botswana is AIDS. All the statistics are true but not a single shot has been fired. However, AIDS is taking a toll as profound as any military confrontation around the globe, and it is a security threat to countries it assaults as well as its neighbours (quoted in AIDS: Security Implications for Africa, 2001: 1).

Botswana is a country of paradoxes. On the one hand, it is often regarded (and portrayed) as an 'African Miracle', with one of the most successful economies on the continent and an oasis of political stability in a sub-region characterised in the past (and, regrettably, present) by conflict, economic collapse and political repression. Yet at the same time, Botswana has one of the highest HIV/AIDS infection rates in the world. This combination, of a burgeoning economy and burgeoning infection rate, makes the country of profound interest to any discussion of the political implications that the AIDS pandemic might have on Africa. This paper will proceed in three parts. First, we discuss briefly the economic trajectory post-1966 and the tangible economic and social benefits that accelerated economic growth has brought to the country. We then discuss the extent of the pandemic in Botswana, putting it into a regional comparative perspective. Finally, we discuss the implications, political and economic, that such a scenario may have for Botswana in the future.

'The African Miracle'

In mapping out his own view of Botswana's developmental trajectory, President Festus Mogae has advanced the view that 'Batswana [inhabitants of Botswana] know that diamonds plus development equals democracy' (quoted in 'Clean Cut',

Kutlwano (Gaborone), vol. 41, no. 3, April/May 2001: 33). Botswana, since independence in 1966, has been governed uninterruptedly by the Botswana Democratic Party (Tlou and Campbell, 1997). This party has pursued state capitalist policies, even during the heyday of African experimentation with socialism. Both the growth and developmental record of independent Botswana has been impressive (for a good overview of Botswana's economic history, see Murray and Parsons, 1990). From being one of the poorest countries in the world at independence, Botswana has enjoyed rapid economic growth and is now classified by the World Bank as a middle income country, with a per capita GDP of more than $6000. Yet, when Botswana became independent, it had a per capita income equivalent then to roughly US$80 (Republic of Botswana 'Economic Snapshot', 2001).

Table 9.1: Real GDP growth (annual percentage change) of Botswana and Mauritius compared with Africa as a whole, plus selected countries

	Av. 1982-91	1992	1993	1994	1995	1996	1997	1998	1999
Africa	2.2	-0.7	0.4	2.3	3.2	5.6	2.9	3.1	2.3
Botswana	10.8	3.0	2.0	3.4	4.7	6.9	7.8	6.0	5.0
Mauritius	6.4	4.8	6.7	4.3	3.5	5.1	5.5	5.6	5.4
Nigeria	3.5	2.6	2.2	-0.6	2.6	6.4	3.1	1.9	1.1
S. Africa	0.9	-2.1	1.2	3.2	3.1	4.2	2.5	0.6	1.2
Zimbabwe	3.7	-9.0	1.3	6.9	-0.6	8.7	3.7	2.5	0.5

Source: International Monetary Fund, 2000: 205

Botswana enjoys a comprehensive and increasing infrastructure, such as tarred roads and a growing rail network. Botswana now has about 18,300 kilometres of roads (compared to 13 kilometres at independence). This road network links all settlements with a population of over 100 people, which represents over 90% of the national population. This does not include internal roads in cities, towns or villages which are public roads maintained by local governments (Republic of Botswana 'Growing Infrastructure', 2001).

Educational and health services absent at independence—as well as an effective civil service and reliable banking and financial institutions—have all been developed (for an overview, see Botswana: Review of Commerce and Industry, 2000). A combined enrolment ratio of first, second and third education levels is around 70%, compared with an average of 44% for the rest of sub-Saharan Africa. This has resulted in a literacy rate of 74%, contrasting with 58% for the rest of the continent. Ninety percent of Botswana's children are enrolled in primary school, and primary health care is available to 80% of the rural population who are within 15 kilometres radius of a health clinic (Republic of Botswana, 1997a: 17). Households with access to potable water went from 56% to 83% between 1981 and 1994. Poverty has declined considerably: the numbers of the national population who are poor and very poor declined from 59 to 47 percent between 1985/86 and 1993/94, and the numbers of poor and very poor households declined from 49% to 38% during the same period (Siwawa-Ndai, 1996: 28).

The source of this has been the use of fortuitous deposits of diamonds and minerals, a welcoming posture towards quality FDI and a tourism policy that has courted the top-end of the market. A beef export industry that has preferred status with Europe further contributes to state receipts. It is certainly true that diamonds have been the engine of growth. The domestic cost of production is low compared to their overseas sales value and as a result, diamond sales for Botswana are extremely profitable (Jefferis, 1998). Furthermore, in 1975 the Botswanan elite successfully negotiated with De Beers Diamond Company for a 50-50 share ownership in all of the country's diamond mines (compared to the previous 85-15% share in favour of De Beers). This more equitable share holding has provided the state with influence over the mines' wage policies as well as the ability to authorise to expand when deemed needed to advantage both Botswana and the private De Beers. This would never have been possible if Botswana had not taken a more forceful stance vis-à-vis De Beers, i.e. private capital.

By the early 1980s, diamonds had replaced beef as Botswana's leading foreign exchange earner: in 1981, diamond exports accounted for 40% of total exports—in 1999 it was 74% (Republic of Botswana Central Statistics Office, 1999: 3). This has allowed the government to invest considerably in a wide variety of development schemes. In addition, beef exports have given the state extra income for development schemes. The Beef Protocol with the European Union allows Gaborone to acquire considerable revenue from its beef exports, as agreed prices are actually higher than world market prices. The EU has accepted a 90% rebate of the variable levy to all beef exports from the Afro-Caribbean Pacific (ACP) group of countries. Concomitant with this, the EU purchases more beef from Botswana than from any other southern African country.

But, as has been said before, an abundance of natural resources such as diamonds or cattle is no guarantee of success and does not explain Botswana's developmental record. Certainly, Botswana has avoided the pitfalls of the 'Dutch Disease' i.e. the effect of a large change in wealth resulting from a sudden and dramatic change in the price of a primary product or of a sudden and dramatic discovery of a primary resource. As Clark Leith has remarked, 'the growth of the Botswana economy is not simply a story of a mineral enclave with an ever growing government, attached to a stagnating traditional economy' (Leith, 2000: 4). So what have been the economic underpinnings that have helped turn Botswana into a relative success story and have made it a developmental state? Derek Hudson (ex-Deputy Governor of the Bank of Botswana) has listed a number of macro-economic priorities that the state has maintained over time:

• A policy that does not spend all of its revenue when it enjoys boom periods (mostly located during times of high diamond sales), whilst at the same time not borrowing heavily during bust periods.

- A conscious policy to build up foreign exchange reserves to provide a cushion during lean times. Foreign exchange reserves are, in per capita terms, one of the highest in the world and are sufficient to pay for 26 months of imports.
- The maintenance of a liberal exchange control regime.
- Ensuring that the currency is not over-valued.
- Development projects are properly planned so that any future recurrent spending budgets are accounted for within the project's costs (Hudson, 1991: 52-53).

Explanations and accounts of Botswana's development trajectory are diverse. One school of thought may be called the 'African Miracle' school (originally coined by Penelope Thumberg-Hartland), which is mainly positive and largely economistic in its approach and misses the inherently political nature of Botswana's post-independence experience (see Thumberg-Hartland, 1978; Picard (ed.), 1985; Picard, 1987; Harvey and Lewis, 1990; Danevad, 1993; Stedman, 1993; Dale, 1995). Though of course this 'school' is varied, it does in the main approach Botswana's post-independence from a positive and often uncritical stance, asking whether Botswana is indeed 'A Model for Success?' (Picard, 1987). Those working more from a political economy perspective have been more critical. Such analysts do of course acknowledge the rapid economic growth and efficient state machinery, as well as the long-running liberal democracy. However, they are more critical of the profound contradictions that have developed alongside Botswana's developmental trajectory (see Colclough and McCarthy, 1980; Parson, 1984; Tsie, 1995; Gulbrandsen, 1996). These scholars question the scenario where there is 'Poverty in the Midst of Plenty', blaming it on deliberate policy choices made as part of the developmental state project (Gulbrandsen, 1996).

Perhaps the most persuasive work that has thus far emerged in the literature, and that attempts to account for why Botswana's developmental record is so radically different from most other African states, is Abdi Samatar's book *An African Miracle* (Samatar, 1999). Touching on one of the main factors in accounting for Botswana's relative success, Samatar asserts 'a key force that distinguishes successful from failed states is the social chemistry of the dominant class and the discipline of its leadership' (ibid.: 6). Like many of the political economists, Samatar is critical of the social polarisation and disparities of income within the country. But, and I think this is where Samatar's approach is superior to the overly negative accounts provided by some, he argues that Botswana's wealth grants the elite a certain space that can be used in order to resolve the more iniquitous inequalities through determined policy choice and implementation.

According to Samatar, Botswana's success as a developmental state is located in a professional bureaucracy that has conducted and implemented policy-making efficiently. This has been made possible by an essential oneness that links a web of cattle-ranchers, politicians, bureaucrats and various chiefs together. Most of these actors can be located in two or more of these ranks. There exists a sort of 'alliance' between the political and bureaucratic elite, with both dedicated towards development. In doing so, the elite has privileged policies that aim to attract private FDI and then seek to divert receipts into national development (Hill and Mokgethi,

1989). The Botswanan state was able to do this because of a number of factors: the traditional power and legitimacy that the first president, Seretse Khama, was able to draw upon and the decision to strip chiefs of their power meant that there was little opposition to building up a strong state apparatus. Daron Acemoglu et al (Acemoglu et al, 2001, p. 44) have put it thus:

> [T]he members of the BDP and the political elite that emerged after 1966 had important interests in the cattle industry, the main productive sector of the economy. This meant that it was in the interests of the elite to build infrastructure and generally develop institutions…which promoted not only national development, but also their own economic interests. This development path was considerably aided by the fact that the constitution and policies adopted by the BDP meant that there were no vested interests in the status quo that could block good policies.

Furthermore, the post-colonial elite have dominated the National Assembly in such a way that state resources were not diverted to maintain patronage networks but rather were able to be deployed for development. Crucial to this was the disqualification by law of civil servants contesting for public office. According to Mpho Molomo, whilst 'this practice deprives political parties of the chance to field educated and experienced candidates, it nonetheless reinforces the demarcation between the state and the government. It adds to the autonomy of the state because it insulates the state bureaucracy from party politics' (Molomo, 2000: 77). Thus there has been a relative autonomy that has allowed the political and bureaucratic elite to formulate policies that have benefited national development (even whilst benefiting traditional elites e.g. policies vis-à-vis cattle production). However, all of this is likely to be threatened by the HIV/AIDS pandemic.

The HIV/AIDS Pandemic

Africa in general, and eastern and southern Africa in particular, continues to dwarf the rest of the world in terms of HIV prevalence, HIV incidence, and AIDS deaths. Each year, in Africa, there are millions of new cases of HIV as well as AIDS deaths. No country, sector or individual is unaffected and certain groups are particularly hard hit, especially children and the elderly living in AIDS-affected households. The human immuno-deficiency virus (HIV), which causes AIDS, has resulted in a global pandemic. In 1991, UNAIDS and the WHO's Global Programme on AIDS estimated that by 2000 some 9 million people would be living with HIV/AIDS and that 5 million would have died. By the time the December 2000 UNAIDS report was released the true figures were considerably worse: 36.1 million living with HIV/ AIDS, of which 1.4 million were children under 15 years; and 21.8 million deaths, comprising of 17.5 million adults (9 million of whom were women) and 4.3 million children.

In 2000 alone, 5.3 million people were newly infected with HIV (including 2.2 million women, who are likely to pass on the virus to any children they may bear, and 600,000 children), and 3 million died (including 1.3 million women and

500,000 children). Although the pandemic has stabilised and even decreased in some countries the general trend is still increasing.

Globally, there is a great deal of variability in the trend of infections (increasing, stabilised, decreasing), mode of transmission and the extent of the spread of the pandemic in the general population. In Africa, and increasingly in south and south-east Asia and Latin America the epidemic is becoming generalised, i.e. most infections are due to heterosexual and mother-to-child transmission. In parts of Latin America, eastern Europe and high-income countries the epidemic is still concentrated in sub-populations, in particular intravenous drug users (IDU) and homosexual men.

The developing countries are by far the worst affected, with sub-Saharan Africa having the highest prevalence. This region has accounted for 83% of all deaths since the epidemic began (a quarter of which were children), although it only contains 10% of the world's population. Other than in Senegal and Uganda, this situation is still worsening. Although prevalence elsewhere in Africa is lower, especially in west Africa, indications from countries such as Côte d'Ivoire and Nigeria suggest the infection rate is also increasing there. It is within the countries of the Southern Africa Development Community (SADC) that HIV/AIDS is at its worst: in seven countries more than one in five adults is HIV-positive (Botswana, Lesotho, Namibia, South Africa, Swaziland, Zambia and Zimbabwe); Botswana has the world's highest adult prevalence (35.8%); South Africa is the nation with the largest HIV-positive population (4.2 million) and the largest fraction of global new infections (50%); and without preventive therapy, around 30% of all babies born in the region will be HIV-positive and will die by the age of eight.

The epidemic is worsening faster than humanity can mobilise action against it and two decades after its discovery, some would argue that we have not yet reached the peak of the epidemic. Certainly, we have not felt the full consequences of an epidemic that is slow in taking its toll. Many people continue to be frustrated by the apparent lack of action and success in dealing with HIV/AIDS. This is attributed to a number of factors including: lack of political will and commitment; lack of resources and infrastructure; limitations in our understanding of the virus and biomedical technologies; hidden agendas preventing effective action; the stigma and shame still attached to HIV/AIDS; lack of knowledge and education; and people having limited options for prevention and management.

HIV/AIDS Epidemiology with Reference to Southern Africa

Epidemics typically follow a path where the number of infections rises slowly at first and then rapidly once the pool of infected individuals exceeds a certain threshold. Prevalence levels fall off once the majority of susceptible individuals have become infected and, ultimately, begins to fall either because of the development of natural resistance, changes in behaviour, rising mortalities or the appearance of a cure. The development of a threshold population of HIV-positive individuals and the subsequent rapid increase in HIV prevalence is extremely likely, because the time lag between the epidemic curves for HIV and AIDS is several years. In the southern African context the epidemic is therefore largely unstoppable.

Any persistent large-scale variations in prevalence tend to reflect factors such as geographic isolation or differences in sexual practices, youth behaviour, stigma, the nature and effectiveness of prevention and treatment initiatives and, possibly, reporting errors.

Evidence based on interviews with early HIV cases suggests that the epidemic has spread southwards through southern Africa. The first infections tended to occur as a result of sexual contact between sex workers and 'foreigners', who are often truck drivers plying international routes. Once established within groups of high-risk women, the virus is then transmitted to local clients, including mineworkers who are predominantly migrant single men, who subsequently transferred the virus into rural and urban communities via their partners and families. The speed of this spread is largely a function of the quality of transport infrastructure, which is very good throughout much of the region. Cultural practices, including a predilection amongst older men for younger women, is further accelerating intergenerational transmission.

Prevalence varies significantly between southern African countries that, with the exception of Mauritius, all have significant HIV-infected populations. Countries are mainly in the rapid growth phase of the HIV epidemic or approaching a plateau, but several more years of monitoring will be required before it will be possible to establish the levels at which prevalence will ultimately peak. Based on the most highly affected countries, i.e. Botswana, Swaziland and Zimbabwe, it is likely that at least 25%-35% of the entire adult population of SADC will eventually become infected, although in places prevalence may well reach 40%-50%.

Table 9.2: Selected prevalence data for SADC member states – 2000

	Adult prevalence (%)	Est. no. infected people	Adults and children	Women (15-19)	Children (0-14)
Angola	2.78	160 000	150 000	82 000	7900
Botswana	35.8	290 000	280 000	150 000	10 000
DRC	5.07	1.1 mill.	1 100 000	600 000	53 000
Lesotho	23.57	240 000	240 000	130 000	8200
Malawi	15.96	800 000	760 000	420 000	40 000
Mauritius	0.08		500		
Mozambique	13.22	1.2 mill.	1 100 000	630 000	52 000
Namibia	19.54	160 000	150 000	85 000	6600
South Africa	19.94	4.2 mill.	4 100 000	2 300 000	95 000
Swaziland	25.25	130 000	120 000	67 000	3800
Tanzania	8.09	1.3 mill.	1 200 000	670 000	59 000
Zambia	19.95	870 000	830 000	450 000	40 000
Zimbabwe	25.06	1.5 mill.	1 400 000	800 000	56 000

Source: UNAIDS Epidemiological Fact Sheets
http://www.unaids.org/ hivaidsinfo/statistics/ june00/fact_sheets/

Regional AIDS data provides further insights, although it is incomplete and in some cases doubtful (e.g. DRC in 1999). AIDS cases take about 5 years to begin rising significantly and by analogy the initial phase of the HIV-epidemic must also take about as long. A crude estimate of the time needed for the epidemic to begin to plateau can be made using the year in which the number of AIDS cases exceeds 0.1% of the adult population. In Zimbabwe, Botswana and Swaziland (which for argument's sake are assumed to be close to their prevalence plateaus) this occurred in 1992, 1993 and 1996, respectively. The corresponding point in HIV prevalence would have been reached 4-7 years earlier, i.e. in 1985-88, 1986-89 and 1989-92, respectively.

Countries in southern Africa therefore have no more than 15 years and perhaps as little as 8 years after the onset of rapid prevalence growth before the epidemic has affected the bulk of the susceptible adult populations. As the former point was passed by the mid-1990s in most countries, the region's HIV epidemic is likely to peak around 2005 and AIDS mortalities around 2010. Preventative measures have the potential to reduce the prevalence at which the HIV epidemic plateaus, but there is little time left for southern African countries to achieve major successes during this period. The political and social implications of the pandemic will thus be felt: there is virtually nothing Botswana can do to avoid this reality.

Implications for Botswana

Drawing out the political implications for Botswana of the HIV/AIDS pandemic is, obviously, a speculative exercise at this point in time. Having said that, it is quite clear that HIV/AIDS is having a major and negative impact on Botswana, at a variety of levels. Indeed, at the purely economic level, both the production and the consumption levels of the Botswanan economy is continually touched, having ramifications for future foreign direct investment (FDI) and undermining investor confidence in making long-term investments in the country. One need only realise the extent of the pandemic in Botswana: if the U.S. had a similar proportion of infections there would be 50 million infected people. In Botswana, as many babies are infected in four days as are infected in one year in the United States.

In addition, the pandemic will take people out from the workplace whilst sick, leading to increased absenteeism and a fall in productivity. The country needs its educated and trained people to work for at least 10-15 years if economic decline is to be averted; yet because of HIV/AIDS many skilled workers are economically active for only 5 years. Where mothers and fathers have already died, children may well have to leave school in order to look after ill parents. Household spending power will decrease, labour productivity will suffer, the corporate memory or skills base within companies will literally die out. The economy as a whole, the state and the private sector, will have to pick up the tab for training new workers, paying health bills and so on, which will drain the state budget from any capacity to spend on other fundamental services.

HIV/AIDS will also likely reverse the decades of development enjoyed by Botswana after independence. By eroding the knowledge base of society and weakening production sectors, it destroys social capital. By inhibiting public and private sector development and cutting across all sectors of society, it weakens national institutions. By eventually impairing economic growth, the epidemic has an impact on investment, trade and national security, leading to still more widespread and extreme poverty. Indeed, the political implications of HIV/AIDS is likely to be seen in an indirect fashion—particularly stemming from the impact the pandemic will have economically. One area where the impact is probably more direct is in the field of education. The loss of large numbers of teachers is a major blow to Botswana's future development: a generation of Batswana face the prospect of a lesser-quality education and reduced job prospects. It is axiomatic that there can be no true economic development without education. If HIV/AIDS affects school enrolment (perhaps as children stay at home to look after ailing parents), the impact will be massive—a generation of ill-educated youths with no job prospects and no parental support will have to be accommodated by society. Already, about 10,000 children under 14 carry the virus. Roughly 66,000 children have lost one or both parents to the disease. With major segments of the educated population lost for one or two generations and with the educated portion of the population so small to begin with, political instability is a likely consequence. The crisis in education caused by AIDS will inevitably become an economic crisis and in turn a political crisis.

This political crisis will take place within the broader context of a country that is having its administrative capacity decimated. The HIV/AIDS pandemic strikes at the ranks of skilled administrators, diminishes the reach or responsiveness of governmental institutions or reduces their resilience. This will detrimentally affect the operational effectiveness of such institutions as the armed forces, police, prosecution service and judiciary. Beyond a reduction in human resources, the epidemic will result in a reduction in public revenues and budgets will be diverted towards coping with the epidemic's impact. The capacity of governments to serve their citizens is among the casualties of the epidemic as budgets shrink and civil servants are killed by AIDS. In Botswana, for example, the government will lose 20% of public revenue by 2010 because of AIDS. According to the World Bank, HIV/AIDS and the impending death of up to 25% of all adults in some African countries will have an enormous impact on national productivity and earnings. Labour productivity is likely to drop, the benefits of education will be lost, and resources that would have been used for investments will be used for health care, orphan care, and funerals. Savings rates will decline, and the loss of human capital will affect production and the quality of life for years to come (World Bank, 1999). USAID estimates that Kenya's GNP will be 14.4% smaller in 2005 than it would have been without AIDS. The disease is similarly expected to hinder growth prospects throughout southern Africa as well.

Botswana's Democracy in Peril?

Samantha Willan has addressed the potential of HIV/AIDS to undermine democratic governance itself. Although her study was on South Africa, it has pertinence for Botswana. According to Willan, a few aspects of the pandemic, taken together, might lead to the breakdown in democracy. It can certainly cripple a country's attempts to establish and maintain democracy and equity because the next generation of political and economic leaders is being wiped out; a magnitude of orphans poses a long-term threat to stability and development; family structures and social society are breaking down due to their inability to cope; the increase in the budgetary demand on governments is projected to increase to the nth degree— cutting down on delivery in other sectors of society; and citizen support and participation in democratic governance will wane, as more people develop terminal diseases and are removed from the public sphere. This will also affect civil society's capacity to take part in public debates, translating into a loss in society's ability to build a sense of national cohesion (Willan, 2000:14).

Replacing skilled professionals is a top priority, especially as Botswana has traditionally relied upon a relatively small number of skilled and educated policy-makers and managers for public management and core social services. Losing such personnel reduces capacity, while raising the costs of recruitment, training, benefits and replacements. However, one aspect that is likely to emerge and undermine the democratic credentials of Botswana is the rise in xenophobia. This is likely to occur as expatriates will be more and more needed to fill positions vacated by sick and dying Batswana. Already, xenophobia and racism in Botswana is quite a serious issue. The speaker of the House of Chiefs, Chief Tawana Moremi, has expressed openly racist rhetoric in public on a great number of occasions, once actually saying he 'hate[s] foreigners, especially Whites' (Midweek Sun (Gaborone) June 6, 2001). Importantly, his comments were not met with howls of protest by the general public or media—indicating, perhaps, a tacit approval of such sentiments. There is a palpable feeling within Botswana that ordinary Batswana have somehow missed out on the 'Miracle'. Touch paper issues such as 'citizen empowerment' are very serious in today's politics in Botswana and there is an increasing readiness to blame foreigners for most of the country's ills. But with local citizens succumbing to the illness in greater numbers, the country must be run somehow—and expatriates are the only people to do this. Political instability and the opportunities afforded to cheap populists over the role of non-citizens within Botswana may well be exacerbated by the HIV/AIDS crisis. These attitudes can contribute to the eruption of violence, not just spontaneously, but in some cases as the result of exploitation by ethnic, religious or national elites to serve their narrow interests.

Families, businesses and communities now have to cope with the extra burden caused by the epidemic—they are further impoverished by the costs of widespread illness and death from AIDS. Worsening economic conditions make it more difficult to care for the ill, more difficult to mount effective education campaigns and more likely that some women and a few men exchange sex for money, food or shelter, thus increasing the likelihood of further HIV transmission.

At the same time, mass poverty stimulates increased migration, with large amounts of people moving from rural to urban areas in search of work. In many circumstances, traditional community relations and social networks are undermined or broken in the process. This helps create an environment where behavioural patterns favourable to the spread of HIV/AIDS develop—a vicious circle.

Gender Issues

Of the 34.7 million adults living with HIV/AIDS, 47%—or 16.4 million—are women. A number of telling statistics indicate the ongoing situation vis-à-vis women and HIV/AIDS: 46% of adults newly infected with HIV in 2000 were women; 52% (1.3 million) of all AIDS deaths in 2000 were women; since the beginning of the epidemic, over 9 million women have died from HIV/AIDS-related illnesses; the percentage of women infected in 1997 was 41%; in 2000, it had risen to 47%; 55% of all HIV-positive adults in sub-Saharan Africa are women; teenage girls are infected at a rate 5 or 6 times greater than their male counterparts. The issue of gender and the spread of the epidemic is vital to understand. It is likely that if women had control over their bodies and were able to negotiate safe sex, the epidemic would not have reached such vast proportions. Obviously, HIV/AIDS itself is a health issue, but the epidemic is not: knowledge on how the virus is transmitted and who is most vulnerable is widespread, but this knowledge does not seem to stop practices that increase the rate of infection, particularly among women. Why this is so relates largely to how values and traditions often prevent women and girls from being able to resist unwanted and unprotected sex. But all of this is political: gender is not merely socially constructed, it is political and the heavy impact of the pandemic on women is a profoundly political affair that will also further undermine political stability.

Finally, a US National Intelligence Council report concludes that there is a definite link between infectious disease epidemics (in particular HIV/AIDS) and security (National Intelligence Council, 2000). The report found that the impact of HIV/AIDS is likely to aggravate and even provoke social fragmentation and political polarisation in the hardest hit countries in the developing world; the relationship between disease and political instability is indirect but real. Infant mortality (likely to more than double in a number of southern African states because of HIV/AIDS by 2010) correlates strongly with political instability, particularly in countries that have achieved a measure of democratisation. In addition, the severe social and economic impact of HIV/AIDS, and the infiltration of the epidemic into the ruling political and military elites and middle classes of developing countries are likely to intensify the struggle for political power to control scarce state resources. This will hamper the development of a civil society and other underpinnings of democracy, and will increase pressure on Botswana's democracy. Whilst Botswana may indeed enjoy economic growth and political stability that is the envy of the continent, the HIV/AIDS pandemic threatens to undermine this and roll back the achievements the country has made since independence.

References

Acemoglu, Daron, Simon Johnson and James Robinson (2001) 'How Botswana Did It: Comparative Development in Sub-Saharan Africa', unpublished paper.
'AIDS: Security Implications for Africa' (2001) *African Security Review*, vol. 10, no. 4.
Colclough, Christopher and S. McCarthy (1980) *The Political Economy of Botswana: A Study of Growth and Distribution*, Oxford: Oxford University Press.

Dale, Richard (1995) *Botswana's Search for Autonomy in Southern Africa*, Westport: Greenwood Press.

Danevad, Andreas (1993) *Development Planning and the Importance of Democratic Institutions in Botswana*, Bergen: Christian Michelsen Institute.

Edge, Wayne and Mogopodi Lekorwe (eds.) (1998) *Botswana: Politics and Society*, Pretoria: Van Schaik.

Good, Kenneth (1993) 'At the Ends of the Ladder: Radical Inequalities in Botswana', *Journal of Modern African Studies*, vol. 31, no. 2.

Gulbrandsen, Ornulf (1996) *Poverty in the Midst of Plenty*, Bergen: Norse Publications.

Harvey, Charles (1991) 'Botswana: Is the Economic Miracle Over?', *Journal of African Economics*, vol. 1, no. 3.

Harvey, Charles and Stephen Lewis (1990) *Policy Choice and Development Performance in Botswana*, London: Macmillan.

Hill, Catherine and D. Nelson Mokgethi (1989) 'Botswana: Macroeconomic Management of Commodity Booms, 1975-86' in *World Bank Successful Development in Africa*, Washington DC: World Bank.

Holm, John and Staffan Darnolf (2000) 'Democratising the Administrative State in Botswana' in York Bradshaw and Stephen Ndegwa (eds.) *The Uncertain Promise of Southern Africa*, Bloomington: Indian University Press.

Hope, Kempe Ronald (1996) 'Growth, Unemployment and Poverty in Botswana', *Journal of Contemporary Studies*, vol. 14, no. 1.

Hudson, Derek (1991) 'Boom and Busts in Botswana', *Botswana Notes and Records*, vol. 23, 1991.

International Monetary Fund (2000) *World Economic Outlook 2000*, New York: IMF.

Jefferis, Keith (1998) 'Botswana and Diamond-Dependent Development' in Wayne Edge and Mogopodi Lekorwe (eds.), op.cit.

Jefferis, Keith and T.F. Kelly (1999) 'Botswana: Poverty Amid Plenty', *Oxford Development Studies*, vol. 27, no. 2.

Leith, Clark (2000) 'Why Botswana Prospered', unpublished paper, November.

Mhone, Guy (1996) 'Botswana Economy Still an Enclave', *Africa Development*, vol. 21, nos. 2 and 3.

Molomo, Mpho (2000) 'Understanding Government and Opposition Parties in Botswana', *Commonwealth and Comparative Politics*, vol. 38, no. 1, March.

Murray, Andrew and Neil Parsons (1990) 'The Modern Economic History of Botswana' in Zbigniew Konizacki, Jane Parpart and Timothy Shaw (eds.) *Studies in the Economic History of Southern Africa*, vol. I: Frontline States London: Frank Cass.

National Intelligence Council (2000) *The Global Infectious Threat and its Implications for the United States*. NIE 99-17D. Washington DC: NIC.

Owusu, Francis and Abdi Ismail Samatar (1997) 'Industrial Strategy and the African State: The Botswana Experience', *Canadian Journal of African Studies*, vol. 31, no. 2.

Parson, Jack (1984) *Botswana: Liberal Democracy and the Labour Reserve in Southern Africa* Boulder: Westview Press.

Parsons, Neil (2000) Botswana History Pages 'Ethnicity', www.ubh.tripod.com/bw/bhp13.htm#ethnicity

Parsons, Neil, Willie Henderson and Thomas Tlou (1995) *Seretse Khama, 1921-1980*, Gaborone: Macmillan/Botswana Society.

Picard, Louis (1987) *The Politics of Development in Botswana: A Model for Success?* Boulder: Lynne Rienner.

Picard, Louis (ed.) (1985) *The Evolution of Modern Botswana*, Lincoln: University of Nebraska Press.

Republic of Botswana (1996) *Presidential Task Group—A Framework for a Long Term Vision for Botswana*, Gaborone: Government Printers.

Republic of Botswana (1997a) *National Development Plan 8 1997/8-2002/03*, Gaborone: Government Printers.

Republic of Botswana (1997b) *Presidential Task Group—Vision 2016: Towards Prosperity For All*, Gaborone: Government Printers.

Republic of Botswana (2000) Central Statistics Office 'Stats Update December 1999'.

Republic of Botswana 'Economic Snapshot', 2001, www.gov.bw/economy/index.html

Republic of Botswana 'Growing Infrastructure', 2001, www.gov.bw/gem/growing_infrastructure.html

Robi, Modibedi (1994) 'Economic Policy for the 21st Century' in Sue Brothers, Janet Hermans and Doreen Nteta (ed.) *Botswana in the 21st Century* Gaborone: Botswana Society.

Samatar, Abdi Ismail (1997) 'Leadership and Ethnicity in the Making of African State Models: Botswana Versus Somalia', *Third World Quarterly*, vol. 18, no. 4.

Samatar, Abdi Ismail (1999) *An African Miracle: State and Class Leadership and Colonial Legacy in Botswana's Development*, Portsmouth: Heinemann.

Siwawa-Ndai, Pelani (1996) 'Some Facts and Figures about the Quality of Life in Botswana' in Doreen Nteta, Janet Hermans with Pavla Jeskova (eds.) *Poverty and Plenty: The Botswana Experience*, Gaborone: Botswana Society.

Stedman, Stephen John (ed.) (1993) *Botswana: The Political Economy of Democratic Development*, Boulder: Lynne Rienner.

Thumberg-Hartland, Penelope (1978) *Botswana: An African Growth Economy*, Boulder: Westview Press.

Tlou, Thomas and Alec Campbell (1997) *History of Botswana*, Gaborone: Macmillan.

Tsie, Balefi (1995) *The Political Economy of Botswana in SADCC*, Harare: SAPES Books.

Tsie, Balefi (1996) 'The Political Context of Botswana's Development Performance', *Journal of Southern African Studies*, vol. 22, no. 4, 1996.

UNAIDS (2000) *AIDS Epidemic Update: December 2000*, New York, United Nations.

USAID 'Initiative for Southern Africa', http://www.info.usaid.gov/pubs/cp98/afr/zz-isa.htm

Willan, S. (2000) 'Will HIV/AIDS Undermine Democracy in South Africa?', *AIDS Analysis Africa*, vol. 11, no. 1, June/July.

Woo-Cuming, Meredith (ed.) (1999) *The Developmental State*, New York: Cornell University Press.

World Bank (1999) *Intensifying Action Against HIV/AIDS in Africa: Responding to a Development Crisis*, www.worldbank.org/html/extpb/abshtml/14572.htm.

Chapter 10

Uganda and the Challenge of HIV/AIDS

Daniel Low-Beer and Rand Stoneburner

On the banks of Lake Victoria in the early 1980s, Ugandans started talking about a new disease, at the same time it was being discovered in the large teaching hospitals in the United States. Ugandans gave the disease the real and evocative name 'SLIM', linked to connotations of wasting and the consequences of the disease. It communicated more than the split term 'HIV/AIDS' used later and elsewhere. Ugandans related the disease directly (and indirectly) to sexual behaviour, and soon had to deal with the consequences of the epidemic – young people infected, death, and orphans (Barnett, Blaikie 1992). A village chief[1] in the villages that first responded to the epidemic told me that what disturbed them most was that SLIM went against nature – the elders were now caring for the young. This is where the Ugandan response to HIV/AIDS began, and the elements that led to its success were formed: communication, behaviour change and care. In 1983 SLIM was 'discovered' by epidemiologists in these same villages (Serwadda et al. 1985) and named AIDS. The disease was acknowledged by the government who put in place a response to the disease as early as 1986 (Kaleeba et al. 2000). Yet there have always been qualities in the community response in Uganda that preceded and exceeded any set of interventions that could be delivered to the population.

Ugandans have a simple way of communicating HIV prevention. They talk of an anthill with a snake inside. If you put your hand inside, you take a risk, and you may well get bitten. Awareness campaigns began with the beating of a drum, the basic and traditional method of warning a community of imminent danger. The government communication program was direct and focused on avoiding risk, and sticking to one partner or 'zero grazing' ('zero grazing' was publicized with a simple picture of a cow). True, they dealt with HIV in their own way, but they dealt with it as a nation, within communities and as individuals. The messages put across, largely ignored internationally, may have wide relevance for HIV prevention elsewhere.

In the early 1990s, there were the first signs of stability and a decline in HIV prevalence in Uganda (WHO 1994, Asiimwe-Okiror et al. 1995, Stoneburner et al. 1996). The early 1990s, like today, were an exciting time for HIV prevention, yet with more limited resources and options. There had been successes in Europe and the United States among gays and intravenous drug users, and then evidence of declines at the national level from Africa (Uganda) and Asia (Thailand). The success in Thailand was accepted almost immediately, and correlated with increasing condom use (Brown et al. 1994, Mason et al. 1995, Mastro et al. 1995; Rojanapithayakorn et al. 1996). In contrast there has been confusion for a decade over the timing of the declines in Uganda, and the basis for changes in sexual behaviour (Asiimwe-Okiror *et al.* 1997, Mbulaiteye *et al.* 2002, Korenromp, E. *et al.* 2002, Parkhurst 2002). This has hindered our learning the general lessons of an African success.

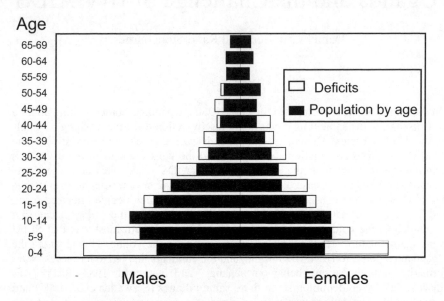

Figure 10.1: Demographic impact of AIDS on a local community in Uganda

An African 'Success': Basic yet Universal Lessons

Uganda remains the best example of changes in population behaviours and communications reducing HIV. The data is relatively clear and conclusive. HIV prevalence declined nationally from 21.1% to 9.7% nationally across 15 antenatal clinic states, during the period 1991–98. These declines are repeated in other national datasets, army recruits and blood donors, as well as data from all strata of society, urban and rural. The major mechanism was a reduction in non-regular sexual partners by 60% over the period 1989–95, and an associated contraction of sexual networks. The scale of these changes is equivalent to a 'social vaccine' of 75% efficacy (Stoneburner, Low-Beer 2000, 2003). It is more effective than any available medical approach or proposed vaccine, and has been available for almost a decade from Africa.

What does it tell us about HIV prevention? Firstly, that it can be highly successful, changing the course of an epidemic over a matter of years, even in resource-poor settings. Secondly, it is built on behavioural change, a response at the population level both to the epidemic and to avoiding risk. This can be supported and catalysed but cannot be delivered as a traditional intervention. Other interventions, for example the demand for voluntary counselling and testing services (VCT) and care support networks, are greatly enhanced if this basic population response is mobilised. Communication programmes in Uganda were clear and direct. AIDS kills but many of the behaviours and situations that put people at risk can be avoided. The response was strengthened by basic care among health personnel and the community. The care provides support for people with AIDS but also involves people in the reality of the epidemic. However, in almost all other countries, HIV prevention has fallen short of that seen in Uganda.

To explain why the lessons of an African success have not been better incorporated into international HIV policy (Schwartzlander *et al.* 2001; Stover *et al.* 2002), it is necessary to consider the political economy of AIDS and of AIDS in Africa, dealt with in this book. Presented first will be the evidence and data on epidemiology, behaviours and communications in Uganda and other countries. At the same time, the academic and political debate explaining this data will be followed, to assess why it has been so difficult to accept an African success. This will the lead to a closer assessment of the Ugandan context, policy components in relation to the timing of declines in HIV, and communications about AIDS and people with AIDS.

The Ugandan context has lessons that are basic yet universal, and often forgotten or overlooked elsewhere. Much more needs to be added, but they are the building blocks for HIV prevention. However, they cannot be delivered in a traditional policy manner, through a magical set of costed interventions. They require real human, community, public health and political urgency in addition to financial capital.[2] Crucially this must be guided by independent national, rather than advocacy driven, surveillance and evaluation, with prevention and care integrated by communities. It necessitates a shift in epidemiological and policy thinking. At stake is nothing less than a social vaccine for AIDS, far more successful than any medical approach, gel, vaccine, or testing service we are likely to provide from experience outside.

Declines in HIV Prevalence in Uganda: When and by How Much?

Uganda had a severe epidemic by 1991, with over 20% of adults infected and evidence of changes in the population structure in the worst affected areas, Figure 10.1 (Low-Beer *et al.* 97). This was associated with increased orphan rates, mortality and social and economic impacts (Barnett, Blaikie 1992, Hunter 1990). To begin with, the term 'success' in Uganda must be qualified. Ugandans did not avoid or prevent an epidemic, but by the quality of their response, they overcame it. When talking about this response, we are not talking about an issue on which many models of behavioural change have been built, like heart disease or teenage pregnancy or sexually transmitted disease. AIDS in Uganda was a condition that could challenge in a relatively short time, the integrity of an individual or community.

While working at the World Health Organisation (WHO) in the early 1990s, the first evidence of stability in AIDS cases and declines in HIV prevalence[3] in Uganda took us, researchers, and international agencies to a great extent by surprise. Demographic projections of AIDS published at the same time were based on 20–30 year epidemic curves, following an inevitable path towards stability in the 2010s and 2020s (WHO 1991). In Thailand, observed declines could be correlated with increased condom use. However, what had either interventions or Ugandans themselves done to reduce HIV in a 'full-blown' African epidemic?

Our initial analysis, performed while at WHO on limited data, suggested a decline in HIV incidence in Uganda from the late 1980s (Stoneburner *et al.* 1996, WHO 1993). Further modelling and birth cohort analysis showed a very different HIV incidence curve to those published at the time. There was rapid spread of HIV across a population, unlike the successive stages across risk groups from sexually transmitted disease modelling. This was then maintained by demographic conditions that were important in Africa in fuelling HIV, and epidemiological processes. However, HIV could also respond quite rapidly to changes in sexual behaviour. We tentatively (on limited data) hypothesised a decline in risk exposure from 1988. This was seen in the youngest ages first, which were most affected by recent HIV incidence. However the changes were population wide and occurred across all age groups, seen by successive declines by cohort over time.

Further data was soon released such as HIV prevalence data among pregnant women attending antenatal clinic sentinel surveillance sites (ANC), and demographic and health surveys, including that for Uganda in 1995 (Macro International 96). Crucial HIV surveillance and behavioural data appeared from other countries, although AIDS case surveillance was effectively discarded. We expected similar HIV prevalence declines to be seen in other countries, but as the 1990s continued we were disturbed to see that Uganda was relatively unique.

To evaluate the declines in HIV prevalence and their determinants, the methods we used were a comparative analysis of HIV prevalence and HIV behavioural data by age and sex in countries with high HIV prevalence. The countries investigated were in East and Southern Africa (Uganda, Kenya, Zambia and Malawi with additional behavioural data for Zimbabwe and Tanzania). The aim was to assess what distinctive determinants of declines in HIV prevalence characterised Uganda, and whether they could be seen even to a lesser degree elsewhere.

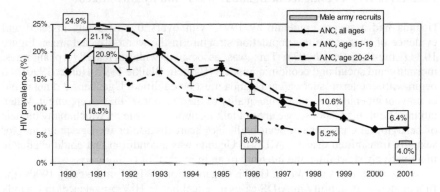

Source: Uganda AIDS Control Programme; Low-Beer, Stoneburner 2003

Figure 10.2: HIV prevalence in Uganda among antenatal clinic surveillance sites

We analysed HIV prevalence among pregnant women attending antenatal clinic sentinel surveillance sites (ANC) over the time period 1990–98, supplemented with data from army recruits and population cohorts (Figure 10.2). We also analysed population-based demographic and HIV behavioural data collected in Demographic and Health Surveys (DHS III) and knowledge, attitudes and behaviour surveys (KAPB). This included a KAPB survey performed in Uganda in 1989 on a representative sample of 3,118 persons aged 15–55 (Ankrah *et al.* 1993).

First, the early timing and scale of the HIV prevalence declines in Uganda were distinctive. HIV prevalence rates among pregnant women surveyed at ANC sentinel sites crested in the early 1990s, peaking in 1991 at 21.1% (95% C.I. (confidence interval), 25.1% to18.1%) and then declined 54% to 9.7% (95% C.I., 10.7% to 8.7%) by 1998 (Figure 10.2). The age-stratified analyses of these data reveal greater declines among younger age cohorts, which best reflect recent HIV incidence. HIV prevalence rates declined 75% in 15–19 year olds (from 20.9% to 5.2%) and 59% in 20–24 year olds (from 24.9% to 10.2%) between 1991 and 1998.

There are questions of bias, particularly in antenatal clinic data, discussed later. However, declines were also seen in male army recruits (aged 21), from 18% to 6% between 1991–96 (and to below 4% in 2002) (Mugenyi 1998, 2003). Blood donor data also shows significant declines, even among replacement donors from 24% to 7% (1989–98),[4] who are least affected by selection bias. There are 50% declines in rural districts, for example in Gulu from 27.1% to 12.8% (1993–98) among pregnant women, and from 2% to 0.8% (1994–98) among secondary school students; and in rural sentinel sites from 4.2% to 2.3% in Mutolere and 2.8% to 0.9% in Matany (1993–99). In a study in Kabarole of all young women, an area away from the epicentre and the trans-African highway, there were also declines in all strata over the period. There were greater absolute declines in urban areas, but comparable relative declines in rural areas: 30% to 10% in urban; 18% to 9% in semi-urban; 10% to 5% in rural, 1991–96 (Kaleeba *et al.* 2000).

There have also been declines in rural population cohorts in Masaka and Rakai (Mbulaiteye *et al.* 2002; Mulder *et al.* 1995; Wawer *et al.* 1997), as well as declines in HIV incidence in the Masaka MRC cohort among adults of all ages from 7.6 per 1000 person years in 1990 to 3.2 per 1000 person years in 1998 (a decline of 58%). The decline was greater among males by 75% (from 9.4/1000 to 2.4/1000) than females (6/1000 to 4/1000). If the data is grouped from 1990–94 and 1995–98 a decline in HIV incidence of 37% is reported (Mbulaiteye *et al.* 2002). As discussed below, the data from these cohorts suggest HIV incidence was higher in the 1980s than the 1990s (Low-Beer 2002; Korenromp *et al.* 2002), and the data may capture the tail of earlier incidence declines. This is supported by HIV incidence declines from Kagera over the border in Tanzania (with strong links to these districts) which declined 88%, from 47.5 to 5.6 per 1000 person years, 1987–89 to 1993–96 (Kwesigabo, G., *et al.* 2000). While there is geographical heterogeneity, rural as well as urban sentinel sites showed declines by 1998, with the exception of Tororo on the Kenyan border (which appears to behave, culturally and epidemiologically, more like Kenya than Uganda, yet has subsequently declined since 1998).

Comparison to Kenya, Malawi and Zambia, between 1990–98 revealed that statistically significant declines in overall HIV prevalence rates were largely unique to Uganda at this stage. More recently further declines have been indicated in

Zambia, Rwanda and possibly among youth in South Africa, but these have not been population wide or of the scale of Uganda (Agha, S. 2002; UNAIDS 2002; Fylkesnes 2001). It is important to define accurately the timing of the unique declines in Uganda, if we are to assess what interventions have worked. The data shows declines in HIV prevalence of over 50% from the early 1990s, suggesting earlier declines in HIV incidence from the late 1980s or early 1990s. Despite confusion in their interpretation, the data on these declines are relatively clear, and supported from other sources across the country.

Behavioural Determinants: Changes in Primary Sexual Behaviours

When Ugandans were asked how they had changed their behaviour due to AIDS by 1995, they responded with the following: 48% of men and women reported that they stuck to one partner; 11% of women and 14% of men stopped all sex; and 2.9% of women and 12.5% of men started using condoms.[5] In many other situations, increased condom use was frequently shown as an indicator of prevention success, for example in Thailand (Mastro et al. 1995, Rojanapithayakorn et al. 1996). However while condom use had increased in Uganda, it was not comparatively higher than in other countries (Figure 10.4). Unlike the Ugandans themselves, foreign researchers had been surprisingly reluctant to highlight the precise changes in basic sexual behaviour.

There were differences in 'ever having sex', and marriage rates in Uganda compared to other countries. However, by far the biggest difference was in the number of sexual partners. People with non-regular sexual partners[6] declined by 60% in Uganda, from 1989–95 (Figure 10.3). Other countries in the mid to late 1990s had similar sexual partner rates to Uganda in 1989, and did not show this shift. While there had been a focus on distant determinants and even more proximate determinants like condom use, the major difference was in primary sexual behaviours. This had not been highlighted in previous analyses by WHO and UNAIDS, which will be discussed below (Asiimwe-Okiror et al. 1997). There seemed to be a basic behavioural response to avoid risk associated with HIV, resulting in a reduction in sexual partnerships and associated sexual networks.

According to WHO GPA data, people with non-regular sexual partners decreased in urban areas, by 52% among men (from 41% to 20%) and 65% among women (from 22% to 8%), and in rural areas by 63% among men (from 37% to 13.5%) and 68% among women (from 17% to 5%). The sampling of these surveys was designed to be compared based on World Health Organisation GPA guidelines. There is therefore quite clear evidence of a substantial decline in sexual partners, if we look at Uganda over time (1989 compared to 1995), or evaluate it comparatively to other countries. When comparing DHS data among 15–24 year olds, 19.1% of men and 6.5% of women report casual sex in Uganda in 1995, compared to 56.8% and 20.1% in Kenya in 1998; 55.9% and 20% in Zambia in 1996; 55.9% and 20% in Malawi in 1996; and 47.8% and 14.9% in Uganda in 1995. Similar differences are apparent in all age groups, with other countries in the mid to late 1990s having similar levels of non-regular partners to Uganda in 1989, and substantial reductions uniquely in Uganda by 1995.

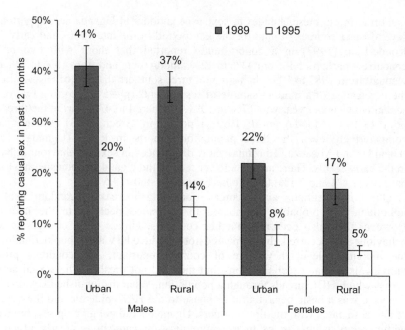

Source: Comparison of the WHO GPA/Uganda AIDS Control Programme, KABP surveys in 1989 and 1995

Figure 10.3: Percentage of men and women reporting non-regular partners in the last 12 months

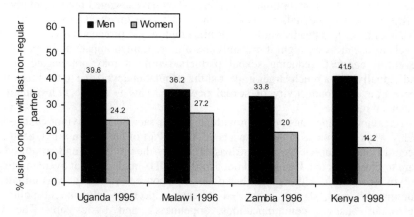

Source: KAPB survey for Uganda from 1989

Figure 10.4: Condom use with last non-regular partner

Furthermore, these changes to sexual behaviours in Uganda are supported from several other sources of data for the key period in the late 1980s and early 1990s. Konde-Lule (1993) in a cohort study reported that those with two or more concurrent partners fell from 43% to 12% among men, and from 13% to 1% among women, from 1987 to 1992. In a study of three southern districts of Uganda in 1991, the percentage of a random sample of respondents (n=954) reporting two or more sexual contacts per year was 17% in 1991, compared to 43% during the three years prior to this (Moodie *et al.* 1991, reported in Green 2003). When analysed comparatively even the three population cohorts in Rakai (Uganda), Masaka (Uganda) and Mwanza (Tanzania) show differences in sexual behaviour at baseline in the early 1990s. There are 78% fewer men in the Ugandan studies with 5+ sexual partners (1.4% and 2.1%) than in the Tanzanian study (9.6%).

Other interventions and changes (including increasing condom use) were important, and probably contributed to continued declines in the late 1990s. However they also occurred in other countries. Unless basic changes to sexual behaviour also occurred, they appeared not to reduce HIV at the population level. At the individual level they were of course important, and condoms protected individuals in many real situations, but they did not break up the sexual networks across which HIV spreads through a population. What distinguished Uganda in this analysis, was a basic behavioural response to the HIV epidemic and the avoidance of risk associated with multiple partners. Ugandans did not give up sex, but had sex within relationships, or as their communication campaigns clearly urged 'zero grazed' and 'loved carefully'.

Ugandans were quite clear about how they changed their behaviour, and the debate has really only been heated at the international level.[7] If you go into a village in Uganda, they will talk to you about AIDS, how they have dealt with it, and normally their recommendations on what to do. The changes they have made are not piecemeal, life has not continued as before. They have engaged fundamentally with AIDS, in the way they talk, think and behave. This has involved a basic response of risk avoidance to a deadly epidemic. While condom use protects individuals, unless levels of use are very high, it probably has a more limited impact at the population level. In contrast, reducing sexual partners (while it may not negate all risk individually) has a much larger impact at the population level, due to the break up in the scope and connectivity of sexual networks. This is a crucial lesson of the Ugandan response.

Behaviour change has not been without loss or sacrifice. Behaviour change is in many ways a response to these aspects of AIDS. Part of the response in Uganda has been a basic acknowledgement of loss caused by the epidemic, and an attitude of care to those affected. Uganda did not avoid an AIDS epidemic, but overcame and is still overcoming it. Although the behavioural response occurred and was initiated at community level, it was supported in each aspect by government policy on behaviour change, communications, 'openness', and basic care. The way community and political efforts have reinforced each other (yet the impetus still comes from the community level) is relatively rare in a national response to AIDS.

Both approaches were open to the fact that they were facing an epidemic, but an epidemic in which risk behaviours for many people were largely avoidable. Even in 1989, when there were limited options and condoms were not widely distributed,

85.2% of Ugandans thought AIDS could be avoided. We often provide examples of the exceptions, women trapped in relationships, street kids, or forced sex workers, and these are important. But realistically, multiple partners was a risk behaviour that many people felt they could reduce and largely avoid in an epidemic. It was primarily a very basic response of risk avoidance.

A major reason in 1989 for not using condoms among 68% of men and 67% of women was that they found them dangerous. At first, this appears a strange response, and it may well be cultural: many people found condoms offensive at this stage of the epidemic. However there is a difference between removing yourself from a risk situation (if possible) rather than entering a risk situation with protection. The approach of risk avoidance is important, as condoms were seen by most as being good for casual relationships but not for marriage. Qualitative material from South Africa also shows high levels of anxiety (around acceptance, chances of breaking, quality of condoms) in going into a high risk situation protected by a condom in contrast to avoiding risk situations.

The simple HIV prevention test you often hear among Ugandans is to ask yourself, would you recommend to your daughter, son, or family to carry on with casual sex but use a condom when facing a deadly epidemic? In an epidemic that affects 20% of the population, personal communications in such situations would be: first, avoid risk situations; and only second if you enter them protect yourself with a condom, gel, or whatever else is provided and available.

A (abstinence), B (be faithful or behaviour change), and C (condoms) are all important in HIV prevention, but the foundation in Uganda was B, behaviour change with a reduction in sexual partners. This is the building block to which other interventions can be added. These other interventions should not detract from the fundamental need in an epidemic to respond behaviourally at the population level. Often our attempts to modify and reduce transmission in risk situations (however interesting medically) may give a false sense of security. There is great unease in many African populations about measures not based on risk avoidance, even if like condoms they are relatively effective. DHS data in 19 African countries shows greater priority for primary sexual behaviour change to avoid AIDS than starting or increasing condom use, despite the promotion of the latter (Green 2003). It is a very different context to the reproductive health policies in the developed world, or to family planning. Both the prevalence of HIV risk and its consequences are much worse. This is not a moral judgement, but a response to an emergency and population threat, which as illustrated at the start of this section can challenge the integrity of an individual or community in a relatively short time. Certainly a response needs to encompass a full range of services and interventions, but many countries that have utilised these, without the basis in behaviour change, have, despite their other interventions, seen HIV prevalence increase consistently throughout the 1990s.

Communicating AIDS

The differences in communications are noticeable on the ground, before encountering them in the data. Working for WHO, one frequently has to pick up fieldwork experiences in taxi rides to and from airports. However superficial the method, it was striking how Ugandans talked about AIDS. Once you explained you were working on AIDS, there would often follow a stream of opinions, stories and questions – personal about families and communities, sometimes outrageous and even with a bit of stigma, but also a great sense of reality and realism. Without getting a word in edgeways, you would open the door of the taxi at your destination, leaving a tip to quieten things down.

In the 1990s, I found if you took a similar taxi ride in Kenya, and said inevitably that you worked on AIDS, there would be silence or a swift change of subject. In Southern Africa, there would be similar disinterest, occasionally taking you to the side at the end of the trip to ask you what can be done for a relative who has AIDS, or ask whether government condoms are safe – often with a slight whisper, rather than the open and exuberant conversations from the Ugandan taxi driver. It was striking, and we thought important, but not something that epidemiologists usually include in their analysis.

Once we asked the question of what catalysed this basic behavioural response in Uganda, we started to assess communications: how people talked about AIDS and people with AIDS. Basic knowledge and awareness indicators (ever having heard of AIDS) were high and similar across the countries. There were knowledge deficits, and some false rumours, for example that AIDS could be cured by sex with a virgin in South Africa.[8] We did not think knowledge characteristics distinguished Uganda, but were similar to other countries. One of the problems empirically, is that we tend to look at knowledge indicators rather than to capture the communication process by which information and opinions are transmitted. The DHS data provides limited insight into the communication process, but we can distinguish vertical communication channels (mass media and institutional) from horizontal channels (personal channels through social networks, friends and family).

When analysed by the communication channel for acquiring and communicating AIDS information (personal, institutional and mass media), there were differences by country. In Uganda, personal networks of friends and family were dominant, unlike all other countries. 82% of women had heard of AIDS from this source, compared to 40–65% in other countries. Communication through social networks also dominated in Uganda when stratified by urban areas (74%), rural areas (84%) and among men (70%). In Kenya, mass channels still dominate, as they do in Malawi, Tanzania, Zambia, and Zimbabwe (and even in Uganda in 1989). There was a unique shift in Uganda, 1989–95, in the dominant channel for communicating about AIDS, from formal to informal channels.

Why were personal channels important? They show that the issue of AIDS had taken root in social and personal networks in conversations between friends, families and in communities. This was important because knowledge of AIDS would be communicated with advice, or an opinion, and possibly imparted with a sense of trust. It led to a greater sense of realism and the personal risks of the epidemic. This is important given general scepticism to vertical messages from media or institutional sources.

A second communication component that is distinctively high in Uganda, is knowledge of someone with AIDS through social networks (Figure 10.5). This draws people close to the reality and consequences of the epidemic. A higher proportion, 91.5% of men and 86.4% of women, know someone with AIDS or who has died of AIDS in Uganda. In urban areas 94% of women and 96% of men know someone with AIDS or who has died of AIDS. In most districts a vast majority know someone personally who has died of AIDS, greater than 85% except those in the far North East near Kenya or in the North West (Figure 10.5). This is higher than in all other countries, and significantly higher than in South Africa, which reported 14% knowing someone with AIDS in 1998 and 50% in 2002 (HSRC 2002, also see chapter in this book by Whiteside, Willan, Mattes, Manning). Although the stage of the epidemic played some role initially, no country has reached the levels in Uganda of knowledge of someone with AIDS through social networks.

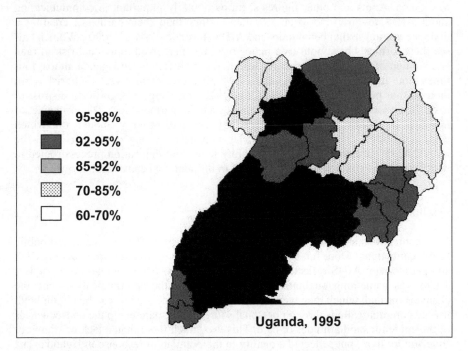

Figure 10.5: Personal networks: knowing someone with AIDS

There are a number of factors to take into account in interpreting this data: stage of the epidemic; openness of communication; and reporting of HIV/AIDS including AIDS case diagnosis and HIV testing. Our modelling has suggested that communication networks are very multiplicative (Low-Beer 2000, 2002). If there is openness in communication networks to AIDS, a high percentage of people will know someone with AIDS early on in an epidemic. Over 90%, 40% or under 20% will know someone with AIDS before peak HIV incidence, depending on whether AIDS and people with AIDS can be discussed through personal networks. We also believe that AIDS case diagnosis by public health personnel at local level was important in Uganda, discussed later.

Two further aspects are age and gender barriers to communications. Knowledge of someone with AIDS is distinctly lower in the youngest ages, 15–19, than the older ages, 20–54, in all other countries, in Kenya (by 22%), Tanzania (23%), Malawi (17%), Zambia (22%) and Zimbabwe (27%), except Uganda (by 2%). This is partly because AIDS mortality is lower in these younger ages. In Uganda this age difference and communication deficit among the youngest ages, has been bridged. It suggests the importance of communication at community level, linking younger people (who experience the risk behaviours) to the consequences of AIDS in older groups. There is bridging social communication across age groups.

Gender barriers to communicating about AIDS within couples are still important in Uganda. Aunts and other figures seem particularly important in communicating about AIDS to girls and young women (rather than their partners), creating a dialogue around sexual behaviours and AIDS (Kyaddondo et al. 2000). Women still see their partner's behaviour as a major risk. The perceived individual risk of men and women of the same partnership are often very different. In Uganda almost four times more men (27.4%) than women (7.4%) perceive themselves at low risk when their partner perceives themselves at high risk. This suggests significant distrust of male behaviour, and limits to 'openness' within partnerships. The principle of negotiation within partnerships may not be the primary model on which communications and behaviours in Uganda have changed. Rather than the individual or partnership, it is a community level communication process rooted in wider social networks which is significant in influencing behavioural norms.

Qualitative Components of Communications

Communications are often reduced to the provision of messages, media and public health campaigns. More fundamentally, how Ugandans communicated about AIDS and people with AIDS reflected and influenced the way the population responded. There was something qualitative to the content of the communications and the channels through which they were communicated. Three aspects can be highlighted: trusted communications through personal sources, transparency to the consequences of the epidemic, and attitudes of care. This was much more than a lack of stigma or 'live and let live', but reflected a quality to the population response in Uganda. The qualitative components were central to catalysing a behavioural response in Uganda.

Firstly, the communication process about AIDS in Uganda should not be romanticised or made superficial (as in many media and public health campaigns, deflecting the force of its impact on behaviours). It was a difficult and real engagement with AIDS and people with AIDS in Uganda. The vast majority of Ugandans said they would care for people with AIDS: 86.2% of women and 77.4% of men. When men where asked in 1995, what the government should do for AIDS victims, many proposed treatment and helping relatives care. However, 29% also said people with AIDS should be isolated, quarantined or jailed, and 3.5% said they should be put to death. Opening up communications did not lead to clean, open conversations, and stigma remained tied up if not opened out, in the communication response.

This is reflected in the death of the famous Ugandan musician Philip Lutaaya. Once he found out his AIDS status, he toured Uganda in 1989, performing his music and giving testimonies at schools, colleges, churches and other places. While he attracted large crowds, many people also accused him of pretending to have AIDS to make money from his concerts (Kaleeba *et al.* 2000). There was an acrimonious national debate, with all types of response aired, and some of his concerts degenerated as sceptics shouted accusations at him. As he became progressively ill, there was a difficult national process that culminated after his death in December 1989, in a wave of public admiration following his funeral. The video, *Born in Africa*, which tells the story of his last months, has been sold in millions in Uganda and other countries in Africa.

Personal communications are important because they involve trust, opinions, sanctions, stories and a more personalised form of knowledge. This is against a background of widespread scepticism about sources of AIDS and other information, from the media and public sources (rarely acknowledged in policy), however healthy and bright the messages are. Political leadership is often emphasised in Uganda, and was important. Yet it is rare that we get really trusted communications from leaders, without them being connected to horizontal personal communications. Museveni may well be an exception rather than provide a general lesson.

As important were cultural, community and religious figures. Religion certainly played an important role, and there was something of a religious revival in Uganda in the 1990s, together with an engagement of religious leaders in areas of AIDS policy and care. Of the three chairpersons of the Uganda AIDS Commission, one was an Anglican and another a Catholic Bishop. Trusted communications about AIDS and people with AIDS were important qualitative elements: as a South African boy stated '*the majority especially the youth, the majority don't take AIDS seriously .. no they just talk about it .. I think people who make us clear about this are our parents when they tell us about somebody who died of Aids*' (Brookes, Low-Beer 2003).

Secondly, there was great transparency about the AIDS epidemic in Uganda, and direct knowledge of people with AIDS through social networks. In other countries, even when there is AIDS mortality, it often does not lead to openness and secondary conversations. Here is an example after a funeral of someone with AIDS in South Africa in 2002 (collected in a collaborative study with Heather Brookes of the HSRC, South Africa):

Then the neighbour [T's best friend] came over as we were talking… She came asking for washing powder soap.
My mother-in-law asked her, 'How did the funeral go?'
The neighbour said, 'It went well.'
My mother-in law asked, 'What did she die from?'
The neighbour said, 'She had piles.'
My mother-in-law said, 'Oh shame she had piles. Why didn't she consult a doctor?'
The neighbour said, 'She went to the doctor but she still died.'
My mother-in-law said, 'Shame now who will look after the child, at least the grandmother is still alive it won't be such a big hassle.'
Then the neighbour went.
That's when my mother-in-law said, 'AIDS is killing children.'

Although there is recognition of AIDS among the immediate family, this has not created the same community knowledge and secondary communications in South Africa. In particular there is not a definite diagnosis of the cause of death, important at the public health level, but even more because it feeds into communities. The reality of the epidemic (and secondary conversations around risk and behaviour) is contained within the family, and does not reverberate in this case to the extended family, neighbours or the wider community.

This is in comparison to a later funeral in the same community in 2002, also collected with the HSRC (Brookes, Low-Beer 2003):

> *I attended a funeral of 'Brenda'. It was so sad when her uncle pleaded with the youth to change their behaviour. He said 'Our youth please change the ways in which you behave about your future... The future of this country is in your hands, you can be happy because you still have a chance to change. Go to your churches and be strong because the nice time has no ending, instead it ends your life...'*
> *When we came back from the graveyard everyone was talking about what her uncle said. It was so touching everyone was talking freely about the dangers of the virus... we in my group, we approved of what the uncle said. We know it was AIDS. He was giving us guidance as an elder.*

The funeral is an extreme but significant event in many communities, and the structure of these conversations is reflected in many other situations, casual, hanging out on street corners, in families. It shows the varying levels of transparency, and their effect on the important secondary conversations in a community around risk, opinions and behaviours.

The third important component of Ugandan communications is an attitude of care. The role of the AIDS support organization (TASO) and other NGOs were essential in creating these social networks and resources for care, and have been described elsewhere (Kaleeba *et al.* 2000). The first lady, Mrs Janet Museveni urged support for families with AIDS, lending support to Uganda Women's Effort to Support Orphans (UWESO). The AIDS support organization (TASO) was formed in 1987 by a group of 16 volunteers in Kampala, 12 of whom had HIV/AIDS. They debated hard whether to use the word AIDS in their name (due to stigma), and in the end decided not to compromise on the open approach symbolised by the word 'AIDS' (Kaleeba *et al.* 2000). Initially people asked them not to park their vehicles with TASO on them near their houses, so as not to be associated with AIDS. However their commitment to promote openness and 'living positively with AIDS', increasingly involved people with AIDS in their communities, and mobilised social networks of support, counselling and care. They promoted 'shared confidentiality', openness about HIV status with a limited circle of trusted people, opening up channels of support and care. TASO grew rapidly, and worked in developing other NGOs. By 1997, there were 1020 organisations working with HIV/AIDS in Uganda (Uganda AIDS Commission, 1997). The approach of organizations like TASO (reflecting as well as catalysing the Ugandan response and 'social capital') are apparent in the quality of the communication process (trusted personal communications, transparency, attitudes of care), involvement and internalisation of the epidemic, and the basic behavioural response.

These activities were also reinforced by a basic government policy of care at home, within communities and through the health sector. However there was also a community response that was sustained by but also invigorated all these activities, and led to the success of care networks and later uptake of counselling and testing. Again the attitude of care involved a difficult engagement with the epidemic and people with AIDS. Here is an example of a young girl caring for her cousin (Brookes, Low-Beer 2003):

She is my cousin... she got HIV/AIDS... When I came from school, I used to help her...
Sometimes she could not do things and I had to take her to the toilet, I didn't even like to look at her.
We were saying there is someone in the room who is sick, who is HIV positive, we were not hiding it.
During her last days she said to me, 'My cousin... You must be away from men and you must be away from sex because look at me, AIDS kills'.
You could see the bones.

Communication and even public health campaigns can gloss over these experiences, and it is a difficult balance to capture the realism of the epidemic and the humanity of those infected often leading healthy lives but also suffering. However, we must not negate or shy away from the reality of the epidemic, because it is real and because it changes behaviours. It is also a very different attitude to the slogan 'live and let live',[9] indifference being replaced with a difficult engagement not without stigma, but overcome in the example above by a basic attitude of care.

There were distinctive communication characteristics to the Ugandan success in HIV prevention that catalysed and reinforced behaviour change. There were more open personal communication networks for communicating about AIDS and people with AIDS. There was also a quality to the communications and Ugandan response: trusted conversations, transparency to AIDS and its consequences at the local level, and attitudes of care. This resulted in a greater personalisation of the epidemic, and enhanced HIV prevention, behaviour change and many AIDS activities. We believe it was a community communication process, particularly around knowing people with AIDS. This is different from individual knowledge, or even communication between partners (for example after VCT), and creates rippling social pressures in a community, which in Uganda elicited a quality to their behavioural and communication response.

The Political Economy of the Ugandan Success

Debates over whether the declines in Uganda are real and what the causes are, have divided approaches to epidemiology and HIV prevention for a decade (Asiimwe-Okiror *et al.* 1997, Mbulaiteye *et al.* 2002, Korenromp *et al.* 2002, Parkhurst 2002; Schwartzlander *et al.* 2001; Stover *et al.* 2002; Attaran, Sachs 2001). This is surprising given the clarity in the data on the declines and on the changes in sexual partners, comparatively and from 1989 to 1995. It raises questions about the political economy of allocating AIDS intervention resources, alongside the analysis of the data we have presented. We therefore ask two related questions in this section: What policy lessons can we learn from the Ugandan success, and why have the lessons of an African success been so difficult to incorporate into international policy?

We were certainly surprised in 1993/94 that an African success was not accepted more enthusiastically and immediately internationally. The Ugandan AIDS control program did initially publish evidence of declines in HIV prevalence, the large reduction in sexual partners and their basis in primary behaviour change in 1995 and 1996 (Asiimwe-Okiror 1995, 1996, Opio 1995). However, a succession of UNAIDS reports played down the role of a reduction in sexual partners in the same data from 1997 (Asiimwe-Okiror *et al.* 1997; UNAIDS 1998, 1999), and questioned the validity of the changes in HIV prevalence and underlying HIV incidence (UNAIDS 1999, Wawer 1997, Parkhurst 2002).

Firstly, biases related to fertility were suggested as explaining declines in HIV prevalence among pregnant women. These do not explain similar declines, from 18% to 6% (1991–96) continuing to under 4% in 2002, among male army recruits nationally (Mugenyi P (1989, 2003)), or age trends. A UNAIDS funded model then attributed the declines almost entirely to mortality (UNAIDS 1999). Although mortality is important, it does not explain the age trends, and declines in the younger groups that reflect recent HIV incidence. It is also very difficult to model such a rapid decline in HIV prevalence without assuming a substantial decline in HIV incidence. The model appeared to use a fixed incubation length (so all people with HIV died a fixed time after infection) rather than the realistic incubation distribution, which accentuated the effect of deaths. Our analysis of HIV data suggests Uganda is at most 2 to 3 years in advance of the comparison countries in terms of epidemic stage (Stoneburner *et al.* 2003). Yet these countries have not shown similar declines in risk behaviours or HIV prevalence up to a decade later. This suggests mortality or stage of the epidemic are not the determining factors, though positive trends are developing in some countries, for example Zambia (Agha S. 2002).

Most recently, articles in *The Lancet* suggested declines in HIV incidence in Uganda since the late 1990s (Mbulaiteye *et al.* 2002) and in recent years (Grulich, Kaldor 2002), and that they are concentrated in urban areas (Parkhurst 2002). It is now clearer that these cohorts probably had higher HIV incidence in the 1980s than the 1990s, given the high ratio of HIV prevalence to incidence at baseline in the early 1990s, and that behaviour change played an important role (Low-Beer 2002, Korenromp *et al.* 2002). The article by Parkhurst raised important points about the political process and the independence of evaluation of data, particularly in official and media sources. However it failed to take into account the wealth of data showing national declines in HIV prevalence, from army cohorts, blood transfusion, rural cohorts, rural population surveys, declines in all sentinel sites (rural or urban) by 2000, as well as behavioural data. Epidemiological understanding was limited in suggesting a decline in HIV incidence has to occur 7 years before a decline in HIV prevalence, though in Uganda HIV incidence does probably decline from the late 1980s or early 1990s.

The basic thesis that there has been intense international political pressure on interpretation of the data is interesting. It may well be that, particularly recently with the global fund, the success in Uganda has actually been underestimated in relation to the internationally packaged and costed interventions like Sexually Transmitted Disease treatment, condoms, media promotion or counselling and testing. Much of this debate appears to occur at the international level. The recent articles in *The Lancet* around the Barcelona 2002 AIDS conference (on the timing and questioning the validity and scale of earlier declines), led to disbelief in Uganda in local newspapers (*Economist* 2002, *New Vision* 2002). The Ugandan Minister of Health commented, '*they don't believe that any country in Africa can do anything positive*' (*New Vision* 2002). He/she emphasised the quality of their own national evaluation and surveillance capacity, which first identified HIV declines in 1993 and the behavioural changes by 1996 (noting a 60%+ decline in sex with non-regular partners in the initial Ugandan report of the KAPB study, Uganda Ministry of Health 1999, p.19). Perhaps the most fitting response came from the Ugandans themselves who, urging their population to take little notice of the international debate, showed that HIV prevalence was now below 5% nationally (*New Vision* 2002).

Secondly, there has been confusion regarding the behavioural determinants. Most influential was the early UNAIDS study, showing condom use increasing and a decline in sexual partners by only 9% in male youths 15–24, 1989–95. This created a novel indicator of non-regular partners, which was not used in other surveys, and greatly underestimated sexual partner reduction (Stoneburner *et al.* 2003, Green E *et al.* 2002). The data from these surveys has only been narrowly circulated (within UNAIDS). Figure 10.3 shows declines in sexual partners in this data, using the standard DHS and WHO indicator, PI-4. It shows declines in casual sex of over 50%, 1989–95, much higher than in other countries using the same indicator. The influence of this study, playing down sexual partner reductions (an HIV prevention focus that if replicated could save several tens of millions of infections in Africa in the 1990s), puts into question the independent role of surveillance in relation to advocacy and policy.

Finally, population cohorts have been established in the south east of Uganda, Rakai and Masaka, since the early 1990s. They have focused on cofactors like sexually transmitted diseases, and have had great prominence in international policy for most of the 1990s. However, together with the Mwanza cohort, they have not emphasised changes in behavioural patterns and HIV dynamics. The focus on cofactors and comparison between sub-groups in a population underplays that HIV declined across the community (in both arms of the study) before in Rakai and Masaka, and after the study in Mwanza. There are also large differences in sexual partners at baseline, 4.5 times more men in Mwanza with 5+ sexual partners (9.6%) compared to the Uganda cohorts of Masaka (2.1%) and Rakai (1.4%), and 1% compared to 0.1% and 0% among women. Despite a decade of analysing these datasets, this has not previously been highlighted (Low-Beer 2002). The data within these studies seems to point to behaviour change and HIV declines across the community, similar to the population surveillance data available since the early 1990s. However it also suggests there is a blind spot in epidemiological approaches when it comes to assessing the determinants of population changes in a key epidemic like Uganda. Despite first and second-generation surveillance, and rigorous controlled population studies involving UNAIDS and major western medical schools over a decade, they failed to highlight a decline by 60% in a primary indicator of HIV risk, like sexual partners in Uganda.

It appears that to learn the lessons from Uganda will require more than a closer evaluation of the HIV prevalence declines and their causes. The challenge requires a shift in the policy and epidemiological approaches to HIV prevention, and much greater independence of surveillance from advocacy and policy. In many ways, the Ugandans led the way in this area, bringing together local epidemiologists and social scientists in the late 1980s in their AIDS control programme. They implemented population HIV and behavioural surveys in 1988, 1989 and 1995 (beyond second-generation surveillance) and produced innovative insight and recommendations from social scientists and epidemiologists into their epidemic as early as 1993[10] (Ankrah *et al.* 1993; Opio A. 1995, Asiimwe-Okiror *et al.* 1996; Konde-Lule 1995).

HIV Lessons for the 21st Century out of Africa

If we asked the village chief on the banks of Lake Victoria what his community did about AIDS, he would stress: communication, behaviour change and care. The story is embellished with tales of mythical women bringing AIDS across the waters[11] in the early 1980s, and epidemiological experts arriving soon afterwards. The fundamentals of their response are not told with an air of great success, rather that they overcame a deadly epidemic. Nevertheless, there are universal lessons in the prevention fundamentals, and how it was built on in public health and politically in Uganda. HIV prevention successes are often attributed to a set of interventions or to a figurehead like Museveni, although he would not assume the credit for AIDS reduction. The first international lesson out of Uganda is that the response preceded and exceeded HIV interventions. Ugandans managed their epidemic, took credit for success, and national and international policy provided support, rather than the other way around. HIV policy and prevention started in these villages, and political and public health interventions built on this.

Local communications were supported by a clear national AIDS communication programme, based on the reality and realism of the epidemic. There were myths to be dispelled, but campaigns supported a communication process underway in Ugandan communities, rather than disrupted it. The key messages were 'loving carefully' and sticking to one partner or 'zero grazing', which seemed to resonate with Ugandans of most ages. It made people think about primary sexual behaviour, the consequences of HIV infection, and avoiding the risks they were able to avoid. The communication programme did not play down or make superficial the reality of AIDS, the risks of sex, or the problems of stigma. Ugandans did not shy away from the harsh realities of the epidemic, with personal rather than symbolic representations of risk, and many personal testimonies from cultural and political figures.

Community level interventions and support networks flourished, in part because of political commitment, but also because they built on the basic communication and behavioural response. This integrated local, religious and cultural leaders and most importantly people with HIV and AIDS, an obvious example being TASO growing from a local to a national initiative. There was always a dual commitment to delivering an intervention alongside mobilising a population level response supporting these activities.

Basic care, and care was very basic at this stage of the epidemic, was a priority; involvement of people with HIV; and acknowledgement of death due to AIDS. This was bolstered by a public health system, which acknowledged and diagnosed AIDS at a local level, often simply based on the symptoms. Unfortunately AIDS case diagnosis lost momentum after 1994, and was replaced by anonymous sentinel site blood testing,[12] which does not have the same connection with local health personnel, communities and families.

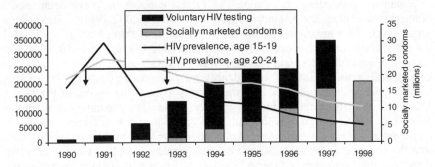

Figure 10.6: Increase in socially marketed condoms and voluntary counseling and testing in relation to declines in HIV prevalence

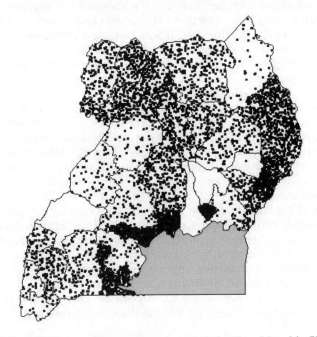

Figure 10.7: AIDS cases diagnosed and reported at local level in Uganda by 1990

Public health surveillance and national attempts to independently evaluate and understand their epidemic from the government down to local communities, were critical. They constituted an intervention in themselves (Okware *et al.* 2001). AIDS reporting at local level meant most communities acknowledged AIDS, and health personnel probably discussed it with individuals and families affected before 1992. Figure 10.7 shows the number of AIDS cases reported in most communities by 1990. Public Health surveillance allowed Ugandans to define and deal with their epidemic nationally, within communities, and individually.

Voluntary counseling and testing (VCT) and condom use have been used in hindsight to explain the Ugandan success (UNAIDS 2002; VCT efficacy study group 2000). They are important, but the time trend shows they were at low levels in the early 1990s, and increased most in the mid to late 1990s (Figure 10.6). In some ways, the demand and uptake of VCT was the result of the communication and behavioural process (85% of Ugandans were ready to be tested, 97% of these wanted to know the results, and 87% their family to know the results, in 1989 before VCT was available), rather than a primary cause. The communication process following AIDS case diagnosis and VCT may be very different. AIDS case diagnosis provides community level knowledge from local health personnel, passing into the community through discussions and formal events like funerals. It relates directly to the continuum of care and support, however basic in most communities.

Secondary communications around VCT provide information to the individual or couple, which is more restricted and problematic. The VCT study group showed evidence of behaviour change, with a 35% reduction in unprotected sexual intercourse with non-primary partners after individuals received VCT (VCT efficacy study group 2000). However, it was much less conclusive with primary partners. With primary partners, providing health information was more successful than VCT after first follow-up for men. They had similar outcomes among women. Even when individuals knew they were HIV+ a majority carried on unprotected sex with their primary partners (62.5% of men, 46.6% of women).

The communication process after VCT has been problematic in these and other studies (Van der Stratten *et al.* 1995; De Zoysa *et al.* 1995), often leading to a break-up of relationships (a significant factor in the reported behaviour change). VCT is an important service, particularly as treatment is improved. However the Ugandan success can not be packaged into an intervention that can be delivered 'scientifically' and with enough money, when it is really grounded in personal and social communications.

The basics of the Uganda success have to be built on with condom provision, treatment for STDs and HIV, and a range of further interventions. However, the fundamental blocks also have to be in place: communication, behaviour change, and care. HIV prevention is integrated by communities that need to maintain a basic continuum from prevention to care, in order to deal with the epidemic and their friends and relatives with AIDS. This is a very different way of integrating HIV prevention from the extensive, costed set of disparate interventions, which claim credit as an international package for large declines in the epidemic (Stover *et al.* 2002, Attaran, Sachs 2001).

While this is an African success, based on behaviour change, it has much in common with other population level successes, in very different contexts. The basic behaviour changes of reducing sexual partners and risk aversion were also present in the gay community in USA in the 1980s, among youth in Zambia, and in Thailand (Winkelstein *et al.* 1987; Agha 2002; Okware *et al.* 2002; Kwesigabo *et al.* 2000; Green 2003; Sittitrai *et al.* 1992). Even in Thailand visits to sex workers declined by over 50% – as important as the publicised increase in condom use when with a sex worker. One must be careful in generalising, there are many differences and barriers in other countries. Nevertheless, there is a basic building block of HIV prevention in the quality of the Ugandan response: based on primary sexual behaviour change, open communications about AIDS and people with AIDS, and community level structures of support, contact and care.

The scale of the decline in HIV in Uganda is equivalent to a 'social vaccine' of 75% efficacy (Stoneburner, Low-Beer 2000). It has been available for ten years, and has greater efficacy than present or planned medical interventions, gels, treatments, even condoms and vaccines. If applied more widely in Africa it would save several tens of millions of infections. We know its components, the basis of HIV prevention in sexual behaviour change, a reduction in non-regular partners – and the continuum from communication, behaviour change to care integrated by communities that have to deal with AIDS and people with AIDS. As our approaches and treatments become ever more sophisticated, we should also highlight the responses of communities in Uganda (the simple symbol of the 'zero grazing' cow) that preceded, exceeded and greatly enhanced other prevention efforts.

The difficult challenge of this section, is that an international response requires mobilisation nationally, among communities and individuals. As the locus of decisions move to the global level (for example with the Global Fund), the most difficult and primary priorities are decided among communities affected by AIDS. Uganda certainly used international support, but it set its own priorities, many of which we need to learn from internationally. As Museveni comments, '*I am not too sure about this global village, but I know I have my village. If I need advice I go to my village, and see what is going on and can talk to people I trust, it is where my politics start*'.[13] There are lessons from these Ugandan communities for HIV prevention, which we must learn globally. We need to look at these real communities, which hold together a continuum of communications, behaviour change and care, developing the most successful social vaccine to come out of the AIDS response globally, and available to us now.

Notes

1   The conversation occurred in 1995 in a village in Rakai district. The village chief, when he heard we were from WHO, made us give real health support insisting on a full medical checkup, before describing in animated detail the arrival of HIV, the response in the community, and the age and sex patterns of impact more accurately than we were able to in a later publication in *Nature Medicine* (validated in part by his insight).

2   The costs may be more related to elements of social capital, as developed in Stoneburner, Low-Beer et al. 2001. Social capital is mobilised rather than delivered as a pure investment, but if there is not a correct mix of these terms of capital, investments in HIV prevention can dramatically underperform.

3   The first evidence of declining HIV prevalence was from 6 sentinel sites in 1993, two in Kampala and four in other urban areas. These were reported by the Ugandan AIDS Control Program to WHO immediately. Surprisingly, reported AIDS cases had already stabilised and were starting to decline (in part due to the decreased effort in AIDS reporting). However a full understanding of HIV dynamics (incidence, prevalence and mortality) is needed to relate trends in AIDS, HIV incidence and prevalence, and it does not follow as argued later (UNAIDS 1999; Parkhurst 2002) that AIDS and HIV prevalence declines occur 7 years after HIV incidence declines.

4   Replacement donors are less affected by selection bias, as they are generally related to the patient on the basis of need rather than selected in terms of risk behaviours.

5   Breaking this down by marriage status: among unmarried men, 38% stopped all sex, 17% stuck to one partner, and 20% started using condoms. Among married men 65% stuck to one partner, 1% stopped all sex, and 8% started using condoms. In all these situations, 55–65% of people reported changes to primary sexual behaviours (reducing partners or stopping all sex, with a different balance depending on marital status). This conforms with the Ugandan AIDS policy which focused on delaying sex among youth and sticking to one partner among adults, and despite being largely ignored as a best practice has had much success.

6   A non-regular partner follows the PI-4 indicator developed by WHO GPA (see Stoneburner et al. 2003 for the discussion).

7   Which the Director General of Health in Uganda (referring to *The Lancet*) urged the Ugandan population to ignore as much as possible (New Vision 2002).

8   Although the Human Sciences Research Council report found that only 1.7 percent of South Africans believed this to be true. *Nelson Mandela/HSRC Study of HIV/AIDS South African National HIV Prevalence, Behavioural Risks and Mass Media Household Survey 2002*, Human Sciences Research Council, Cape Town 2002, Page 82.

9   'Live and let live', the theme for AIDS day 2002, was launched in South Africa with an MTV concert, and as it is a slightly MTV slogan, the danger is that such media and slogan based approaches can drain away the force from the real experiences and responses to the AIDS epidemic, and we no longer experience or communicate about AIDS in the primary way that may change behaviour. 'Talking about it' can prevent really talking about it; as there is a quality as well as quantity to communications (Philip Lutaaya communicates AIDS very differently than fashionable US rap groups). I am exaggerating slightly, in response to what was a popular music concert.

10 Ugandan social scientists were teamed with epidemiologist from November 1986, sitting on the advisory National Committee for the Prevention of AIDS (NCPA) and on its various committees, including the clinical research subcommittee.

11 Seen as coming from an island in Lake Victoria on the border with Tanzania: outside the control of the government, it became a locus for smuggling and trade between the two countries.

12 A special session on AIDS surveillance at the Vancouver International AIDS conference in 1996 sealed the fate of AIDS case surveillance. It stressed its cost (its main component was a piece of paper with boxes to tick at the health personnel's end, and a computer to store and analyse the data centrally); inaccuracy of the data (though like much surveillance data it was seldom analysed in detail); and delay in reflecting changes in HIV incidence (in fact it is the measure closest linked to HIV incidence in analysis through a fixed incubation period, thus allowing back calculation). AIDS case reporting had been introduced partly to provide data, but also to catalyse political behaviour change, so that each country would record and admit that they had at least one real, AIDS case, and have to respond. It was overlooked that as it expanded, AIDS case reporting may have a similar impact on behaviour change and the reality of the epidemic at district, local and community level.

13   Quoted in a speech by Museveni at the International Conference on Racism, Durban, South Africa.

References

Agha S. (2002) 'Declines in casual sex in Lusaka, Zambia: 1996–1999', *AIDS* **16**, 291–293.

Ankrah E., Asingwiire N., Wangalwa S., Misanya-Gessa A. (1993) 'AIDS in Uganda: Analysis of the Social Dimensions of the Epidemic: Uganda Population AIDS KABP 1988–89' (Makerere University, Kampala Uganda).

Asiimwe-Okiror G., Musinguzi J., Opio A., Tembo G., Biryahwaho B. *et al.* (1995) 'Declining HIV prevalence in women attending ANC sentinel surveillance sites, Uganda, 1989–1995' IX International Conference on AIDS and STDs in Africa, Kampala, Uganda.

Asiimwe-Okiror G. *et al.* (1996) 'Declines in HIV prevalence in Uganda pregnant women and its relationship to HIV incidence and risk reduction', XI International Conference on AIDS; **MoC905**.

Asiimwe-Okiror G., Opio A., Musinguzi J., Madraa E., Tembo G., Carael M. (1997) 'Change in sexual behaviour and decline in HIV infection among young pregnant women in urban Uganda' *AIDS* **11**, 1757–1763.

Attaran A, Sachs J. (2001) 'Defining and refining international donor support for combating the AIDS pandemic', *The Lancet* **357**, 57–61.

Barnett T., Blaikie P. (1992) *AIDS in Africa: its present and future impact*, London, Belhaven.

Berkley S., Okware S, Naamara W (1989) 'Surveillance of AIDS in Uganda', *AIDS* **3**, 79–85.

Brookes H., Low-Beer D (2003), *HSRC study into communication patterns around HIV and behaviours in South Africa*, preliminary material (funded by Health Systems Trust and Cambridge University).

Brown T, Sittitrai W, Vanichseni S, Thisyakorn U (1994) 'The recent epidemiology of HIV and AIDS in Thailand', *AIDS* **8** (suppl 2), S131–S141.

De Zoysa I, Phillips KA, Kamenga MC *et al.* (1995) 'Role of HIV counseling and testing in changing risk behaviour in developing countries' *AIDS* **9** (suppl A), S95–101.

Economist (2002) 'AIDS in Uganda: was the miracle faked ?', August 15th.

Fylkesnes K. *et al.* (2001) 'Declining HIV prevalence and risk behaviours in Zambia: evidence from surveillance and population-based surveys' *AIDS* **15**, 907–916.

Green E. *et al.* (2002) *What happened in Uganda ?*, USAID case study paper.

Green E. (2003) *Rethinking AIDS Prevention*, Westport, Praeger Press, Greenwood Publishers (*in the press*).

Grulich AE, Kaldor JM (2002) 'Evidence of success in HIV prevention in Africa' *The Lancet* 2002; **360**: 3–4.

Human Sciences Research Council (2002) *Nelson Mandela/HSRC Study of HIV/AIDS South African National HIV Prevalence, Behavioural Risks and Mass Media Household Survey*, HSRC, Cape Town.

Hunter S (1990) 'Orphans as a window on the AIDS epidemic in sub-Saharan Africa: initial results and implications of a study in Uganda', *Social Science and Medicine* **31**, 681–90.

Kaleeba N., Kadowe J, Lalinaki D Williams G (2000) *Open Secret, People facing up to HIV and AIDS in Uganda*, Strategies for Hope Series No. 15, ACTIONAID, London.

Kelly K. (2000) *Communicating for Action, Summary of Findings of Sentinel Site Monitoring and Evaluation Project*, Department of Health, South Africa.

Kengeya-Kayondo J.F., Carpenter L.M., Kintu P.M., Nabaitu J., Pool R., Whitworth J. (1999) 'Risk perception and HIV-1 prevalence in 15000 adults in rural south-west Uganda' *AIDS* **13**, 2295–2302.

Kilian A., Gregson S., Ndyanabangi B., Walusaga K., Kipp W. *et al.* (1999) 'Reductions in risk behaviour provide the most consistent explanation for declining HIV-1 prevalence in Uganda' *AIDS* **13**, 391–398.

Konde-Lule J.K. (1995) 'The declining HIV serprevalence in Uganda: what evidence ?' *Health Trans Rev* **5**, 27–33.

Konde- Lule J.K. (1993) 'The social and demographic impact of AIDS in a rural Ugandan community: results of a 5 year follow-up study, 1987–92', Population Association of Uganda Annual Conference, Kampala, Uganda.

Korenromp E., Bakker R., de Vlas S. *et al.* (2002) 'HIV dynamics and behaviour change as determinants of the impact of sexually transmitted disease treatment on HIV transmission in the context of the Rakai trial', *AIDS* **16**, 2209–2218.

Kwesigabo, G., *et al.* (2000) 'Monitoring of HIV-1 infection prevalence and trends in the general population using pregnant women as a sentinel population: 9 years experience from the Kagera region of Tanzania', *AIDS* **23**, 410–417.

Kyaddondo D., Rwabukwali C., Achom M., Nakabilito C. (2000), Proceedings of XIII International Conference on AIDS, Durban, South Africa, 9–14th July, **MoPeD2524**.

Low-Beer D, Stoneburner R (2001) 'In Search of the Magic Bullet: evaluating and replicating prevention program', Leadership Forum on HIV prevention, Kaiser Family Health Foundation, Gates Foundation, New York (accessible from kff.org).

Low-Beer D, Stoneburner RL, Mukulu A (1997) 'Empirical evidence for the severe but localized impact of AIDS on population structure', *Nature Medicine* **3(5)**, 553–557.

Low-Beer D, Stoneburner RL (1997) 'A new age and sex structure HIV model: Features and applications', *Bulletin of the WHO* **75(3)**, 213–221.

Low-Beer D, Stoneburner RL, Mertens T, Burton A, Berkeley S (1997) 'The Global Burden of AIDS' in *The Global Burden of Disease*, World Bank/WHO, Cambridge, USA.

Low-Beer D, Stoneburner RL. (2002) 'Evidence of distinctive communication channels related to population level behaviour changes and HIV prevalence declines in Uganda', XIV International Conference on AIDS; **WePeD6263**.

Low-Beer D (2002) 'HIV incidence and prevalence trends in Uganda', Low-Beer D, *The Lancet* 360 (9347).

Low-Beer D., Stoneburner R.L., Whiteside A.,Barnett T. (2000) Proceedings of XIII International Conference on AIDS, Durban, South Africa, 9–14th July, **ThPeD5787**.

Macro International (1996) *Uganda Demographic and Health Survey 1995*, Calverton, MD, USA.

Mason C, Markowity L, Kitsiripornchai S, Jugsudee A, Sirisopana N, Torugsa K, Carr J, Michael R, Nitayaphan S, McNeil J (1995) 'Declining prevalence of HIV-1 infection in young Thai men', *AIDS* **9**, 1061–1065.

Mastro T, Limpakarnjanarat K (1995) 'Condom use in Thailand: how much is it slowing the HIV/AIDS epidemic ?', *AIDS* **9**, 523–525.

Mbulaiteye SM, Mahe C, Whitworth JAG *et al.* (2002) 'Declining HIV-1 incidence and associated prevalence over 10 years in a rural population in south-west Uganda: a cohort study' *The Lancet* **360**: 41–46.

Moodie R., Katahoire A, Kaharuza F, Balikowa D, Busuulwa J, Barton T (1991) *An evaluation study of Uganda AIDS control programme's information education and communication activities*, Uganda Ministry of Health AIDS Control Programme, and WHO GPA, July-December 1991.

Mugenyi P (1989, 2003), unpublished data.

Mulder D., Nunn A., Kamali A., Kengeya-Kayondo (1995) 'Decreasing HIV-1 seroprevalence in young adults in a rural Ugandan cohort', *British Medical Journal* **311**, 833–6.

New Vision (2002) 'Ignore negative HIV/AIDS campaign – Omaswe (Director General of Health)', Saturday 13th July.

New Vision (2002) 'AIDS infection rate down to 5%', Thursday 24th October.

Okware S, Opio A, Musinguzi J, Waibale P (2002) 'Fighting HIV/AIDS: Is success possible?' *Bulletin of the World Health Organisation* **79**, 1113–1120.

Opio A (1995) 'Behaviour change? Results of a population survey in Uganda', IX International Conference on AIDS and STDs in Africa, Kampala, Uganda. Supplementary session on 'Declining HIV prevalence'.

Parkhurst J. (2002) 'The Uganda success story ? Evidence and claims of HIV-1 prevention', *The Lancet* **360**:78.

Parkhurst J. (2001) 'The crisis of AIDS and the politics of response: the case of Uganda', *International Relations* **15**, 69–87.

Rojanapithayakorn W, Hanenberg R (1996) 'The 100% condom program in Thailand', *AIDS* **10**, 1–7.

Schwartlander B, Stover J, Walker N *et al.* (2001) 'Resource needs for HIV/AIDS', *Science* **292**, 2434–2436.

Serwadda D, Mugerwa R, Sewankambo N *et al.* (1985) 'Slim disease: a new disease in Uganda and its association with HTLV-III infection', *The Lancet* **2**, 849–852.

Shuey D., Babishangire B, Omiat S, Bagarukayo H (1999) 'Increased sexual abstinence among in-school health education in Soroti district, Uganda', *Health Education Research* **14(3)**, 411–419.

Sittitrai W., Phanaphak P., Barry J., Bronw T. (1992) 'A survey of Thai sexual behaviour and risk of HIV infection', *International Journal of AIDS and STDs* **5**, 377–388.

Soderlund N, Lavis J, Broomberg J, Mills A (1993) 'The costs of HIV prevention strategies in developing countries', *Bulletin of the WHO* **71(5)**, 595–604.

Stoneburner R, Low-Beer D, Barnett T, Whiteside A (2002) 'Enhancing HIV prevention in Africa: investigating the role of social cohesion on knowledge diffusion and behaviour change in Uganda', Presentation at the World Bank, October 2000.

Stoneburner R, Carballo M, Bernstein R, Saidel T (1998) 'Simulation of HIV incidence dynamics in the Rakai population-based cohort, Uganda' *AIDS* **12(2)**: 226–228.

Stoneburner R, Low-Beer D, Green E (2003) 'Population level HIV declines and behavioural risk avoidance in Uganda: evidence for a largely successful (and economical) public health prevention program – but why doesn't it sell ?' (submitted for publication).

Stoneburner RL, Low-Beer D, Tembo GS, Mertens TE, Asiimwe-Okiror G (1996) 'Human immunodeficiency virus infection dynamics in East Africa deduced from surveillance' *American Journal Epidemiology* 1996; **12**: 435–49.

Stoneburner R.L., Low-Beer D. (2000) 'Elements of sexual behaviour change associated with HIV prevalence declines in Uganda: comparative analyses of HIV and behavioural data in Uganda, Kenya, Malawi and Zambia' Proceedings of XIII International Conference on AIDS, Durban, South Africa, 9–14th July 2000, **ThOrC721**.

Stoneburner R., Carballo M (1997) 'An assessment of emerging patterns of HIV incidence in Uganda and other East African countries', Family Health International AIDS Control and Prevention Project, Arlington, Virginia.

Stover J., Walker N., Garnett G. et al (2002) 'Can we reverse the HIV/AIDS pandemic with an expanded response ?', *The Lancet* **360**, 73–77.

Uganda AIDS Commission (1997) *Inventory of agencies in HIV/AIDS related activities in Uganda.*

Uganda AIDS Commission (2001) *Status and impact of HIV/AIDS in Uganda.*

Uganda Ministry of Health (1995) *Knowledge, attitude, behaviour and practice study*, Kampala, Ministry of Health AIDS Control Programme.

Uganda Ministry of Health (1999) *An overview of HIV/AIDS in Uganda*, Entebbe, Uganda.

Uganda Ministry of Health (1999), *HIV/AIDS Surveillance Report*, Entebbe, Uganda.

Uganda Ministry of Health (2000) *HIV/AIDS situational summary Report*, Entebbe, Uganda.

UNAIDS (1998) *Case study: A measure of success in Uganda*, UNAIDS, Geneva, Switzerland.

UNAIDS (1999) *Best Practice Collection: Trends in HIV incidence and prevalence: natural course of the epidemic or results of behavioural change?*, UNAIDS, Geneva, Switzerland.

UNAIDS (2002), *AIDS epidemic update* (UNAIDS, Geneva, December 2002).

Van der Stratten A, King R, Grinstead O, Serufilira A, Allen S. (1995) 'Couple communication, sexual coercion, and HIV risk reduction in Kigali, Rwanda,' *AIDS* **9**, 935–44.

Van Griensven G, de Vroome E, Goudsmit J, Coutinho R (1989) 'Changes in sexual behaviour and the fall in incidence of HIV infection among homosexual men', *British Medical Journal* **298**, 218–221.

VCT efficacy study group (2000) 'Efficacy of VCT in individuals and couples in Kenya, Tanzania and Trinidad: a randomized trial', *The Lancet* **356**, 103–112.

Wawer MJ., Serwadda D., Gray RH., Sewankambo NK., Li C., Nalugoda F., Lutalo T, Konde-Lule JK. (1997) 'Trends in HIV-1 prevalence may not reflect trends in incidence in mature epidemics: data from the Rakai population-based cohort, Uganda', *AIDS* **11**, 1023–1030.

Winkelstein W, Samual M, Padian N, Wiley J, Lang W, Anderson R, Levy J (1987) 'The San Francisco men's health study: reduction in HIV transmission among homosexual/bisexual men 1982–86', *American Journal of Public Health* **77**, 685–689.

World Health Organisation (1991) *The AIDS epidemic and its demographic consequences: Proceedings of the UN/WHO workshop on modeling the demographic impact of the AIDS epidemic in pattern II countries*, United Nations ST/ESA/SER.A/119.

World Health Organisation (1993), *Internal memo on stabilization in HIV/AIDS and possible decline in HIV incidence in the 1980s*, Stoneburner R., Low-Beer D – initial report from Uganda on declines in HIV prevalence in 6 sentinel sites.

Chapter 11

The Impact of HIV/AIDS on Democracy in Southern Africa: What Do We Know, What Do We Need to Know, and Why?

Robert Mattes and Ryann Manning

From Botswana to Zimbabwe, the present state of democratic politics across Southern Africa surely leaves much to be desired. Yet as imperfect as it may be, few people would wish to go backwards. Too many people remember what life was like under the former colonial, settler, one party or military regimes that this region has endured. But the persistence of democracy, as imperfect as it may be, cannot be taken for granted. While HIV/AIDS kills people, damages households, and strains national economies, there are many reasons to believe it may also threaten the existence of democratic government. The purpose of this chapter is to sketch out the potential challenges that the HIV/AIDS pandemic may pose to southern Africa's young and fragile democracies, assess the state of our knowledge about that threat, and identify priority areas for future research: that is, those areas where the potential threat to democracy is greatest but where our knowledge is lowest.

Social scientists are only beginning to understand the range of potential impacts that the HIV/AIDS pandemic may have on Southern African societies. Researchers are beginning to systematize propositions and compile evidence about the demographic, economic and social impacts of the disease on infected people, their households and communities, national populations and national economies (Hamoudi and Sachs 2001). They have only recently begun to develop propositions about the impacts of HIV/AIDS on the broader processes of governance (Parker et al. 2000; Cheek 2001; Heinecken 2001; Fourie and Schonteich 2001). However, the implications of the pandemic for the survival and consolidation of democratic government, in particular, remain largely unexamined. While there is a growing, though unorganized, body of theoretically informed speculation about the impact of HIV/AIDS, there is virtually no body of substantive evidence.

But why a specific research focus on the impacts of HIV/AIDS on democracy? Would not any disease of this scope – for example malaria, which currently kills more people than AIDS – threaten the stability of any political regime? We believe, the answer is 'no.' HIV/AIDS is not just any pandemic. Its primarily sexual mode of transmission allows it to spread quickly and silently throughout a population. The relatively long time span between HIV infection and death due to AIDS complications imposes a virtual death sentence on significant portions of a population. And its sexual mode of transmission brings a range of social stigma that adds to the suffering of its victims.

But if HIV/AIDS has unique characteristics, is it not true that we should seek to understand the threat it would pose to the security and governance of any state? Again, the answer is 'no.' Democracy is not just any regime. Researchers should be especially interested in the plight of democracy, as opposed to other types of political regimes. Over the past two centuries, democracy has come to enjoy a privileged normative status as *the* preferred type of political regime because it uniquely recognizes the moral agency and dignity of human beings, and thus their right to determine their individual and collective fates (Sen, 1999). Yet it is precisely this moral agency and human dignity that may be most severely challenged by HIV/AIDS, an argument that will be fleshed out more fully below. But while they may be normatively privileged, democracies are fragile and more difficult to sustain than non-democratic regimes (Przeworski et al. 2000). Of the 71 democracies that were established by or after 1950, 33 had died by 1990, lasting an average of just 5.1 years (compared to the 9.4 years of dictatorships that were born after 1950 but died prior to 1990). The 38 democracies surviving after 1990 had an average life span of 13 years (compared to 26.2 years for surviving dictatorships).

In Southern Africa, the 1990s saw eight countries achieve a successful transition from an authoritarian regime to a founding democratic election, joining the two existing multi-party systems in Botswana and Zimbabwe. Yet many of these democratization processes are incomplete and some have even undergone reversals. Even where states have implemented regular elections and secured the conditions for political competition, pluralism, and the protection of human rights, democracy remains far from consolidated.

As defined by Larry Diamond (1999), continental Southern Africa presently contains three emerging 'liberal democracies' (countries that combine genuine political competition with a full range of political freedoms and civil rights). Based on their ratings of political and civil rights, South Africa, Botswana, and Namibia are all labelled by Freedom House as 'free', thus falling into this category. Yet even these countries run the risk of eventually degenerating into what Diamond has called 'semi' democracies because the existence of single dominant political parties may over time limit effective competition. The region also contains four functioning 'electoral democracies': that is they combine genuine political competition with an insufficient protection of rights. Malawi, Tanzania, Mozambique and Lesotho are rated as 'partly free' by Freedom House, thus falling into this category. Finally, for our purposes, Southern Africa has two of what Diamond (1996) calls 'pseudo' democracies or what Richard Joseph (1998) calls 'virtual' democracies. These countries hold elections and allow opposition parties, but competition, pluralism and rights of association, speech and media are actively constrained by the state. Zambia and Zimbabwe are rated as 'partly free' by Freedom House but score sufficiently badly on political rights that they fall into the 'pseudo-democracy' category. An over time analysis of the Freedom House ratings shows retrograde trends in political freedom and civil liberties in Zimbabwe, but also Malawi (Karatnycky 2002).

Thus, even without the presence of HIV/AIDS, the future of democracy in the region is far from certain. None of Southern Africa's democracies can yet be considered to be consolidated: defined here as meaning little or no probability of breakdown or reversal to some authoritarian regime. We believe that it is possible that HIV/AIDS not only makes the probability of consolidation even more remote, it may even heighten the possibility of breakdown and reversal. This chapter is an attempt to systematize the various arguments about why this may be so, and to identify how much we actually know.

HIV/AIDS and Democracy: A Brief Overview

Social scientists have identified three key factors crucial to sustaining and consolidating democratic rule. The first factor has to do with *economics*. While wealthier countries are no more likely than poorer ones to have transited from authoritarian to democratic rule, wealthier countries are far more likely to maintain democratic rule. Poor countries can, however, increase the prospects of democratic endurance if their economies grow steadily, and if they reduce inequalities (Przeworski et al. 2000).

The second factor has to do with *political institutions*. That is, sustainable democracies require a professional civil service and strong, viable and autonomous courts, legislatures, executives and electoral systems at national and local levels. The 'institutionalization' of such bodies and processes requires skilled personnel with sufficient resources, developing specialized areas of expertise, and developing and following clear and predictable rules and procedures. As such the rules of democratic governance become routinized and independent of the forces of clientelism, corruption or the whims of the ruling political party.

The third factor has to do with the *attitudes* of rulers and citizens. Put simply, democracies require democrats. Democracy can only be considered consolidated if it has been legitimated. That is, all relevant elites and the overwhelming majority of citizens must see democracy as 'the only game in town' (Linz and Stepan 1996).

Reaching the appropriate thresholds across each of these factors will be difficult for Southern Africa's nascent democracies even under normal circumstances. However, across each factor, the HIV/AIDS pandemic threatens to make consolidation even more difficult, if not completely unobtainable. It may threaten the economic growth that seems so vital to sustaining democracy in low to medium income countries. It may threaten the processes of political institutionalization that are so vital to young democracies. Finally, the burden, illness and death that the pandemic places on individuals and households may be so great that the value of popular self government pales in existence to mere survival.

The Economic Impact of HIV/AIDS on Democracy

Declining Growth and Increasing Inequality

Ever since the pioneering work of Seymour Martin Lipset (1959) social scientists have been aware of the strong correlation between wealth and democracy. The most recent work by Adam Przeworski and his colleagues (2000) has given us the clearest specification of the linkages between economic development and democratic endurance. Wealthy democracies do not die. The wealthiest democracy to ever revert to authoritarian rule was Argentina, in 1974, with a GNP per capita of $6,055.

Under that threshold, the death rate of democratic systems increases monotonically as national wealth declines. While those with a GNP per capita between $6,001 and $7,000 have a probability of reversion in any single year of 0.0080 (or an average life expectancy of 125 years), those with a GNP per capita of $1,000 or less have a probability of reversion of 0.1216 (or an average life expectancy of around just 8 years).

Given these findings, none of Southern Africa's multiparty systems could be given a very long 'life expectancy.' Botswana and South Africa are the region's wealthiest countries, yet all other things being equal, their GNP per capita would suggest a democratic life expectancy of just thirty six years. Democracies with Namibia's level of wealth have lasted, on average, just eighteen years. The national wealth of the rest of the region's multiparty systems would have average endurance of just eight years.

Table 11.1: National wealth and life expectancies of continental Southern African democracies

Country	GNP Per Capita (1999)	Rank (1999)	Probability of Democratic Breakdown	Average Life Expectancy
Botswana	3240	84	0.0278	**36.0**
South Africa	3160	86		
Namibia	1890	105	0.0556	**18.0**
Lesotho	550	152	0.1216	**8.2**
Zimbabwe	520	154		
Zambia	320	176		
Tanzania	240	190		
Mozambique	230	193		
Malawi	190	199		

Source: World Bank (2000) and Przeworksi et al. (2000)

But Przeworski et al. (2000) also demonstrate that poor countries can sustain democratic rule if they grow and reduce inequalities, India being the most prominent example. Where a democracy's economy has contracted, its probability of extinction is 0.05 (around 1 in 20), but when incomes are growing, it decreases to 0.015 (or 1 in 66). If growth is 5% or higher, the probability of reversal declines even further to 0.013 (or 1 in 77). The odds of a democratic reversal fall to just 1 in 135 if its economy grows for three or more consecutive years.

However, the opposite is also true. In the words of Diamond and Linz (1989) 'economic crisis represents one of the most common threats to democratic stability.' Where incomes have contracted in the preceding year, a democracy is three times as likely to break down in the following year compared to a democracy that experienced growth (1 in 20 versus 1 in 66, respectively). When incomes decline for two or more consecutive years, the chances of democratic breakdown rise to 1 in 13. Of the 39 'democratic deaths' observed between 1950 and 1990, 28 were accompanied by a fall in per capita income in either one or two years preceding the end of democratic rule (Przeworski et al. 2000).

Democracies are more sensitive to economic stagnation and crisis than authoritarian regimes, and poorer democracies are more sensitive than richer ones. Poorer democracies, those with per capita GNP under $2,000, broke down in approximately one out of every ten occasions where incomes had declined in the previous year (12 times of 116 country years). Middle income democracies, those between $2,000 and $5,000, fell approximately one out of every 16 times that incomes declined (17 out of 113 country years). As stated earlier, above $6,055 (Argentina, 1974), no democracy has ever died (Przeworski et al. 2000). None of this bodes well for Southern Africa's low to lower middle income democracies. As of 1998–1999, growth was generally low with only one country (Mozambique, 6.6 percent) above the 5 percent threshold. Positive growth rates were also recorded in Malawi (4.4), Tanzania (3.1), Botswana (3.0), Namibia (0.6) and Zambia (0.4). However per capita income declined in Lesotho (-3.0 percent), Zimbabwe (-1.8 percent) and South Africa (-0.9) (World-Bank 2000).

Finally, Przeworski et al. have found that inequality reduction is also an important factor in poorer democracies. While the available data is limited, they found that out of 358 country years where a democracy had a GINI Index below the international mean (.35), there was only one reversal. However, of the 379 occasions where a democracy had a GINI index above .35, five democracies broke down. Democracies are less stable when the income share of the bottom 40 percent declines (Przeworski et al. 2000).

While data is incomplete, inequality (as measured by the GINI Index) is extremely high in at least three countries in the region: South Africa (59.3), Zimbabwe (56.8) and Lesotho (56.0). But it is still above the international mean in three other countries: Zambia (49.8), Mozambique (39.6) and Tanzania (38.2) (World-Bank 2000). And indications are that income inequality is increasing in South Africa where income of the bottom two-fifths has declined since 1994 (Whiteford and Seventer 1999).

Again, this is not encouraging news. It becomes even more depressing once one considers that the HIV/AIDS pandemic is widely expected to limit growth, increase inequality and reduce national wealth across the region. Because HIV infection is spread predominantly through sexual activity, AIDS related illness and death occurs disproportionately amongst younger, more mobile, economically active people. This is expected to reduce household earnings and personal savings, as well as human capital and the size and skills of future work forces. Firms are expected to face higher wage bills due to increased employer contributions to pension, life and medical benefits, as well as higher training and replacement costs. Productivity is expected to decrease due to a decreased skills base, lower worker morale, increased absenteeism and the necessity of constantly replacing skills.

Based on these assumptions, economists project an average reduction in per capita income growth of between 1 and 1.5 percentage points per annum for the entire sub-Saharan sub-continent (Over 1992). For South Africa, studies forecast declines between 0.2 to 0.3 percentage points until 2005 and between 0.3 and 0.4

points thereafter (Quattek and Fourie 2000). In cumulative terms, growth would be 0.5 points lower in year two of the projection and 2.6 points lower by year eleven (Arndt and Lewis, in Parket et al. 2000: 17; and Parker et al. 2000: 10–12). However, the impact on overall per capita income, is less clear. While AIDS is expected to slow income growth, it will also slow population growth. *If* populations fall faster than national incomes, GDP per capita income may actually *increase* (Nattrass 2002).

Economists also expect the pandemic to increase inequality, at least in South Africa. While relatively skilled workers may benefit from greater demand and higher wages for their labor, a larger supply of goods produced for their niche market, and a possibly longer life span due to access to anti-retroviral drugs provided by their firms, the relatively unskilled and unemployed will face declining income, less and more expensive goods produced for them, and greater morbidity and mortality. While total GDP shrinks, the skilled may enjoy an increasing share (Nattrass 2002).

However, these are all *projections* based more on *assumptions* about how people, firms and governments will react to HIV/AIDS than actual evidence. But Nicoli Nattrass (2002) has demonstrated how projections may vary in important ways depending upon the assumptions underlying the model. Take for example, assumptions about the how the costs of HIV infections affect firms' decisions on investment, projection, pricing and hiring. The costs of anti-retrovirals has plummeted so much that firms may soon be able to share costs with workers and provide access to medication, at least to their highly skilled personnel. If this happens, existing models will have over-estimated effects on the workforce. At an even more fundamental level, economist have assumed that firms have the necessary basic information to calculate the labour costs of AIDS and its impact on their profits, and that they do in fact perform such calculations. However, recent research in South Africa suggests that firms either have not collected or used existing information and thus have only the vaguest sense of indirect costs. Moreover, direct costs may comprise less than 5 percent of the total wage bill, mostly because most firms provide so few pension and medical benefits to unskilled workers in the first place, but also because many employees choose to leave their job once they discover they are HIV positive (Nattrass 2002; Kennedy 2002). In fact, a DFID sponsored survey of South African firms found that most firms expected either a moderate (53 percent) or little or no (38 percent) impact on their business (Beresford 2002a).

Nattrass (2002) also notes that existing projections fail to 'trace through' the 'second order' impacts that occur after people, firms and governments respond to the 'first order' impact of AIDS on things like consumption, investment, savings and the size of the labor force. These are things that we simply do not know, but need to find out. Will firms respond to higher medical costs by replacing workers with machines, raising costs, reducing profits or sharing costs with workers? Will governments increase health spending, and if so will it come at expense of other items, and if so which ones? Will they finance this through increased taxes or increased borrowing? However, while these are necessarily future-oriented questions, there is almost certainly enough evidence provided by current and recent behavior across the region to provide social scientists with firmer guidance to what is likely to happen in the future. The fact that the pandemic has a different age, severity and curve in each country across the region, and even in differing provinces and regions within countries, provides fertile ground for cross sectional and some limited longitudinal research.

On a different point, Alex de Waal (2002) observes that existing models are linear, in that they model the particular economic impacts of a range of factors and then sum them. However, he argues that we need to understand development as a *process*, modeling the interactions amongst these effects, as well as second order reactions to first order effects. Dynamics may accelerate if they reach critical thresholds or co-occur in specific combinations. This may prove to be more difficult to assess, at least at present, since the pandemic is still so young. However, it does shift our attention to longitudinal analysis in countries where the disease is oldest, such as Zambia and Zimbabwe.

Perhaps more fundamentally, De Waal (2002) notes that no models attempt to forecast the way in which sharply decreased adult longevity may reshape economic rationality and thus the decisions of firms, household and individuals. Virtually all economics, rooted firmly in the logic of developed economies, is based on the principle that individuals rationally consider future expectations, which in many ways is based on one's anticipated life span. He argues that over the past century, most people in developed societies – once they have reached their teens – have been able to expect to live into their 70s. But under conditions of a highly uncertain adult life span, the rationale to invest time and resources in one's own education or training, or to save and invest becomes questionable. As he puts it: 'Why save for a future that does not exist?' 'Just as a doubling of longevity would entail major structural transformations of developed economies, a halving of adult lifespan in much of sub-Saharan entails a structural change in the region's economies that make it impossible for it to follow existing models for economic development' (De Waal 2002: 9). In contrast to the assumptions of *homo economicus*, De Waal (2002) argues that people's emphases turns to spending and consuming, to liquidating assets to pay for health care, but also to enjoy one's short life span.

If true, this would seem to have fundamentally important implications, not only for micro-economic behavior but also for citizenship behavior, as we discuss below. We may be able to begin to assess the relationship of adult longevity and individual behavior in a few different ways. We could use cross-national survey data, such as the Afrobarometer or the World Values Study, to examine the link between national rates of life expectancy and individual attitudes and behavior. But we can also imagine innovative scholars approaching this question through innovative experimental designs that observe subjects' behavior under different life-prospect scenarios.

Budgets and Taxes: Increased Demands and Decreased Supply

Existing levels of HIV infection mean that Southern African societies will experience drastically increased levels of severe illness and increasing demands for access to government clinics, medical stocks and available hospital beds that threatens to push the region's limited public health systems to, and past their limits. Thus, as governments increase health spending to catch up with the increasing demand for medicine and hospital beds, a growing wage bill as they struggle to replace dying nurses and doctors from an increasingly scarce labor pool, and as they attempt to alleviate the burden of families caring for orphans, public spending on HIV/AIDS related matters may come to consume the entire health budget and, or increase the overall national budget.

Evidence, albeit often anecdotal and episodic, is beginning to accumulate that suggests these impacts are already occurring. In South Africa, recent government reports have admitted that substantial increases in AIDS patients are steadily displacing other patients (Ensor 2001). In its industrial heartland, Gauteng province, Soweto's Chris Hani Baragwanath Hospital, the country's largest, has seen a 500 percent increase in HIV patients since 1996. One half of all beds in the province's public hospitals are occupied by AIDS patients (Cheek 2001). Yet the country's health system is unable to meet these increased demands. A 2002 survey of AIDS affected households in four South African provinces found that between 40 to 60 percent of people living with AIDS had never been admitted to a hospital (Beresord 2002b). Just sixteen percent of households were able to obtain a state grant, even though they were eligible (Clarke 2002). Current government estimates see the number of orphans rising from the current 150,000 to 2,000,000 by 2010, far outstripping the existing welfare system (*Business Day*, 2001).

While much of this is certainly a problem of institutional capacity, we focus here on what these demands entail for national budgets in the region's multi-party systems. Economic policy makers will come under increasing pressure to larger and larger shares of the national budget to public health and welfare for AIDS orphans and the families or institutions who care for them. Significant shifts have already occurred. By 1997, public health spending on AIDS exceeded 2.5 percent of GDP in seven of 16 sampled African countries, an extremely high proportion since total health spending accounted for only 3 to 5 percent of GDP in these same countries (Heinecken, 2001: and Cheek 2001). As of 1998, 12 percent of South Africa's national budget went to health, but 21 percent of provincial budgets went specifically to HIV/AIDS spending (*Budget Watch* 2001a; *Budget Watch* 2002b). The total proportion of the South African government's budget devoted to AIDS will increase by 22 percent (1.4 billion to 1.8 billion) just between 2003 and 2004 (Proceedings 2002). Yet recent government reports admit that even with current levels of real growth in future health budgets the system would not be able to keep pace with increased demand for services (Ensor, 2001).

Zambia's AIDS spending rose from $1.7 million in 1990 to $12.9 by 1995, and is expected to rise to $21 million by 2005 (Cheek 2001). Zimbabwe currently spends almost half of its health budget on treating AIDS patients (Heinecken 2001), a figure expected to rise to almost two-thirds by 2005 (Cheek 2001). In Malawi, Grace Hiwa, a senior government health official, has publicly worried that one half of their health budget would soon have to be devoted to treating AIDS patients (cited in Cheek 2001: 21). Regardless of whether or not they decide to go down the path of providing drugs that reduce mother-to-child transmission, or anti-retroviral therapies, all countries with any form of public health system will be ultimately forced to confront these costs. As Nattrass and Jolene Skordis (2001: 2) conclude from their costing of mother-to-child transmission drugs in South Africa, 'unless the government is planning to deny hospital care to children with HIV/AIDS (which would be unconstitutional in South Africa), it costs the government more to let the children contract HIV from their mothers, get sick and die, than it does to save them' (also see Geffen, Nattrass and Raubenheimer 2003).

While relatively wealthier countries like South Africa or Botswana may be able to redistribute expenditures between budget sectors, or embark upon limited, disciplined deficit spending, the poorest countries in the region will be forced to increase their dependence on foreign assistance. International donors already account for approximately two thirds of HIV/AIDS budgets in low and middle income countries across the world, largely accounted by overseas development assistance. As of 1996–97, sub-Saharan African governments were contributing an average of just 9 percent of all HIV/AIDS spending in their countries. Even in South Africa, which is much more able to support its own efforts, a 2000 Futures Group International study found that it still received around one half of its total HIV/AIDS funding from external sources (*Budget Watch* 2001a).

This will mean a sharply increased demand on the international community. Zimbabwe's foreign assistance needs in the next few years have reportedly already increased by 27 percent due to AIDS (Bollinger et al. 1999, cited in Youde 2001: 26). Such increased demand for donor assistance in health may crowd out other development assistance funds that countries badly need (Youde 2001). And if widely known, such dependence on donor funding may also reduce the recipient government's popular legitimacy because of the conditionalities with which donor funds usually come. The current controversy over the UNAIDS Fund grant to the South African province of KwaZulu-Natal illustrates some of the potential complications this reliance can generate.

At the same time that the HIV/AIDS pandemic results in increased public demands for increases in public health expenditures, increased levels of death and severe illness will simultaneously reduce the tax base from which governments finance their budgets. HIV/AIDS has a disproportionate impact on the most productive part of the labor force, which disproportionately reduces the numbers of those most able to contribute to the national treasury through payroll taxes. How will government pay for such increased budgetary allocations in the face of decreasing tax bases? If they choose deficit financing, they may crowd out the private investment that could otherwise increase employment and growth. If they choose expenditure switching, they may crowd out the government investment in infrastructure or development programs (e.g. housing, education or land redistribution) that might otherwise help reduce inequality and build public confidence in democratic government.

Again, we are left with much more conjecture and anecdote than real evidence. In order to understand the ability of governments across the region to meet these challenges we need far more systematic macro level, cross-national research on national budgets and the proportions allocated to health in general, and HIV/AIDS in particular, as well as the additional amounts contributed by foreign donors. Again, given the variation in the age, scope and speed of the disease across the region, cross-national analysis would enable some basic tests of propositions about how and whether budgets respond to the actual pandemic, or to other institutional and political factors. Over time analysis of budgetary trends throughout the 1990s might provide social scientists with useful guidance to how government will respond in the future as the pandemic proceeds.

Political scientists and economists could contribute quite a lot with intensive, country specific research into the political, economic and ideological constraints on national governments. Do they have the will, predisposition and political space to expand their budgets to fight the disease? Is there room for increased taxation on surviving taxpayers? Is there any possibility of improving tax collection systems to enhance national revenue? To what extent do governments across the region actually respond to citizen demands? Can we simply assume that a rise of X percent in sick people will result in a concomitant rise in health spending? National spending on health care may be more determined by levels of wealth and government allocation than objective need. Survey research could help us understand whether it actually matters that countries come to depend increasingly on foreign donor assistance: do people really care where their government receive financial support, especially if the funds are used for the purpose of fighting AIDS?

The Institutional Impacts of HIV/AIDS on Democracy

Democracy, above all, is a system of rules and procedures by which free and equal people elect representatives to make decisions for them, and a system of rules and procedures by which those representatives make those decisions. A consolidated democracy is one in which these rules are widely known, and predictable – where the processes of democratic governance become a matter of habit. These rules are given effect through political institutions – such as legislatures, executives, courts and regulatory and security agencies – who both embody and enforce these rules. To work effectively, these institutions require people with sufficient skills, expertise and resources to develop sufficient political autonomy and power to fulfill their functions, whether it is to make laws, oversee the executive, prosecute criminals, or deliver public services impartially. In this sense, the development of a strong and effective state is a necessary, though certainly not sufficient condition for the consolidation of democracy.

There is little reason to believe that state employees across southern Africa are any more immune to HIV infection than the rest of the population. While the greatest number of infections and deaths are projected to occur in the unskilled and semi-skilled part of the workforce, skilled and highly skilled sectors will be hit heavily. In South Africa, HIV infection rates have been projected to peak at 23 percent of skilled and 13 percent of highly skilled workers by 2005. This would result, by 2015, in a skilled work force that is 18 percent smaller, and a highly skilled force that is 11 percent smaller (Quattek and Fourie 2000). Thus, the pandemic is likely to devastate large portions of policy-makers, national legislators, local councilors, election officials, soldiers and civil servants – including doctors, nurses, teachers, ambulance drivers, firefighters and police. Internal South African government reports have concluded that AIDS will become the leading cause of death among public servants by 2002, totaling to as many as 250,000 deaths in the public service by 2012, or 23 percent of a workforce presently of 1,100,000 (*Business Day* 2001a; Youde 2001).

At senior political levels, South Africa has already lost – according to newspaper reports – one senior presidential advisor, a sitting cabinet minister, and an influential legislative back-bencher in the ruling party to the disease, and Zimbabwe is believed to have lost at least three cabinet ministers to AIDS in the recent past (Youde 2001). However, some of the first systematic research has been done at the local council level by Ryann Manning (2003) who recently analysed the Durban Metropolitan Council's records over a 21 month period and found sharp increases in the extent of Councilor absenteeism due to illness (from less than one in the first half of 2001 to over four in mid 2002) as well as in the proportion of total absenteeism due to illness (from less than 5 percent in the first half of 2001 to 37 percent in late 2002). She also found a 32 percent turnover in personnel in the previous six months in its Parks, Recreation and Culture department. The electricity department estimated that for the past two years, they had four to five employee deaths and two medical boardings per month, double their previous rates.

However, beside killing increased numbers of public servants and elected officials, the pandemic could severely damage the process of political institutionalization in several ways. First, increasingly smaller proportions of civil servants, policy-makers and legislators will be at their jobs long enough to develop the specialized skills, expertise and professionalism needed to do their job. Second, it will be increasingly difficult for legislatures, ministries and agencies to pass on the skills that they do have. There will be fewer experienced officials available to train younger personnel in key formal skills (such as program design, budgeting, cost/ benefit analysis, monitoring and evaluation, or personnel management), or pass on more informal standard operating procedures or norms such as ministerial accountability, bureaucratic neutrality, or official ethics. It will also be difficult for managers to generalize from existing ante-natal clinic prevalence data to their own departments to anticipate future hiring and training requirements. Identifying training needs and grooming replacements is likely to be made even more difficult by the stigma of AIDS which means that civil servants may leave work and die with little warning (Manning 2003).

In South Africa, recent government reviews have concluded that the country is not training enough nurses and teachers to cope with current demand, and pointed to similar problems looming in the police and justice system (Ensor 2001b). In Zambia and Malawi, deaths among doctors and nurses have exceeded the rate at which replacements can be trained (Cheek 2001). Again, however, besides newspaper reports, there is little in the way of serious systematic evidence on these questions. Manning (2003) found in her Durban research with fire department managers that while it takes three months to train a firefighter (and Durban officials note that their training section is already severely understaffed), it takes years to create one with enough skills to pass knowledge onto younger members through informal training. When asked about their ability to coordinate and plan the recruitment and planning or replacements, several city managers related stories of processing applications for medical boarding on a Friday only to find out on Monday that the person had died over the weekend.

Third, where civil servants do endeavor to deliver public services according to rational principles of need or merit, the rapidly changing demographic impacts of the HIV/AIDS pandemic on the citizenry may make it increasingly difficult to anticipate demand accurately and plan the types, amounts and locations of services to be supplied. National and local governments may invest in services that end up under utilized because of an unanticipated fall in demand, or they may face unanticipated demands because their ability to supply has fallen faster than the decline in the overall population. Manning (2003) found that Durban's municipal housing program managers admitted that they had little knowledge about how HIV/AIDS would affect patterns of household formation. South Africa awards subsidies to households, not individuals. Thus, even if they could make a relatively accurate projection of decreases in eligible individuals, it would be difficult to know whether the number of households would actually decrease or not. The pandemic may reduce demand for housing if splintered families combine into new households; but it may also increase demand if families splinter and scatter into new, smaller households, or if the spurs increased urban migration. The housing department estimates that approximately 20 percent of awarded deeds are in the names of people who have either already died or simply disappeared. The likely increase in orphans also places new challenges on housing planners who must find new ways to increase the capability of communities to absorb these children.

All this is even more worrying since the region's nascent democracies are not known for strong political institutions. The dominant view of political institutions across the region, and indeed most of sub-Saharan Africa is one of neo-patrimonialism whereby 'strong man' political leaders manipulate patronage, region and ethnicity to gain and hold political loyalty. Patronage relationships shape the behavior of legislators and civil servants as much as any legal-rational principles of a bureaucratic state (Bratton and Van de Walle 1997). A civil service characterized by a high degree of turnover and increasingly larger proportions of inexperienced personnel will be even less likely to develop and enforce institutional boundaries and autonomy, and more likely to succumb to the short term patronage or corruption payoffs of neo-patrimonial executive branch and party officials or business people.

While the pandemic will affect all state institutions, there are at least two that are intrinsically important for the development of young democracies. The first are the set of institutions responsible for organizing and conducting regular free and fair election, the irreducible minimum of democratic government. The loss of non-partisan supervisory officials, combined with the complicated voter registration procedures of southern Africa's multi party systems may increase opportunities for voter fraud. This will necessitate more regular vetting of voter rolls, otherwise rapidly increasing death rates may increase opportunities for governments to utilize hundreds of thousands of 'ghost voters' to inflate vote totals. Increasing proportions of ill voters may also necessitate more, or more strategically located polling places, or greater use of absentee ballots to enable the ill to vote (Costareeli n.d.).

Thus, better electoral administration skills may become more necessary at precisely the same moment that electoral commissions begin to lose skilled personnel. Moreover, the funds necessary to register people, maintain voter rolls and hold free and fair elections may also be crowded out by the increased shares of national budgets going to health care or anti-HIV/AIDS programs (Youde 2001). All of these prospects threaten to damage popular perceptions of the impartiality of elections. Countries with specific types of electoral systems may come under additional pressures. Increased deaths among MPs and local councilors in constituency systems will increase the number of bye-elections that are necessary. A steady flow of bye-elections may increase government sensitivity to shifts in public opinion, but may also be financially unsustainable. Countries may be forced to abandon constituency representation for party list proportional representation. While the list provides for swift and cheap replacement of sick or dead legislators it also removes a fundamental linkage between governors and the governed.

The second set of key democratic institutions are national, regional and local legislative bodies, the *sine qua non* of representative democracy. Legislatures best represent constituent views when they develop institutional autonomy *vis a vis* the executive. This is usually achieved through the development of a seniority system that encourages the accumulation of skills in the use of legislative procedures and rules, as well as substantive specialization and expertise in specific policy areas to enable informed oversight of executive policy. Such skills help create stronger portfolio committees. This applies to both elected members as well as researchers, administrative assistants and clerks. Rapid membership turnover due to AIDS illness and death, however, threatens these processes. But we simply need much more research to find out the actual rate of public service personnel loss and whether it differs across countries, institutions and level of skill. Intra-institutional research is needed to assess the degree to which personnel loss is affecting aspects of institutionalizations such as overall skill levels, training capacity, seniority, role differentiation and autonomy.

In terms of service delivery, we need to know to what extent the loss of personnel and skills actually diminishes delivery capacity, and even if it does, whether that loss is simply matched by diminished demands caused by smaller populations. Education, where more systematic work has recently been done, offers a good example of the caution we should exercise before we make sweeping statements. While a great deal of attention has focused on a possible education crisis caused by high infection rates amongst teachers in places like Botswana, Zimbabwe, Zambia and South Africa (United Nations Integrated Regional Information Network 2001 (in Youde 2001: 36; and Whitelaw 2000 (in Youde 2001: 37)), analysts have often neglected to factor in the reduced demand produced by fewer students, which may simply cancel out the effects of teacher mortality (World Bank, 2000b (cited in Bennell, Hyde and Swainson 2002: Ch. 6). Earlier assumptions that, as relatively well paid professionals often on assignment in remote areas, teachers were especially prone to infection have not been born out. In fact, evidence from a study of schools in Botswana, Malawi and Uganda has found that more poorly paid primary school teachers are more likely to die than much better paid secondary teachers (mortality rates also differed according to gender, marital status and whether they lived in urban or rural areas (Bennell, Hyde and Swainson 2002). The latest evidence seems to suggest that if it ever did exist, the positive relationship of socio-economic status and HIV prevalence has disappeared (Hargreaves and Glynn, 2000 (cited in Bennell, Hyde and Swainson, 2002: 77). If anything, teachers are a relatively low-risk occupation group in sub-Saharan Africa (Bennell, 2001 (cited in Bennell, Hyde and Swainson 2002: 76)). In addition, teacher turnover is already so high in many countries due to low pay and morale that AIDS mortality will not present a serious threat (Bennell, Hyde and Swainson 2001).

Cultural Impacts of HIV/AIDS on Democracy

Democracies require democrats. They require citizens who believe democracy is preferable to all alternatives, and who give life to the democratic processes by obeying the law, participating in democratic life, refraining from supporting elites who would endanger or end democratic processes, and who are willing to stand up and defend democracy if it were under threat (Mattes and Thiel, 1998). As noted earlier, democracy as a political regime uniquely recognizes and is designed to maximize human agency. But the unique combination of HIV/AIDS' characteristics attacks this sense of human agency. First, because it disproportionately affects large numbers of younger age cohorts, it results in a drastically reduced adult life span for those people. Second, the combination of its scope and its incubation period means that at any given moment, a large proportion of society will be living under a death sentence. Third, the length of the incubation period means that many of these people will live under this sentence for a particularly prolonged period. Fourth, at least in southern Africa, HIV infection and the onset of AIDS illness imposes significant economic burdens on individuals and their households in the form of increased medical costs, the prospect of losing a wage earner, as well as the prospects of significant burial costs. And fifth, given that few people can be confident about the HIV status of current or prospective sexual partners, the uninfected are also likely to experience a sense of helplessness and lack of control over their future. For example, where national prevalence is 15 percent and this rate applies throughout one's lifetime, more than one half of today's 15 year olds will die from AIDS (Fourie and Schonteich 2001). Given the lack of any clear, positive message of hope to uninfected people in those age groups about how they can confidently avoid infection over an extended period of time, a large number of teenagers and young adults may conclude that they have little hope of avoiding this death sentence themselves.

Akin to De Waal's (2002) arguments about the need to revise traditional assumptions about *homo economicus*, we also need to consider what such a sharp reduction in adult life expectancy means for our assumptions about the behavior of *homo politicus*. It is likely to recalibrate the context of citizens' rational decision making, in particular reducing the incentives for cooperative behavior and increasing incentives for opportunistic behavior. Thus, the pandemic not only damages the human body, but may also 'damage' the 'body politic' (Whiteside and FitzSimons 1992). This is likely to have several different important political results.

Decreased Citizen Support for Democratic Government

At its most extreme, HIV/AIDS may turn citizens into authoritarians because mounting death and sickness makes them so desperate as to try *any* set of political entrepreneurs who promise to offer a solution, whether they use democratic means or not. De Waal (2002) observes that these could be alternative political or religious movements who seek to place the blame for the pandemic on personal immorality, religious transgressions, minority groups, or external forces. This could become even more likely if the region's democratic governments are widely perceived to be incapable of preventing the pandemic from growing, caring for its victims or preventing a sharp deterioration in quality of life (Brower and Chalk, 2002; Youde 2001). More likely, the pandemic may reduce the importance which people attach to democracy simply because of the competition of more urgent priorities such as simple survival. The degree to which the question of democratic versus authoritarian government matters to someone infected with a fatal disease, or whose life is burdened with caring for such people, or who believes they have little prospect of avoiding infection, is an open question.

Decreased Citizen Participation in Democratic Government

HIV/AIDS may also directly reduce overall levels of public participation in democratic politics. Obviously, mounting AIDS deaths and illness will reduce the absolute number of citizens able to vote or participate in public life. But again, the question becomes whether the death sentence imposed on the infected, or the threat of infection facing the uninfected reshapes traditional incentives to become involved in public affairs. Moreover, the burden of caring for ill family members or friends is likely to reduce those people's time and resources available to participate. Youde (2001) offers the example that many countries in the region require people to make multiple efforts to obtain multiple forms of identification to register to vote, which places both the ill and those caring for them at a severe disadvantage (for a discussion of ways to empower HIV affected people to vote, see Costrarelli, n.d). However, it is also possible that some types of counter trends could occur. As medical research brings down the costs of anti-AIDS medication, or nears an AIDS vaccine, the infected and their loved ones might be galvanized into a strong and active constituency who participate to demand that their governments devote increasing effort and budgets to making these drugs widely available. Though it is composes of a relatively small number of activists, South Africa's Treatment Action Campaign may be one such example a broader type of social movement that could develop in the future.

A Damaged Civil Society

But the level of public participation in any democracy is not determined solely by the choices of ordinary citizens. Mass participation in the political system is also facilitated by civil society organizations and interest groups who mobilize, channel and structure public participation between elections. Civil society across Southern Africa is already quite weak. However, the types of people who form the backbone of most civil society organizations may be especially susceptible to HIV infection: while they tend to be better educated, they also tend to be younger, more mobile, and often spend time away from their home office to do extension work. Many organizations may be very vulnerable to the disease since each lost staff member may have unique skills that took many years to develop. Manning (2002) estimates that a medium to large civil society organization with 30 staff and eighty volunteers, based in South Africa's KwaZulu/Natal province, will lose 1 to 2 employees and 1 to 2 volunteers annually to AIDS by 2009 or 2010 amounting to nineteen staff and twenty two volunteers by 2021. This would mean, by 2009, losing 158 days of staff time and 212 days of volunteer time annually due to AIDS related illness. Thus, the pandemic may indirectly reduce overall levels of public participation in democratic processes by further damaging the capacity of civil society organizations. The loss of long term staff members or volunteers is likely to be particularly devastating because, as the Director of a KwaZulu-Natal democracy promotion organization, they have experience that is vital to understand the culture, traditions and dynamics of the communities where they work, and have build up mutual trust and understanding with communities, churches and traditional leaders, relationships that are the very strength of these organization (cited in Manning 2002: 16).

Macro level evidence supporting this argument can be found in responses to Afrobarometer surveys of representative samples in seven Southern African countries. Those countries with the highest measured levels of severe illness (due to any cause) also have the lowest overall levels of attendance in local community meetings and participation in local service and welfare groups. This relationship persists even after controlling for levels of poverty (Whiteside et al, 2002). This may reflect that fact that AIDS has already killed critical proportions of those who used to perform essential do things such as organize and drive community meetings or local welfare groups. Organizational level evidence to this effect can be found in a survey by the University of Natal's Health Economics and HIV/AIDS Research Division of 59 KwaZulu-Natal civil society organizations. It found that that three quarters reported some form of AIDS related impact on their organization. One third of the Durban based organizations noted increases in absenteeism or loss of staff members to HIV/AIDS (Manning 2002).

The 'Uncivil' Society

Finally, the pandemic may have important effects on the 'civility' of society, by decreasing popular compliance with the law, and increasing violent protest, social intolerance and criminal activity. Those individuals or households who suffer and AIDS illness, or have already lost a wage earner to severe illness or death, will simply be less able to pay local taxes or rates, or for public services such as electricity or user fees for schools or health clinics. However, HIV infection or AIDS illness may reduce or totally remove any incentive to do so, especially if payment is only required after a service has been provided rather than before. In contrast, the incentive would appear to dictate getting whatever you can for as little money as possible. As De Waal notes (2002: 8): 'Those who feel they have nothing to lose cannot be deterred by a judicial system that imposes custodial sentences, or even the death sentence.'

Supporting evidence for this line of reasoning can be found in classic experiments testing derivations of game theory which demonstrated the importance of an uncertain end to any game in maintaining incentives for cooperation. Incentives for 'defection' or uncooperative behaviour increase once players could see the end of a game on the horizon (Axelrod 1984). The seven country Afrobarometer study of survey responses across southern Africa also found that societies with the lowest levels of severe illness also tended to have the lowest numbers of citizens who say they would avoid citizenship duties such as paying rates or taxes for services (Whiteside et al. 2002).

People infected with HIV and ill with AIDS also tend to be lonely and depressed. Such conditions often lead to hopelessness and apathy, but they may as likely lead to frustration and aggression, which could turn into non compliance or even political violence (Shell 2000; also see Gurr 1970, on the relationship of frustration and violence). Paradoxically, the falling prices of some anti-retroviral drugs may aggravate and inflame such simmering frustrations as firms, and eventually governments, have to decide who does and does not receive life prolonging drugs. The crucial period will occur *after* it becomes affordable to provide anti-retrovirals to some employees, but *before* it becomes possible to provide them for all. During this period firms will have an incentive to begin to provide limited drug therapy and to target their most highly skilled workers. If done widely enough, and for a prolonged period, this is likely to reinforce class divisions and inequalities between middle class and everyone else. Even if firms are able to afford universal coverage, in the context of high levels of unemployment, this will still increase inequality and fuel class based conflict between anyone with a decent job and everyone else who either works in the informal sector or is jobless (Nattrass 2002).

Increasing private sector provision may eventually increase pressure on governments across the region to provide therapy to public sector employees (De Waal 2002) and citizens not already covered by their employers. Governments would also confront decisions, at least initially, about where to target drug therapy. As with firms, governments may be tempted to use skills and education as criteria of eligibility for treatment in order to protect its investments in training and education. Alternatively, governments may be tempted to prioritize cronies and or supporters. While these possibilities may seem stretched, we have already witnessed the ability of Zimbabwe's Mugabe government to manipulate the distribution of food aid to favor its political supporters. We also know Zambia already screens applicants for management positions in its mines for HIV, and Botswana restricts its prestigious study-abroad scholarships to those HIV-negative (Cheek 2001).

Whether or not government decisions are based on political expedience, fertile ground for the perception that they are will be provided by the fact that South Africa's highest HIV rates are located in KwaZulu-Natal, political heartland of the opposition Inkatha Freedom Party, or that Zimbabwe's non-Shona population suffer higher infection rates and have less adequate heath care than the Shona, or that Namibia's Herero and Damara have less access to government resources and health care (Cheek 2001). And even if they have the best of intentions, the distribution and infrastructure problems of existing health care systems may privilege certain groups and areas. For example, just one out of every twelve pregnant Batswana women are actually receiving mother-to-child-transmission treatment, most of these living in urban areas (Cheek 2002). In any case, political decisions around AIDS treatment hold the potential to tensions and political conflict between workers and unemployed, urban and rural, or between different ethnic groups.

Another dimension of 'uncivility' may arise not amongst the infected and ill, but in the form of increased public intolerance amongst the uninfected through scapegoating of stereotyped 'high risk' groups such as homosexuals, truck drivers, orphans, sex workers, miners or released prisoners. We know that South Africans, for example, already demonstrate high levels of predisposition to partake in intolerant behaviors against disliked social groups, political tendencies, and foreigners (Gibson and Gouws 2002; Mattes, Africa and Taylor 1999; Mattes, Taylor, McDonald and Poore 2000; and Mattes, Crush and Richmond 2000). Given the fears created by the epidemic, governments may come under increasing popular pressure to deny political and economic rights to these groups. Or, local groups may simply take it upon themselves using terror and intimidation to force these people out of their schools and communities.

One tenth of AIDS affected households in South Africa told interviewers in a 2002 survey that they had faced hostility or rejection from their community. Many specifically complained about the attitudes of health care workers: some reported being chased away, refused help, or confronted with uncaring attitudes (Beresford, 2002b; Beresford 2002c). On the other hand, a three country study of 41 schools in Botswana, Malawi and Uganda found while AIDS orphans were subject to insensitive treatment by teachers and administrators at school, instances of deliberate discrimination were quite rare (Barnell, Hyde and Swainson 2002).

Finally, some analysts are concerned that HIV/AIDS may contribute to lawlessness by orphaning large numbers of children across the region over the next two decades (Fourie and Schönteich 2001).

Without AIDS, orphans in developing countries around the world comprise an average of 2% of all children aged 15 and under (Fourie and Schönteich 2001). According to the United Nations Children's Fund (UNICEF), however, orphans exceed 20% of the under 15 population in Congo-Kinshasa, Malawi, Rwanda, Uganda, Zambia and Zimbabwe. A large part of sub-Saharan Africa's unusually high proportion of orphans has usually been attributed to political conflict. As of 1999, however, UNICEF estimated that just under one-third of all orphans in the sub-continent were AIDS orphans (Hunter and Williamson 2000 (cited in Bennell, Hyde and Swainson 2002)). Within southern Africa, USAID estimated the total number of maternal or double orphans, as of 2000, at 2.9 million, or 8% of all children 15 and under, of which 65% were AIDS orphans (Fourie and Schönteich, 2001).

UNICEF projects the total number of maternal and double AIDS orphans to increase to 14 million across sub-Saharan Africa by 2010. Particularly sharp increases in the orphan population are expected in Botswana, Central African Republic, Lesotho, Mozambique, Namibia, South Africa, Swaziland and Zimbabwe, amounting to 30% to 40% of all children (Bennell, Hyde and Swainson 2002). In southern Africa, USAID expects the total number of orphans to increase to 5.5 million by 2010, by then accounting for 16% of all children 15 and under, of which 87% will be AIDS orphans (Fourie and Schönteich, 2001). In South Africa, a Medical Research Council report estimates that a third of children born in 2002 will be orphaned by 2015, with a total of around 1.9 million orphans under 15 and 3 million under 18 (Smetherham 2002).

All orphans suffer the trauma of losing parents, and of higher levels of impoverishment, exclusion and abuse. The education of orphaned children is often one of the first casualties if extended families suffer losses of income (Fourie and Schönteich, 2001). Demographic and Health Surveys from 15 sub-Saharan African countries in the 1990s found that 'out of school' rates of orphans aged 10 to 14 were on average 19% higher than non-orphans (UNICEF, 2000 (cited in Bennell, Hyde and Swainson 2002: 58)). A Botswana, Malawi and Uganda study of schools in high prevalence districts found that orphans, especially double orphans (i.e. those who lost both their parents), were considerably more likely to interrupt their schooling than other children (Bennell, Hyde and Swainson 2002).

But AIDS orphans are likely to suffer even higher levels of trauma as a result of watching parents endure prolonged, often painful periods of illness and depression prior to death. Social stigmatization may produce even higher levels of discrimination and maltreatment (Fourie and Schönteich 200X). This may lead to higher levels of crime and other anti-social behavior over the next two decades as this growing, and disproportionately large, share of children move through the 15 to 24 age range, the years of greatest propensity to commit crime, and do so with little or no adult guidance Schönteich, 1999; and Fourie and Schönteich 2001). British and South African studies of children or young adults who had committed violent crimes, found that above average proportions of them had been orphaned, abandoned or rejected by parents or guardians (Fourie and Schönteich 2001).

However, analysts need to exercise a great deal of caution in this area. As pointed out above, Southern Africa already possesses an abnormally high proportion of orphans, or children who do not live with both parents and it is not clear whether this has contributed to any of the types of anti-social behaviors projected to result from increased numbers of AIDS orphans. The Botswana, Malawi, Uganda schools survey has yielded several findings that do not conform to the typical expectations. In Botswana primary schools, for example, orphans have lower rates of absenteeism than non-orphans. In poorer societies Malawi and Uganda, absenteeism is already very high amongst all children, though it is slightly higher amongst orphans. But there is no evidence that orphans are any sicklier, or 'needed at home' more often than other children. Neither is there any evidence that they are more likely to repeat a grade (Bennell, Hyde and Swainson 2002). In fact, the economic impacts of AIDS may be so great that they simply affect all children, rather than orphans in particular. A survey of 771 AIDS affected households in four South African provinces found that pressures of losing income have forced families to liquidate their investments in the future, especially the education of their children. Approximately one child out of ten was out of school either because of cost or needed labour at home (Beresford, 2002b). Again, this cautions against making sweeping generalizations about orphans, and reminds us of the need to examine such mitigating factors as overall levels of poverty, the cost of school fees, the presence of school feeding schemes, and the extent to which national cultures value children and education (Bennell, Hyde and Swainson 2002; but also see Bray 2003).

As with almost every other area we have reviewed, what we have is far more informed speculation and proposition than evidence. Psychologists can make an important contribution with basic experimental research examining the impacts of changing levels of adult life expectancy on agency and predispositions to cooperative behavior. Cross-national or even national or sub-national surveys with sufficient cross-sectional variance in terms of the extent of the pandemic is needed to more vigorously test whether those individuals who are infected with, or affected by HIV/AIDS, are any different with respect to their commitment to democracy, trust in government, or satisfaction with the output of government. Do they exhibit lower rates of participation or predispositions to participate? To what extent do people attach importance to the sustenance of democracy as compared to the need to fight HIV/AIDS? Does this differ according to individual or societal levels of HIV infection or AIDS impact? Are infected or affected individuals, or those living in highly infected or affected societies, any less likely to obey the law? How do the uninfected really feel about the infected and the sick? Do they see them as social deviants? Do they blame their condition on their moral flaws? Are they willing to extent them civil and political rights? What do people want firms and government do with regard to anti-retroviral and anti-mother-to-child transmission drugs? Do egalitarian values dictate that their distribution must wait until they all eligible people can be provided, or are they willing to tolerate a targeted and staged roll out? And if so, what criteria do people think should be used to determine who gets these drugs first? While it may be possible to address some of these questions with existing data sets, a specialized regional survey on HIV/AIDS and its possible impacts would be extremely valuable. However, where individual level data does not exist, innovative research designs using aggregate data might be able to test whether national, or intra-national provincial or district differences in voter turnout, tax compliance, or crime rates correlate in any way with HIV infection rates.

We also lack any kind of systematic picture of how HIV/AIDS is affecting civil society organizations. Either through specially designed surveys of a sample of such organization, or through the inclusion of new batteries of questions on ongoing projects measuring the scope and capacity of organized civil society, such as Civicus, we need obtain better information on the extent of organizational AIDS impacts, such as absenteeism, death, replacement and training costs, and estimated skill losses. Alternatively, using snowball sampling, researchers could investigate whether there is any evidence of increased political organization around HIV/AIDS. If so, it would be important to know what these organizations are doing in terms of political advocacy and mobilization and whether such organizations tend to be dominated by professional activists or ordinary citizens.

Finally, while some studies have found abnormally high numbers of abandoned children and orphans amongst selected samples of violent criminals, we need more systematic comparison of orphans and non orphans in terms of school attendance and performance, integration into households, and their basic social values. To what extent is orphanage *per se* a driving force, versus the amount of nurturing provided by either parents or foster care-givers? To what extent can government support to extended families, or effective foster family schemes ameliorate anti-social tendencies amongst orphan? And since abnormally high proportions of children in Southern Africa are already orphaned from other causes, and since so many children already live with only one parent, we need to ensure that we are able to separate the effects of AIDS orphanage from the impact of ordinary orphanage. Panel designs tracking these two groups over time would be invaluable.

Conclusions

Democracy is the preferred political system in the world today. It is the only political regime that is based on and designed to maximize human equality, freedom and agency. Southern Africa was no exception from the 'Third Wave' of democracy that swept the world in the 1980s and 1990s. Beginning in 1990, multi-party systems with regular elections emerged in Namibia, Zambia, Malawi, South Africa, Lesotho, Mozambique, Tanzania joining the existing regimes of Botswana and Zimbabwe. Recent political changes suggest that Angola may not be far behind. However, in none of these countries can democracy be characterized as 'consolidated.' 'Strong man' Presidents and, or dominant political parties threaten political pluralism in the face of weak legislatures, weak party systems, and weak civil societies. Yet with the major exception of Zimbabwe, civil and political rights, and reasonably free and fair elections persist.

HIV/AIDS, however, threatens to block and even reverse democratic development across the region. Lost incomes, sharply increasing health costs, shrinking tax bases, increased labor costs, and decreased productivity all conspire to threaten the economic growth that seems so necessary to sustain democratic practice in poor countries. Increasing death and illness in cabinets, legislatures and government ministries threatens the institutionalization that young democracies need to create the strong and effective states that give effect to the rules of democracy. Sharply decreasing adult life expectancy and increasing proportions of people living with effective death sentences removes incentives for large sections of the populace to participate in democratic politics or comply with the rules of the democratic state. Stigma, discrimination and conflict over scarce resources threaten to increase political conflict and criminal behavior.

However, virtually all of this set of scenarios is based on logic and conjecture, rather than evidence. The truth of the matter is that we know little about why or how citizens, elites and institutions infected, affected or threatened by HIV/AIDS change their political behavior. This paper has attempted to lay out a research matrix into which prospective research can be fitted and researchers can try to specify conjecture into testable hypotheses. Our ultimate objective is to assess the ways in which HIV/AIDS may threaten the survival of democracy, and future oriented questions are inherently not answerable without a crystal ball. However, the advancing but varied state of the pandemic across the region and within each country would seem to provide sufficient data and variance with which to test a large number of questions suggested in this paper through comparative cross-sectional and longitudinal designs. It is only with the knowledge that such research yields that we can offer informed projections about the threats to democracy, and what thus what democrats can do to ensure that government of the people, by the people, and for the people does not perish from this region.

References

Axelrod, R. (1984) *The Evolution of Cooperation*. New York: Basic Books.
Bennell, B.S. (2001) *The AIDS Epidemic in Sub-Saharan Africa: Are Teachers A High Risk Group*? Brighton, Unpublished Manuscript, May.
Bennell, P. K Hyde and N. Swainson (2002) *The Impact of the HIV/AIS Epidemic on the Education Sector in Sub-Saharan Africa*. Centre for International Education, University of Sussex Institute for Education: Sussex, February.
Beresford, B. (2002a) 'The Costs of Doing Nothing.' *Mail & Guardian*, 17 to 23 May.
Beresford, B. (2002b) 'Families Tipped Into Destitution.' *Mail & Guardian*, 27 September to 3 October 2002: 8.

Beresford, B, (2002c) 'Failing to Deliver.' *Mail & Guardian*, 11 to 17 October: 8.

Bollinger, L. J. Stover, R. Kerkhoven, G. Mutangadura and D. Mukurazita (1999) *The Economic Impact of AIDS In Zimbabwe*. Washington D.C.: POLICY Project (www.tfgi.com/Zimbabwe.doc).

Bratton, M. and N. V. d. Walle (1997). *Democratic Experiments In Africa*. Cambridge, Cambridge University Press.

Bray, R. (2003) *Predicting the Social Consequences of Orphanhood in South Africa*, CSSR Working Paper (forthcoming). Cape Town: Centre for Social Science Research, University of Cape Town.

Brower, Jennifer and Peter Chalk (2002) 'The Security Implications of Infectious Disease and Its Impact on National and International Institutions and Policies.' *America's Real Achilles Heal: The Threat of Infectious Disease to National and International Security*. Santa Monica, CA: RAND.

Budget Watch (2002a) 'Focus on Brazil, Thailand, Uganda, Botswana?' *Budget Watch*. Cape Town: Idasa, November: 2.

Budget Watch (2002b) 'Comparing Thailand, Brazil, South Africa, Botswana and Uganda.' *Budget Watch*. Cape Town: Idasa, November: 8.

Business Day (2001a) 'AIDS Could Cripple Public Service.' *Business Day* 29 June.

Business Day (2001b) 'New Priorities Needed.' *Business Day* 10 October: 12.

Cheek, R. B. (2001). 'Playing God With HIV: Rationing HIV Treatment in Southern Africa.' *African Security Review* 10(4).

Clarke, L. (2002) 'Study Highlights Ravages of HIV/AIDS.' *Sunday Independent*, 3 November , p. 4.

Costarelli, E. (n.d.) *HIV/AIDS, Democracy and Citizenship*. Johannesburg: Electoral Institute of Southern Africa.

De Waal, A. (2002) *Modelling the Governance Implications of the HIV/AIDS Pandemic in Africa*, AIDS and Governance Discussion Paper, No. 2. Unpublished Draft, March.

Diamond, L. (1996). 'Is the Third Wave Over?' *Journal of Democracy* 7(3): 20–27.

Diamond, L. (1999) 'Introduction.' *Democratization In Africa*, L Diamond & M Plattner (eds). Baltimore: Johns Hopkins University Press.

Diamond, L. and J. Linz (1989). 'Introduction: Politics, Society and Democracy in Latin America.' *Democracy in Developing Countries: Latin America*. L. Diamond, J. Linz and S.M. Lipset, eds. Boulder, Lynne Reiner.

Ensor, L. (2001) 'AIDS "To Outstrip SA's Future Health Budgets."' *Business Day* 10 October: 4.

Ensor, L. (2001) 'Treasury Sounds the Alarm Over AIDS.' *Business Day* 10 October: 1.

Fourie, p. and M. Schönteich (2001) 'Africa's New Security Threat.' *African Security Review* 10(4): 29–44.

Geffen, N., N. Nattrass and C. Raubenheimer (2003) *The Cost of HIV Prevention and Treatment Interventions in South Africa*. CSSR Working Paper, No. 28. Cape Town: Centre for Social Science Research, University of Cape Town.

Gibson, J and A. Gouws (2002) *Overcoming Intolerance in South Africa: Experiments in Democratic Persuasion*. Cambridge: Cambridge University Press.

Gurr, Ted Robert. 1970. *Why Men Rebel*. Princeton, Princeton University Press.

Hamoudi, A. and J. Sachs (November 2001). *The Economics of AIDS In Africa*. Cambridge, MA., Centre for International Development, Harvard University.

Hargreaves, J.R. and J.R. Glynn (2000) *Educational Attainment and HIV Infection in Developing Countries: A Review of the Published Literature*. London: London Schools of Hygiene and Tropical Medicine.

Hunter. S and J. Williamson (2000) *Children on the Brink: Strategies to Support A Generation Isolated by HIV/AIDS*. New York, UNICEF/USAID, June.

Heinecken, L. (2001). 'Living in Terror: The Looming Security Threat to Southern Africa.' *African Security Review*(10/4): 7–18;.

Joseph, R. (1998) 'Africa, 1990–1997: From *Abertura* to Closure.' *Journal of Democracy* 9(2), April.

Karatnycky, A. (2002). 'The Freedom House Survey.' *Journal of Democracy* 13(1): 99–112.

Linz, J. and A. Stepan (1996). 'Towards Consolidated Democracies.' *Journal of Democracy* 7(2): 14–33.

Lipset, S. M. (1959). 'Some Social Requisites of Democracy: Economic Development and Political Legitimacy.' *American Political Science Review* 53(1): 69–105.

Manning, R. (2002) *The Impact of HIV/AIDS on Civil Society: Assessing and Mitigating Impacts: Tools & Models for NGOs and CBOs.* Durban, Health Economics and HIV/ AIDS Research Division, University of Natal.

Manning, R. (2003) *The Impact of HIV/AIDS on Local Democracy: A Case Study of the eThekwini Municipality, KwaZulu-Natal, South Africa,* CSSR Working Paper (forthcoming). Cape Town: Centre for Social Science Research, University of Cape Town.

Mattes, R. and H. Thiel (1998) 'Consolidation and Public Opinion In South Africa.' *Journal of Democracy* 9(1) (January): 95–110.

Mattes, R., C. Africa and H. Taylor (1999) *Intolerance and Intimidation in South Africa,* Opinion '99 Series, vol. 2, no. 9. Cape Town: Idasa. (www.idasa.org.za).

Mattes, R., D. Taylor, D. McDonald, A. Poore and W. Richmond (2000) 'South African Attitudes To Immigrants and Immigration.' *On Borders: Perspectives On International Migration In Southern Africa,* McDonald, D, ed. New York, St. Martin's Press / Kingston, Ont., Southern African Migration Project.

Mattes, R., J. Crush and W. Richmond (2000) 'The Brain Gain and Legal Immigration to Post-Apartheid South Africa.' *Africa Insight* 30(2) (October): 21–30.

Nattrass, N. and J. Skordis (2001) *Paying to Waste Lives – The Affordability of Reducing Mother to Child Transmission of HIV In South Africa,* CSSR Working Paper, No. 4. Cape Town: Centre for Social Science, University of Cape Town, December.

Nattrass, N. (2002). *AIDS, Growth and Distribution* CSSR Working Paper, no. 7. University of Cape Town: Centre for Social Science Research, March.

Kennedy, C. (2002) *From the Coalface: A Study of the Response of a South African Colliery to the Threat of AIDS.* CSSR Working Paper, No. 5. Cape Town: Centre for Social Science Research, University of Cape Town.

Nattrass, N. (2002). *AIDS, Growth and Distribution in South Africa,* CSSR Working Paper, No. 7. Cape Town: Centre for Social Science Research.

Over, M. (1992). *The Macroeconomic Impacts of AIDS in Sub-Saharan Africa.* Washington D.C, World Bank.

Parker, W., U. Kistner, et al. (2000). *The Economic Impact of HIV/AIDS on South Africa and Its Implications for Governance: A Literature Review.* Washington, US AID.

Proceedings (2002). University of Natal Health Economics and AIDS Research Division (HEARD), University of Cape Town Democracy in Africa Research Unit, and Institute for Democracy in South Africa Workshop On *Democracy in AIDS in Southern Africa: Setting the Research Agenda.* Cape Town, 22–23 April (www.uct.ac.za/depts/cssr/daru).

Przeworski, A., M. Alvarez, J.A. Cheibub and F. Limongi (2000). *Democracy and Development: Political Institutions and Well-Being in the Wolrd, 1950–1990.* Cambridge, Cambridge University Press.

Quattek, K. and T. Fourie (2000). *The Economic Impacts of AIDS In South Africa: A Dark Cloud On the Horizon.* Johannesburg, ING Barings: South African Research.

Schell, Robert (2000) 'Halfway to the Holocaust: The Economic, Demographic and Social Implications of the AIDS Pandemic to the Year 2010 in the Southern African Region.' In

HIV/AIDS: A Threat to the African Renaissance? Konrad Adenauer Stiftung Occasional Papers. Parktown, Kondrad Adenauer Stiftung, June.

Schönteich, M. (1999) 'Age and AIDS: South Africa' Crime Time Bomb?' *African Security Review* 18(4).

Sen, A. (1999) 'Democracy as a Universal Value.' *Journal of Democracy* 10(3): 3–17.

Smetherham, J.A. (2002) '33% will be AIDS Orphans by 2015, says MRC Report.' *Cape Times*. 18 June.

UNICEF (2002) *The Progress of Nations*. New York: UNICEF.

United Nations Integrated Regional Information Network (2001) *Education In Africa Threatened by AIDS*. 27 July (allafrica.com/stories/200107270096.html).

Whiteford, A. and D. E. V. Seventer (1999). *Winners and Losers: South Africa's Changing Income Distribution In the 1990s*. Johannesburg, WEFA.

Whitelaw, K. (2000) 'AIDS In the Classroom.' *US News and World Report* 14 February (www.usnews.com/usnews/issue/000214/aids.htm).

Whiteside, A. and D. FitzSimons, 'The AIDS Epidemic: Economic, Political and Security Implication.' *Conflict Studies* 251. London: Research Institute for the Study of Conflict and Terrorism, May.

Whiteside, A., R. Mattes, S. Willan and R. Manning (2002). *Examining HIV/AIDS In Southern Africa Through the Eyes of Ordinary Southern Africans*, CSSR Working Paper, No. 11. Cape Town: Centre for Social Research, University of Cape Town.

World Bank (2000a). *World Development Report 2000/2001*. Oxford, Oxford University Press.

World Bank (2000b), *Exploring the Implications of the HIV/AIDS Epidemic for Educational Planning In Selected African Countries: The Demographic Questions*. World Bank: Washington.

Youde, J. (2001) *All the Voters Will Be Dead: HIV/AIDS and Democratic Legitimacy and Stability In Africa*. Stockholm: International Foundation for Electoral Assistance.

Chapter 12

Conclusion

Alan Whiteside and Nana K. Poku

This book represents one of the first contributions to the literature on the political economy of AIDS in Africa. As a result it suffers from all the faults that such pioneering literature inevitably faces. As the chapters show there is not much evidence for the political impact of HIV/AIDS, instead we have to rely on informed speculation based on the very little data we do have. The literature is scant (as illustrated in the review chapter by Mattes and Manning) and most of what there is even more speculative than that contained in this book. Perhaps most telling though is that the majority of our authors are not political scientists, they range from epidemiologists through to economists. But what they have in common is a deep concern for the likely effects of AIDS on the body politic of African societies. There is consensus this epidemic could not only halt development in its tracks may in fact, and in the worst circumstances, cause societal collapse.

In the preface we tracked the evolution of the political analysis of HIV/AIDS as we see it. It is not very encouraging. The book looks at the political economy of AIDS in Africa. In this concluding chapter we ask what the critical issues are. We extract the common themes and set a research agenda for political scientists as we move into the new century.

The Tardy Response of Political Scientists

The first theme is that political scientists have been slow to respond to this epidemic. It is not generally been seen as having political consequences. Political scientists have failed to understand what AIDS means for both politics and society at large.

There are three possible reasons for this that we identify. The first is a lack of professional interest in the topic. People are simply not engaged. AIDS is so unique and different that political scientists have been unable to conceptualise what it might mean for their discipline and research. (We will return to this theme). Furthermore it is a sexually transmitted disease and even working on it can be seen as both stigmatising and slightly sordid. Why work on HIV/AIDS when there are so many other areas demanding attention many of which such as state failure and corruption are deeply interesting and relevant.

The second reason for the slow response is the lack of information. We are twenty years into the epidemic but the full impact is only just beginning to be felt in some areas while in others it is still decades away. It is hard to research and write if you lack the necessary information. This is illustrated by the epidemic curves described by Whiteside in his chapter on crisis.

Finally the research terrain, such as it is, is occupied by people with whom most political scientists make uneasy bedfellows. These include the activists and NGOs as described by Webb.

The Unique Nature of HIV/AIDS

The disease is matchless. It is the single most serious infectious disease and the number of people infected continues to rise. The fact is that the majority of people who are HIV positive are young adults: women in their twenties, men in their thirties. The mortality rates are between 90 and 100 per cent over time, current medical treatment does not provide a cure, although it can extend life.

These issues have been extensively discussed and are reiterated in this book. But the overriding point is that AIDS is 'not a shock like any other'. It is unique and it is different and its consequences for economics, development and the politics of African countries are profound and far reaching. This is brought out elegantly by Alex de Waal in his chapter on AIDS and the agrarian crisis. The idea that AIDS is leading to 'a new variant of famine' is profoundly disturbing. De Waal suggests that AIDS means that when a shock such as a drought occurs there is actually very little prospect for recovery for those families affected. This theme is echoed by Whiteside in his examination of AIDS and crisis. He suggests that in certain settings AIDS may actually cause the catastrophe, be a crisis driver. He points to events in Zimbabwe to support his argument.

Perhaps the most unusual of the many features of this disease is the global acceptance that the numbers infected will continue to rise. It is interesting to contrast the reaction to SARS with that of AIDS. Each infection was carefully tracked and every attempt was made to prevent further transmission. With AIDS we accept that there will be new infections.

The Long Wave Nature of the Epidemic

This feature of HIV/AIDS deserves a section on its own. Because there is an incubation period of approximately eight years between infection and the onset of illness this epidemic is a long wave disaster. In South Africa for example the first survey in 1990 found that under 0.5 per cent of women were infected. By the time the most recent (2001) survey was carried out it was estimated that about 25 per cent of women attending ante-natal clinics were infected, and it is likely that prevalence has not yet peaked. From the time that the prevalence peaks to the time when the number of AIDS cases hits their highest level will be at least four to eight years later.

There is evidence from Uganda to show that although the HIV prevalence peaked in 1992 it took to 2003 for the number of orphans to reach its crest. The consequences of the orphaning will be felt over the next generation. For example there will be a generation of children who will not have had the parental love and socialisation that others have had. It is possible many will have not had the education they would have had in the absence of the epidemic. This may have even longer term consequences. For example if girl children are taken out of school due to the epidemic then, because a major predictor of child and infant mortality is girls' education, we might see an increase in this indicator which could last until 2015 or even later.

The long wave nature of the epidemic is a constant theme of all the chapters. Folayan talking about Nigeria and Taylor in his discussion of the AIDS pandemic in Botswana both underline the long wave nature of the disease and the fact that it is still evolving and the major impact will be felt in the future. This is discussed in greater detail by de Waal and Whiteside in their respective chapters. Hard evidence of the lack of visibility of the epidemic though is provided in the chapter by Whiteside *et al* on what we know need and what we need to know. Using the Afro Barometer data they find that in countries such as Lesotho, South Africa, Botswana and Namibia, very few people actually know, or admit to knowing, anyone who has died of AIDS as yet. This may be in part due to the invisibility of the epidemic, but is also probably a result of the fact that AIDS and deaths are still rising.

This long wave nature of the disease goes some way to explaining the difficulty in gauging social, economic and political thinkers in the issue: the evidence is simply not there yet. However the problem is that by the time the evidence is in, it will be too late. What is really required is planning for the increase in morbidity (illness) and mortality (death). We have some evidence for example, that the health care sector is facing an increased burden of patients and demand but sadly there is little to suggest that anyone is actually thinking about what this means in terms of budgets, staffing and facilities. Indeed it is worth noting that were antiretroviral therapy to become widely available then the problems of providing the staff and infrastructure will be considerable. At worst it would mean that other health interventions do not get the sort of attention that they both need and deserve.

Inequality

The importance of inequality both as a driver of the epidemic and as a consequence is repeated many times throughout the chapters. Baylies shows that inequality between men and women, poor and rich means that unsafe sex is maintained despite growing knowledge about the dangers of AIDS. The chapter by Poku on debt shows a grotesque international inequality between countries – an inequality that is maintained by debt. Taylor looks at Botswana, an economic miracle, but notes that it is the nimble political leadership and co-option of many groups that have enabled this country to both maintain its growth and political stability. The inequalities of that society are coming home to roost as the epidemic gains momentum through the country.

Not discussed in this book in any detail is the idea that inequality may result from the epidemic. This is an area which has been addressed by economists and social scientists and needs further attention. For political scientists the question may be framed as 'does the threat to democracy mean that development goals will be under attack and that poverty and equity will receive less attention.' It certainly deserves urgent consideration.

Gendered Impact

The impact of this HIV/AIDS is variable by gender. This is starkly illustrated in the graph in the chapter by Whiteside, Mattes, Willan and Manning which shows estimated increase in death rates for men and women. These have risen three and a half fold for women aged between 25 and 29 between 1985 and 1999/2000. For men the peak is for those aged 30 to 34 but the increase is approximately twice that which it was in 1985.

We know that women are infected younger, that they die younger, and that the burden of care falls on them. Not only are they more likely to be infected (and this theme is taken up in greater detail by Baylies) but they are also the ones that will have to carry the burden of care, deal with the loss of income, and try to hold families together. In his discussion of the famine, de Waal notes that it is on women that societies depend for their recovery after periods of famine. Women are the ones who make the long term plans and have the knowledge to gather wild crops. Women are less likely to die during famines than men.

Gender is a huge issue and we have to acknowledge that it is not properly dealt with in this book. Hopefully the political economy of AIDS and gender will be an area that is further researched.

Response

Most of the chapters in the book make some mention of the response to the epidemic. At the most basic level the discussion of community response in Uganda by Lowbeer and Stoneburner is illuminating. They note that it was the open community response in Uganda that has allowed the epidemic to be brought under control in that country. 'Ugandans were quite clear about how they changed their behaviour, and the debate has really only been heated at the international level. If you go into a village in Uganda, they will talk to you about AIDS, how they have dealt with it, and normally their recommendations on what to do. The changes they have made are not piecemeal, life has not continued as before. They have engaged fundamentally with AIDS in the way they talk, think and behave.' This level of response is lacking across much of the rest of Africa.

The role of NGOs, their legitimacy and purpose is put under the spot light in a number of the chapters but most effectively by Webb. He notes that the mushrooming of national and sub-national NGOs in the past 15 years is in itself a large scale behavioural response. What he asks though, whether NGOs are legitimate actors. What is their role and how can they supplement or in some settings replace the state? Webb asks 'Do NGOs represent the marginalised, are they at the cutting edge in terms of best practice and do they have technical legitimacy?' The answer is a qualified yes. State incapacity and indifference has created a void of service provision and meaningful societal engagement. NGOs have an important function and as Webb suggests this is most clearly seen in Uganda thus supporting the behavioural changes that have taken place there. The role of NGOs is also raised by Folayan although it is not critically examined.

What about government? By and large the government response can be characterised as late, slow, inadequate, and in many cases half hearted. The chapter on Nigeria shows clearly how late this response has been. Mobilising government has been extremely complicated and slow. The reasons for this are alluded to in other chapters. None the less it would be enormously valuable if political scientists were to spend more time on what it is that is required to make government take the leap of imagination that is necessary to respond to AIDS.

Themes for Further Research and Thought

The HIV/AIDS pandemic could keep several departments of political science and all their graduate students busy for many years to come. There are a vast number of areas that require further research. Unfortunately there is not much evidence of this work being carried out and so we will conclude this chapter by proposing a set of themes and areas for further research.

Aids as a Security Issue

The chapter by Ostergard and Tubin looks at HIV/AIDS and South Africa's national security. AIDS as a security issue has been picked up by a number of organisations from the CIA to the United Nations Security Council. This chapter sets out some of the implications of the disease. It is however extremely thin on data. One important research area would be to start looking for hard information as to what is going on in the security apparatus and making informed guesses as to what this might mean for the security of countries and regions. There is a need to assess both internal and external security. As Mattes and Manning show democracy has a short half life in Africa and it would be very valuable to look at AIDS in this context in more detail. It is also worth noting that there are other diseases and crises that we might be able to learn from.

Loss of Life Expectancy

The issue of life expectancy and particularly life expectancy at adulthood is one that merits far more attention. What happens when life expectancy falls from the mid-60s to the mid-30s? What are the mechanisms by which people are made aware of decreasing life expectancy and what role can information and education play here? How do people react to dropping life expectancy in terms of savings, political engagement and the many other mechanisms through which society is regulated and run? The issue is a burning one but is not one where there has been much research or even informed speculation. We would urge this as an item for the research agenda.

Manning and Mattes suggest that we also need to consider what a sharp reduction in adult life expectancy would mean for the behaviour of 'homopoliticus'. The potential political results are decreased support for democratic government from citizens, decreased citizen participation in democratic government, and damaged civil society. Their chapter includes data from the only study thus far on the impact of AIDS on an NGO in South Africa, but again this is based on projections rather than hard data.

Loss of Leadership

What is it that causes states to fail, how important is leadership, what does AIDS mean for this? There is a growing corpus of literature looking at the leadership but this is not applied to the epidemic. This is a glaring omission and we can only hope that in the years ahead it will be rectified. One of the constant themes of the book is that leadership is crucial if we are to make a difference with regard to this epidemic. But where should this leadership come from and how should it be motivated? How do we get people to engage around the epidemic when there is so much difficulty in understanding the long wave nature. Stoneburner and Lowbeer show that political leadership is necessary but not sufficient. This lesson should be clearly understood and we need to develop ways of moving ahead.

Final Thoughts

This book is about the political economy of AIDS and as such is a set of papers that present an academic analysis of a problem. But AIDS is the major development social and political issue facing much of sub-Saharan Africa. It would be no exaggeration to say that development will falter and could be reversed. In some settings life expectancy will revert to levels not seen since the Stone Age. The current global preoccupation with providing antiretroviral therapy is a blind alley. Responding to this epidemic requires action in three areas, and they have to be done together. They are prevention, care and treatment (which include the antiretroviral therapy), and mitigation.

The issue of antiretroviral therapy is however an avenue avenue for political scientists to research. Issues include equity, who gets the treatment and what are the implications of having some people on life saving therapies and others not. That is however not the way we wish to end this book. Rather what we would urge is that political scientists understand that research and addressing this epidemic is not just an academic exercise. There are burning issues which will have huge impact on the lives of many millions. It is an area of theory that requires attention. It has practical consequences. It is our contention that AIDS is a Darwinian event. It means that the world as we know it will change. This will happen first in Africa, followed by parts of Asia and Eastern Europe.

Index